THE
GRAPES
OF WINE

THE FINE ART OF GROWING
GRAPES AND MAKING WINE

Baudouin Neirynck, PhD

SQUAREONE
PUBLISHERS

COVER DESIGNER: Jeannie Tudor
IN-HOUSE EDITOR: Ariel Colletti
TYPESETTER: Jeannie Tudor

Square One Publishers
115 Herricks Road
Garden City Park, NY 11040
(516) 535–2010
(877) 900–BOOK
www.squareonepublishers.com

Library of Congress Cataloging-in-Publication Data

Neirynck, Baudouin.
  The grapes of wine : the art of growing grapes and making wine / Baudouin Neirynck.
      p. cm.
  Includes bibliographical references and index.
  ISBN-13: 978-0-7570-0247-2 (hardback)
  ISBN-10: 0-7570-0247-1 (hardback)
  1. Wine and wine making. 2. Grapes. I. Title.
  TP548.N43 2008
  641.2'2–dc22
                                    2008003794

Printed in the United States of America

10 9 8 7 6 5 4 3 2 1

Contents

This book is dedicated to the Croix family from Beaune, Burgundy.
They were my wine initiators at an early age.

Acknowledgements

My utmost gratitude goes to all the people without whom this book would not have been possible: Ms. Hebe Sun from Hong Kong, the talented illustrator who drew all the grape varieties color pencil illustrations; Professor Georges Halpern, MD, PhD, the author of the chapter on "Wine and Health," for his wise suggestions to a first-time author; Ms. Annabel Jackson, my editor and friend; and Mrs. Geneviève Janssens, Director of Wine Making at Robert Mondavi in California for her review and foreword. My thanks also go to Mr. Bai Zhisheng, Chairman of Dynasty Fine Wines, for his sponsorship toward part of the publishing cost of this book without interfering with the editorial content.

The list of people to whom I am indebted would not be complete without mentioning Mr. Rudy Shur, the publisher; Ariel Colletti, who encouraged me to persevere in the pursuit toward excellence; and Jeannie Tudor, who designed the layout of this beautiful book.

I also thank my wife Cynthia and children Marie and Astrid. Without their patience, I would never have finished this book.

Foreword

Wine has been a companion to the human experience for thousands of years, and yet its mystery and promise continues to captivate us afresh.

Making wine is an art, requiring a skillful touch and a delicate awareness to coax flavor and aroma into perfect balance. It is of course also a science, calling on precise mastery of chemistry and agriculture working in partnership with nature's offerings. As a fifth-generation winemaker, I also consider wine a tradition and connection across generations.

Wine is foremost an experience, an ever-changing and maturing process that brings people together in passion, companionship, and appreciation.

Wine is, in a word, complex. It is my pleasure to introduce this book, which takes a complex subject and presents it in a manner that will appeal to many different kinds of enophiles, whether they are beginning their studies or are further developing their understanding. This tour through the origins, traditions, practices, and qualities of the world of wine will both educate and inspire further research.

Making wine and enjoying wine are two sides of one coin, and this book illuminates both in order to impart a fuller understanding.

Dr. Neirynck's tenacity and thoroughness in producing this work is a wonderful gift to the world's wine-loving community.

Having devoted a twenty-six-year career to the creation and enjoyment of wine, I can say one thing with certainty: There is always more to know about wine. Enjoy your reading.

Genevieve Janssens
Director of Winemaking at Robert Mondavi Winery
Napa, California

Introduction

When Wine Becomes a Passion

In some countries, wine has been considered a daily staple for centuries. Other countries, where wine consumption may have been nonexistent just a few decades ago, have seen the emergence of a wine culture that has grown exponentially. Local wine shops and tasting clubs proliferate, while wines from all around the world are more readily available, thanks to improved distribution networks.

I traveled from Saudi Arabia to Hong Kong in 1987. Only during the last twenty years has wine begun to replace Cognac and other hard liquors as the alcohol of choice at Chinese banquets and wedding parties. The number of specialized wine shops in Hong Kong multiplied by twenty-five between 1987 and 2006. Knowledge and interest is such that a few die-hard amateurs have even been studying for the Master of Wine (MW) examination—the hardest test in the wine trade.

In Beijing in the year 2000, the Chinese government decided that dry, grape-based wine should replace hard liquor and rice wine at all official state banquets. This decision was based on the more economic use of natural resources, including water, for wine production, as compared with the production and distillation of rice (the base grain for the famous rice wine maotai). Regardless, the result was the further advancement of the global wine market.

Figure 1.
Foggy weather above Dynasty Vineyards in Ningxia province, China. Vine leaves absorb moisture supplied by morning fog and mist as water supply is rather scarce in that semi-desertic region.

For Europeans, on the other hand, wine is an integral part of culture. My grandfather had nine children: seven daughters and two sons. In Europe in the 1920s and 1930s, it was customary for the bride's family to organize (and bear the cost of) her wedding. Three to four years after each daughter was born, my grandfather would buy a barrel of a specific wine—usually from Bordeaux—and have it shipped to his home in Belgium, where it was bottled by a local merchant. The bottles belonging to each girl were drank on the day of her wedding. (One of his daughters did not marry—but the wine was consumed anyway!) Every twenty years, the merchant would examine the bottles and taste the remaining stock, top up bottles with wine from the same vintage (to replace any liquid that may have evaporated), and change the corks. Today, this practice is referred to as a Wine Clinic.

At my grandfather's house, the process of choosing a bottle to accompany lunch was a ritual of almost

religious proportions, and visits to the cellar to show his latest acquisitions to business associates were customary. Admittedly, this did not happen in every household. There were many people who could only afford to drink beer.

It was the dedication of my family to wine that inspired me to venture into the food and beverage industry, and restaurant management in particular, where I remained for two decades (1977 to 1997). Today, I am delighted to share my wine passion with you through this book.

A Varietal Approach to the Study of Wine

Typical wine books tend to focus on the acquisition of wine knowledge by presenting information country by country, and region by region. As recently as fifty years ago, a large majority of wines originated from the Old World (essentially from Europe). Since one of the most important influences on the character of these wines was the precise vineyard in which its grapes were grown, this geography-focused approach worked well. After all, these wines are labeled by the vineyard in which the grapes originated. Consumers of European wine rely on the advice of a wine merchant and their own knowledge of wine geography to make a distinction between varying quality, origin, type, and style of wine.

In today's global wine market, however, there are as many popular wines originating from outside Europe as from within. We are seeing two very different approaches between Old World and New World winemakers. Most wines from the New World are *varietals*—wines produced from one or more grapes that are labeled by the name of the grapes used. When looking to buy wine, consumers have shifted their attention toward the comparison of different wines made from the same grape variety, and these wines may even come from more than one country.

Thus consumers now require global knowledge of the multitude of labels and brands, not only from different regions, but also different countries and different continents. As a result, there seems to be an argument for enhancing the information given on a wine label, and a move towards standardizing at least part of worldwide wine production. The result of this argument may

eventually be the production of varietal wines in the Old World. The results of a 2001 study by Jacques Berthomeau, a French wine consultant, suggested that the gradual adoption of varietal naming and stronger branding would improve the position of French wines in an increasingly competitive export market. In other words, he recommended that this ultra-traditionalist country implement a more consumer-friendly system.

There is, after all, consensus in the wine trade that understanding the most important grapes and the resulting wines from around the world is more significant than having specialized knowledge about selected wines from just one or two countries. Apart from some restaurants that are located right in the middle of a wine-producing region and can get away with listing exclusively local wines, the majority of eateries in tourism-oriented areas need to offer a broad choice of wines from across the world. Therefore, *sommeliers*—restaurant wine stewards—need to have generalist, rather than specialist, knowledge.

As grape varieties continue to emerge as more important than place of origin, a different approach to wine education is required. There are calls to shift the paradigm of wine education that was previously centered on geography towards the study of grape varieties across wine-producing regions. With this in mind, the objective of this book is to explain the historical background of wine, viticulture, and vinification, as well as offer a comprehensive exploration of wine through the various grapes cultivated in major wine-producing countries, both Old World and New World. It concludes with information on wine service and storage, as well as ideas on how to approach food and wine matching. However, this book is not intended to be an ampelographic description of all the grapes used in the production of wine but, rather, an exploration of the most popular wine grapes and their origins, development through the ages, and current geographic spread. It also explores the importance of these grapes and olfactory qualities associated with the various regions of production.

I have limited the number of grapes discussed in this book to a little more than twenty. I reached this total by determining both the most significant grapes and those in highest demand in today's market.

Among the white wine grapes, we start with

Chardonnay, which has achieved worldwide recognition and has a cult following among wine drinkers and tasters. Sauvignon Blanc follows, mainly due to the fact it has succeeded in propelling New Zealand to the forefront of wine-producing countries. Next we look at Riesling, the grape that has, with its balance of firm acidity, floral aromas, and varying degrees of sweetness, established the wine reputations of Germany and the Alsace region of France.

Gewürztraminer, although produced only in minute quantities when compared with the other major grapes, is the most aromatic of white grapes, and is a must for beginners in the art of wine tasting. The Semillon grape, responsible for some of the most famous naturally sweet wines such as Château d'Yquem, is also on the list of major grapes. We will also look at Ugni Blanc, which is known as Trebbiano in Italy. This is the most widely planted grape in the world, and is appreciated not so much for its olfactory characteristics but for its ability to produce, when distilled, the best Cognacs in the world.

Then, we will turn to a host of other white grapes. These are all significant either in terms of plantings or due to their specific olfactory characteristics and future development potential.

Of the black grapes, also called red wine grapes, we begin with those utilized in the Bordeaux region of France. Cabernet Sauvignon is the first and foremost, not so much for its aromas and smells as for what it brings to a wine in terms of structure, body, and sophistication. Merlot, the grape of which Château Petrus in Pomerol is made, is a thick-skinned berry capable of producing highly aromatic wines. The two other main grapes of the region are Malbec and Petit Verdot.

The black grape Syrah is called Shiraz in Australia and, sometimes, California. Shiraz is a luscious wine that not only retains all the typical characteristics of the Syrah grape, but adds a depth previously unseen. Pinot Noir, responsible for some of the most prestigious wines in the world, is a more delicate grape that needs certain soils and climatic conditions to give its best. Grenache, also called Canonnau, is one of the oldest grapes officially recognized in ampelographic records. It was originally popular from its usage in French and Spanish wines, but has since been grown with success in California as well.

Sangiovese is the undisputed king of Italian grapes, and an important part of the production of Chianti. Malbec and Tannat are upcoming grapes which have established substantial reputations, not so much in their native country of origin—France—but in their countries of adoption, Argentina and Uruguay respectively. Carignan is one of the oldest-documented grapes, and has spread far and wide on every continent to become one of the most planted grapes in the world. Tempranillo, the Spanish grape, has long been highly regarded for its part in generating famous wines from La Rioja to Ribera del Duero. Lastly, the Venetian grape Primitivo has been adopted by California under the name Zinfandel with such success that Italian winemakers have also begun to adopt this new moniker.

Sideways, a 2004 movie by Alexander Payne, illustrated the current debate in the wine market by epitomizing the myriad of choices facing today's consumers when selecting a wine. Should they go for an oak-influenced, high-alcohol-content Merlot or a super-elegant Pinot Noir with its finesse and higher acidity? In fact, every grape has its own cult following.

Which Wines for Which Consumer

Choice is a matter of preference and price, particularly in the case of wine. The proponents of high-end French, Californian, Spanish, Australian, and Italian wines can make a strong case for their choices. Such wines have been brought to life in a very traditional way, from careful selection of soil and grape type to attentive handling during harvest, vinification, and maturation. They represent the best of the best from each wine region. They are worth their price as well as the years of waiting required before they achieve maturity. These top-notch wines regularly contribute significantly to the bottom line of auction houses because great wines are the subject of much speculation. However, they are reserved for a particular breed of consumer who has the time, financial resources, and facilities to buy and cellar these treasures.

On the other hand, the majority of wine drinkers have neither an appropriate cellar nor the purchasing power to acquire truly exceptional bot-

tles. For them, there exists a range of reasonable and sometimes high-quality wines that do not need to mature. There is usually a price range of between $10 and $15 (£7.47 and £11.20) per bottle.

A Wine for Every Occasion and Budget

You may find that you derive as much pleasure from sharing a relatively good-quality fruity wine with little or no oak flavor and very little tannin, as from opening a 1945, 1959, 1982, or 2003 vintage of a great Bordeaux, or a bottle of Grange or Opus One. After all, not everyone thinks like Marco-Pierre White, the prominent British chef, who said that he would find solace and happiness if he could drink his favorite wine, 1947 Château Cheval Blanc, every day. We can think of numerous wine-drinking occasions—official banquets, weddings, birthdays, funerals, and wine tastings, to name a few—but not everyone wishes to indulge in the most sophisticated red wine every day. Some wines are delightful precisely because they are simple, approachable, and easy to drink. There are as many different wines as there are events at which to drink them. You may find it helpful to peruse a wine magazine or the weekend editions of daily newspapers, as they very often contain a wine section. Such publications usually highlight wines for every budget. Enjoy your reading—as well as your drinking.

PART 1

The Art of Making Wine

1.
Wine and Grapes Through History

When you buy a bottle of wine, you probably don't think about the similarities between it and the wines available more than 2,000 years ago. Yet wine has been around for quite a long time. Its popularity has seen its ups and downs throughout the ages. It is only in recent years that scientists have identified the exact origins of this beverage—some 9,000 years ago. This chapter establishes a timeline from that period to today, and highlights the most important developments in the world of wine.

The Origins of Wine

The production of wine has been around for many, many years. In December 2004, American molecular archeologist Patrick McGovern reported that some Neolithic containers found in Jia Hu, Henan Province in the Peoples' Republic of China and dating back around 9,000 years contained traces of winemaking activity. Laboratory tests revealed residue of wine made with fermented rice, honey, and grapes of hawthorn fruit in these jars. One of the previously known oldest examples was a tannin stain found in a 7,400-year-old *amphorae*—a baked clay container with two handles—that was discovered in 1994 (by the same McGovern). This jar contained residue of tartaric acid, which in nature is rarely found in anything but grapes. It was discovered at the site of Hajii Firuz Tepe, located in the Zagros Mountains of present-day northern Iran, and dates back to 5,400 BC.

Throughout history, various factors have contributed to the propagation of *viticulture*—the study and science of grape growing—with the aim of making wine. Through the Egyptians, the Greeks, the Phoenicians (great traders of the Mediterranean Sea), the Roman legions, and finally priests and monks, winemaking has continued to flourish. Many would use wine as part of religious rituals: where there was a church, there was invariably a vineyard.

WINE AND RELIGION

Vinification originated in countries around the Mediterranean Sea, and it is common to find references to wine in all religions prevailing in the last five or six centuries. While Catholicism and some other Christian religions used wine to represent the blood of Christ in dominical celebrations, the Muslim religion explicitly forbid the consumption of alcohol in any form (and contin-

Figure 1.1.
Italy, Roman Empire: wine-drinking cups made of transparent glass with handles, dated around 250 BC, in the Louvre Museum, Paris, France.

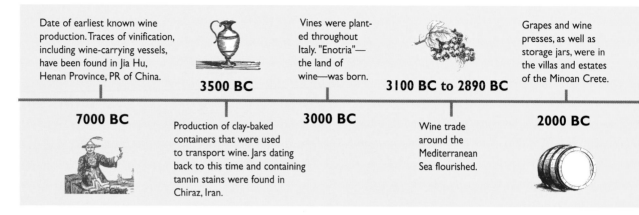

Date of earliest known wine production. Traces of vinification, including wine-carrying vessels, have been found in Jia Hu, Henan Province, PR of China.

Vines were planted throughout Italy. "Enotria"—the land of wine—was born.

Grapes and wine presses, as well as storage jars, were in the villas and estates of the Minoan Crete.

3500 BC

3100 BC to 2890 BC

7000 BC

Production of clay-baked containers that were used to transport wine. Jars dating back to this time and containing tannin stains were found in Chiraz, Iran.

3000 BC

Wine trade around the Mediterranean Sea flourished.

2000 BC

ues to do so). Yet the literature of Sufism (an Islamic spiritual way of life) makes constant reference to wine—if not in its true form, then figuratively, as a symbol of love and affection.

Wine was often referred to as a gift from God, and was offered in return as a sacrifice, in a rite similar to the sacrificial offerings of lambs and chickens practiced by some religions. However, despite some records of overindulgence in wine on the part of the ancient Romans and Greeks during their polytheist religious celebrations, Jewish and Christian communities tended to advocate restraint when dealing with wine consumption, particularly during religious ceremonies.

Christian monks were the main propagators of viticulture, from the early ages of Christianity until the French Revolution in 1789. They were also the first to plant vineyards in California, at Mission San Diego de Alcalá in 1769. In Europe, rich landlords would bequest land to monasteries and abbeys to ensure God's blessing. Monks had the time and knowledge to refine vine-growing techniques, resulting in a dramatic improvement in wine quality. During the Roman Empire, wine was often a concentrated beverage that required dilution and often turned to vinegar. But by the eighteenth century, some of the wines coming out of France, Germany, Hungary, and even South Africa were of an excellent quality, and earned a lofty status in royal courts across Europe.

EGYPT

In the era before the Egyptian dynasties and throughout the dynastic periods (which began around 3200 BC), viticulture was considered an art. Gardeners in charge of vineyards were revered, as exemplified by the hieroglyphs of the time that glorified the "Master of the Vineyards" and the "Master of the Vine-Dresser." Wine labels even included the name of the vintner.

Because vineyards need water for irrigation, most were located in the Nile Delta or around oases in the south of the country. They were owned by the pharaohs. When tombs of the pharaohs were opened in contemporary history, excavators often discovered wine jars with wine residues. Clearly, wine played an important role in Egyptian civilization.

As to prevailing viticulture, the Egyptians already knew how to prune and train the vines. (A discussion on training systems begins on page 23.) The vines were trained on either trellises or in bushes, depending on the climatic conditions of individual vineyards. Vinification, though rudimentary, was advanced enough to allow certain wines to be kept for a few decades. Open-vessel fermentation, racking, and filtering were techniques used in the elaboration of this prestigious beverage.

However, the most impressive aspect of the ancient Egyptian wine industry was the labeling laws, very much in line with those applied in France today. The name of the estate, location, type of wine, date of vintage, vintner's name, and assessment of quality were all found on the labels. This information would be printed under the watchful eye of the "Royal Sealer of Wine."

The Romans valued the wines from Egypt and imported them to various parts of Italy. The best wines came from Mareotis, Menzalah, Tanis, the northern Xois area, and the region of Sile.

ANCIENT GREECE

Wine was very important both culturally and religiously in the lives of the inhabitants of ancient Greece. The origins of wine in this region date back to 1600 BC on the island of Crete—probably the result of trade between the Phoenicians and the Greeks. It was the Greeks who invented Dionysos, the god of wine.

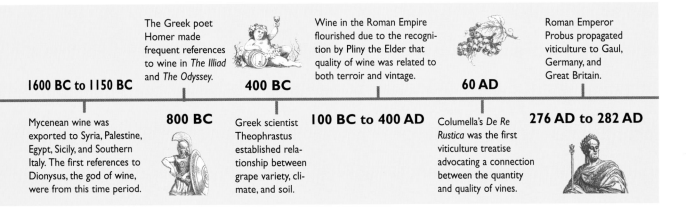

1600 BC to 1150 BC	The Greek poet Homer made frequent references to wine in *The Illiad* and *The Odyssey.* **400 BC**	Wine in the Roman Empire flourished due to the recognition by Pliny the Elder that quality of wine was related to both terroir and vintage.	Roman Emperor Probus propagated viticulture to Gaul, Germany, and Great Britain.

Mycenean wine was exported to Syria, Palestine, Egypt, Sicily, and Southern Italy. The first references to Dionysus, the god of wine, were from this time period. **800 BC**

Greek scientist Theophrastus established relationship between grape variety, climate, and soil. **100 BC to 400 AD** **60 AD**

Columella's *De Re Rustica* was the first viticulture treatise advocating a connection between the quantity and quality of vines. **276 AD to 282 AD**

The Greeks heavily influenced viticulture and vinification techniques throughout Europe, within their colonies of Spain, Portugal, France, southern Russia, and Georgia, particularly around the fourth century BC. Today, for example, DNA fingerprinting allows us to trace some grape varieties found in Spain back to Greece. Similarly, the southern part of Italy still, to this day, cultivates grape varieties that are definitely of Greek origin. These include the Greco family (Greco Bianco, Greco Bianco di Tuffo, Greco Bianco di Novara, Greco Nero, and Greco Nero di Cosenza), the Grechetto, the Aglianico, and the Grecanico, each of which are cultivated in Apulia and Calabria, the regions of Italy geographically closest to Greece.

THE ROMAN EMPIRE

The Romans invented the god of wine Bacchus, their equivalent of the Greek's Dionysus. They were instrumental in propagating viticulture throughout their empire, in as far-flung places as England, Germany, and North Africa. At the same time, Roman writers and agronomists like Pliny, Columella, Virgil, and Cato started what is known today as *ampelography*—the science that studies and documents the classification of grape varieties. They did not attribute names to the grapes, but did describe some of their characteristics.

Finding associations between grapes cultivated 2,000 years ago, and those we know today, is difficult. According to Pierre Galet, probably the most famous ampelographer of our era, the Roman grape variety called *Apianae* attracted bees, and was probably the current Muscat grape in another form. There is also an association between a grape cultivated by the inhabitants of Gaul and Pinot Noir, only realized because of very detailed descriptions by Columella, the great agronomist.

Figure 1.3.
Greek amphora
Peintre d'Androkides
530 BC, in the Louvre
Museum, Paris, France.

At the time, the Gaul region covered most of modern France, Belgium, and a part of Spain.

Some Roman emperors encouraged the cultivation of grapes for winemaking. Marcus Aurelius Probus reigned from 276 to 282 BC, and was famous for having encouraged and propagated viticulture in what is known today as France. On the other hand, the Emperor Domitian, who ruled the empire around 90 AD, was faced with a constant shortage of grain in the cities and tried to revert the cultivation of land from vineyards to grain fields. He banned viticulture to such an extent that half the Roman vineyards disappeared during his reign.

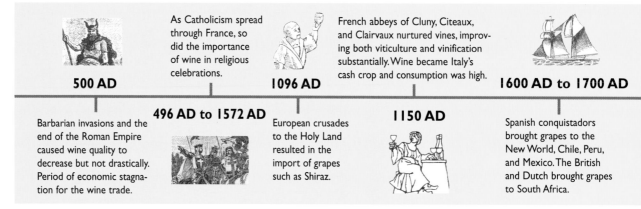

500 AD

As Catholicism spread through France, so did the importance of wine in religious celebrations.

1096 AD

French abbeys of Cluny, Citeaux, and Clairvaux nurtured vines, improving both viticulture and vinification substantially. Wine became Italy's cash crop and consumption was high.

1600 AD to 1700 AD

496 AD to 1572 AD

Barbarian invasions and the end of the Roman Empire caused wine quality to decrease but not drastically. Period of economic stagnation for the wine trade.

European crusades to the Holy Land resulted in the import of grapes such as Shiraz.

1150 AD

Spanish conquistadors brought grapes to the New World, Chile, Peru, and Mexico. The British and Dutch brought grapes to South Africa.

THE FALL AND REVIVAL OF THE WINE TRADE

Starting in 476 AD, the fall of the Roman Empire saw the stagnation of most of the vineyards across Europe. This was mainly due to invasions by the Northern European populations of the Ostrogoths, Visigoths, and Vikings. Then, in the seventh and eighth centuries, came a European revival of viticulture and vinification. This was mainly in France and Germany and largely through the influence of Charlemagne. Italy, on the other hand, had to wait until the thirteenth and fourteenth centuries and the rise of the Frescobaldi and Antinori families to again play a significant role in the wine trade.

The next two centuries were marked by the voyages of the Spanish and Portuguese conquistadors in search of exotic goods such as spices and precious commodities such as gold and silk. Both countries were already producing excellent wines, and began to export their grape varieties to countries that are today at the center of the New World wine production: Chile, Argentina, the United States, and China. Their main objective was to start a wine industry in each new colony to avoid the transportation, by sea, of barrels of wine—which would inevitably spoil after such long journeys. It was not until much later, when the wine fortification process was discovered, that wines were stable enough to travel.

During the Hundred Years' War (1336 to 1453), relations between the British and French became strained. The British sought an alternative wine supply, and found it in Portugal. However, it was the Dutch who first introduced Portuguese wines to the rest of the world, and they were also instrumental in developing the distillation industry in the regions of Cognac and Armagnac.

THE EMERGENCE OF INTENSIVE TRADING

Between the seventeenth and nineteenth centuries, England and Holland became world powers. Their fleets of vessels scoured the world's seas in search of markets from which to import, and to which they could export. Portugal, France, and Spain were natural targets, for they all produced a precious commodity: wine.

Together, the British and Dutch colonized South Africa and, in 1685, established Constantia, the first wine estate of the country. Estates such as Klein Karoo, De Trafford, and Boekenhoutskloof were later established. Elsewhere in the world, the former influence of British and Dutch traders is still evident today in the names of Port wine houses such as Croft, Taylor's, and Sandeman and Cognac houses such as Hennessy, Hine, and Martell.

In the vineyards of Europe, it was a time of experimentation as winemakers sought to improve the beverage's quality. At the end of the seventeenth century and early in the eighteenth century, Dom Pérignon improved the sparkling wines of Champagne by developing the blending method and sealing the bottles with (Spanish) cork. It was also around this time that glass bottles, invented around 1650, became the standard wine container.

FROM *PHYLLOXERA VASTATRIX* TO NEW WORLD WINES

The wine trade flourished until 1867. Then, after 200 years of relatively warm weather, substantial growth of the world population due to medicinal advancements, and the development of large city centers that would become European capitals, the vines were attacked by *louses*—insects that feed on plant juice. These insects, called *Phylloxera vas-*

1700 AD

The Dutch introduced distillation to the regions of Cognac and Armagnac.

During the French Revolution, chaptalization (adding sugar to must or juice before fermentation) appeared throughout Chaptal, glass bottles began to be used, and méthode Champenoise—which yields sparkling wine—was invented.

1789 AD to 1799 AD

1867 AD to 1910 AD

Phylloxera vastatrix devastated European vineyards. Disease-resistant American rootstocks were imported and grafted with European vine cuttings.

Quality wines began to emerge from the New World (United States, Australia, New Zealand, South Africa, and South America).

1980 AD

---

tatrix, devastated vineyards all over Europe. Disease-resistant rootstocks had to be imported from the United States. Replanting the vineyards took a good forty years, during which time production levels decreased substantially.

The 1929 worldwide market collapse, World War II, and the ensuing period of recovery did nothing to help the wine industry. It was not until the 1960s that the wine trade again exploded. Then, the 1970s saw the emergence of formidable competitors for European wines. The new quality wines came from the New World, namely California, Australia, New Zealand, Chile, and Argentina. After apartheid was abolished in 1994, the trade embargo was lifted and excellent wines also began to be exported from South Africa.

Modern Times

During the 1980s, the United States, particularly California, took the world by surprise with its consistently high-quality Chardonnay and Cabernet Sauvignon wines. Both were relatively easy to produce because of the area's favorable and consistent climate. Unfortunately, this led to overproduction by enthusiastic entrepreneurs, and the harvests in the late 1990s suffered as a result.

At the same time, Italy and Spain started their own mini-revolutions in the world of wine. Both countries began to recognize the increasing importance of working with world-class oenologists. The Italian Giacomo Tachis, for example, came to work for the Antinori house, an Italian winemaking family that has been in the business since 1385. Tachis, during his thirty-year employment, revolutionized viticulture for the house. With the encouragement of company head Piero Antinori, he began to create the enduringly popular "Super Tuscans." The Super Tuscans combine Sangiovese grapes with one of the grapes of

Bordeaux, often Cabernet Sauvignon, to make a more modern version of Chianti. (Traditionally Chianti is made from Sangiovese and Canaiolo Nero.)

Until 1960, Italian wines were known as low-quality beverages usually bottled in a *fiasco*—a fat 1.5-liter bottle with a round bottom that was usually wrapped in straw. But excellent wines have replaced them today, not only for domestic consumption, but also for export.

The same kinds of questions regarding ancestral viticultural practices have come up in Spain, particularly during the last twenty-five years. The result is a recognition of the work by innovative winemakers like Peter Sisseck of Dominio de Pingus in Ribera del Duero, Castilla y León. In a region marked by very traditional winemaking techniques, Sisseck, a native Dane, was the winemaker at Hacienda Monasterio winery before he founded Pingus in 1995. Using local Tempranillo grapes from three small vineyards, he prunes aggressively, leaving only a few bunches on each vine. This results in extremely low yields of 0.52 tons per acre (or 7 hectoliters per hectare). The vineyards are cultivated along the principles of biodynamism, and once harvested at ultra-ripe maturity, the grapes are foot-trodden and fermented in stainless steel tanks before being aged in new-oak barrels. Sisseck uses the same barrel supplier as Chateau Petrus in Pomerol. The end result is simply outstanding: a

Dom Pérignon introduced the idea of blending the grapes of several different vineyards. He was also the first to suggest bottling sparkling wine in thicker glass to protect the carbon dioxide bubbles. However, he is often falsely credited with inventing the sparkling-wine production method. This method was actually developed in 1531 in another Benedictine abbey.

Champagne can only be made from grapes harvested by hand from one of three French regions of production. In addition, the yield in the vineyards, the force of the pressing of the grapes to extract the must, and the time the wine has to remain on the lees, concur to make Champagne the most expensive of all sparkling wines.

Around twenty years before the full blow of phylloxera, the Classification of 1855 was developed. It classified the best wines in Bordeaux as established by their quality and market value, and generated an interest that has never abated.

concentrated wine produced only in good years (there is no 2002 Pingus, for example) and which reaches prices of $1,000 (£747) per bottle in specialized wine shops.

A DEVIATION FROM TRADITION

The vision of both the worldwide wine industry and the global wine trade is to continually improve quality standards. This is to not only to satisfy the consumer, but also to support the branding exercises which highlight the growing role of marketing and name recognition in the beverage field. Wine branding has become essential due to the very competitive market. Yellow Tail from Australia, for example, proved that it is possible to develop an annual market of sixty million bottles from scratch in less than five years. Nonetheless, those in the wine world have come to realize that yields above 3.70 tons per acre (or 50 hectoliters per hectare) do not tend to generate quality wine.

At the same time, the internet bubble of 2001 and the ensuing period of financial uncertainty have together shown that sales of high-end and top-quality wines are highly dependent on the strength of prevailing market conditions. Thus, investments required for the drive toward ever-improving quality, and inevitable price increases, must be carefully balanced against economic cycles, and the purchasing power of the target audience. At the same time, there is an ever-growing presence of large companies—such as Australia's Foster's, California's Constellation and Gallo, and France's Pernod-Ricard and LVMH—in the global wine trade. There is, however, no guarantee that these large companies will yield exciting wines.

Instead, innovative wines will remain the privilege of small, independent viticulturists and winemakers. After all, the philosophy of many of the smaller houses is to let the wine and *terroir*—a wine-growing area and its attributes that affect the wine's quality, as defined by the French wine establishment—speak for themselves. For these producers, the process is similar to music: the vineyard is the composer, the grape the instrument, and the winemaker the musician. The end result is hopefully a wine that can draw the best out of these three elements to produce a harmonious product. In the best-case scenario, the wine will also show good aging potential.

The high-end wines of Bordeaux used to enjoy seemingly endless annual price increases. Then, prices for the 2002 vintage plummeted by

Fiaschi (the plural of *fiasco*) are seldom seen today. The task to hand wrap straw around the bottle is no longer economic, and modern wine bottles are strong enough to withstand handling.

European winemakers use different measurements than those in the United States. They use hectares to measure land instead of acres. 1 hectare equals 2.45 acres. 13.5 hectoliters per hectare equal 1 ton per acre.

Figure 1.4.
New vines planted at PB Winery in Khao Yai, Central Thailand. The climate is particularly hot and humid, demanding special vineyard management such as cropping entire yields to avoid a second harvest during the same year.

Winemaking Techniques

The following terms and techniques are important to winemakers who wish to appeal to the niche market with high-quality wines. The techniques are more expensive than those used by mass-market producers, but the resulting wines are considerably more desirable to wine lovers willing to pay more for their bottles.

■ *Organic viticulture* is the process of growing grapes with minimal human intervention in an environment respectful of nature. The main concerns of producers are soil management, animal pests, and diseases. Organic grape growers strive to achieve an optimal balance between animal pests and their predators. *Bacillus thuringiensis,* for example, is a naturally occurring bacterium present in the soil, and is efficient in combating pests such as the grape moth.

■ *Terroir* is a French word used all over the world to describe a wine-growing area and its attributes, including soil and climate, that affect the wine's quality.

■ *Low yield* refers to a comparatively, and intentionally, low volume of bunches. This is achieved through a combination of pruning, canopy management, and green harvest. It is usually expressed in gallons per acre (or hectoliters per hectare).

■ *Old vines*, aged beyond fifteen to twenty years, yield less grapes than young wines. However, the concentration of flavors and aromas increases in old vines, almost always generating higher-quality grapes.

■ *Hand-sorting* occurs after harvest and before pressing. Grapes are laid out on a sorting table, and only perfectly healthy and ripe berries are retained for pressing.

■ *De-stemming* separates the grape berries from their stalks to aid hand-sorting. It also ensures the removal of stems, which can bring harsh tannins to a wine after fermentation. This practice is usually reserved for red-wine grapes.

■ *Thermo-regulated fermentation* enables temperature control during fermentation. The system often consists of cooling coils attached to the fermenting tank, but can also take the form of dry ice thrown into the same tank.

■ *Oak-barrel aging* occurs after fermentation. The wine is transferred into new or one-year-old oak barrels. The wood pores allow for micro-oxygenation and the evaporation of minute amounts of wine (also called "the angels' part"), thus ensuring a safe and steady maturation. At the same time, wood tannins are released into the wine, enhancing aging potential in the bottle.

nearly 40 percent. This was because of an oversupply of quality wines, and the poor performance of the global economy.

The 1980s and 1990s saw the emergence of "wine gurus" such as Robert Parker Jr., whose rating system is based on points out of 100 and has become the most followed in the world. Although still widely recognized, he has since been heavily criticized on the charge of bias.

Spain, France, and Italy remain the largest producers of wine in the world, with a combined planting area of around 6.6 million acres (or 2.7 million hectares). However, according to the results of a 2003 statistical study undertaken by Eurostat (the official statistics agency of the European Commission), the total area of European vineyards has recently decreased by more than 15 percent: from 9.31 million acres (or 3.8 million hectares) in 1989 to 7.84 million acres (or 3.2 million hectares) in 1999. The number of individuals or companies engaged in viticulture has decreased by an even greater degree: it is down 30 percent from 2.1 million down to 1.5 million people. Greece, Italy, and Spain have seen the greatest decrease (nearly 27 percent), whereas

France has seen only a modest reduction (less than 5 percent).

Clearly, a large percentage of the wine market has begun to move away from traditional European terroir wines. In the next twenty to thirty years, there will probably emerge an even bigger split between varietal and terroir wines, and in the consumers who are interested in each. This shift happens around most commodities, or products, that appeal to both a mass market and a niche market at the same time. The wine mass market will make the product affordable and available, thanks to mechanization and viticulture focused on varietal wines. On the other hand, the niche market will target those who can afford wines produced utilizing far more expensive winemaking techniques. These techniques can include organic viticulture, an emphasis on terroir, low yields, old vines, hand-sorting and de-stemming of bunches, thermo-regulated vinification, oak-barrel aging, long-bottle maturation, and classifications lead by wine gurus' ratings. These techniques are defined in the inset above.

CHANGES IN WINEMAKING TECHNIQUES

Concerned by the rise in the use of *genetically modified organisms (GMOs)* in the production of wine, some European grape-growers and wine merchants formed an association to demand a moratorium of at least ten years before such practices are allowed. Yet in the laboratory, GMOs have been found to be capable of trans-forming part of the sugars into lactic acid, thereby acidifying musts in an artificial manner. The *must* is the unfermented grape juice obtained right after pressing. GMOs have also increased the production of glycerol, and allowed *malolactic fermentation*—a second fermentation that reduces the wine's overall acidity—to start while alcoholic fermentation is still unfinished. In theory, there is practically no limit to the potential of GMOs. The main question, however, is whether GMOs have the potential to significantly affect the viticulture and vinification of a product that has remained relatively natural in its elaboration process for centuries.

There is currently a great deal of controversy between advocates of traditional winemaking techniques as opposed to chemically engineered products. There is also controversy between advocates of terroir and non-terroir wines. The twenty-first century has brought traditional terroir wines under tremendous pressure, as Robert Parker ratings have so powerfully influenced how wine-makers work on the extraction and concentration of their wines. Change began in the vineyard, but is now also embraced in the winery. Already, a diluted must caused by rain during harvest can be concentrated by using a reverse osmosis machine to extract excess water content. Enzymes that enhance fruit content or color concentration can be added during alcoholic fermentation to obtain a wine closer to Parker's optimal view of quality. Such interventions boost a wine's rating and thus its price *en primeur*—when bought as a future, or before its release to the market.

As can be expected in any movement in which a predominant force establishes itself on a given market, there has been a reaction to the new wine techniques. In Bordeaux, some wine estates and producers refuse to use concentrators, enzymes, and any other products or techniques for the purpose of achieving a higher Parker rating. Will they succeed in creating an alternative cult following? As Parker himself has always emphasized, people pay too much attention to what he says, and he would welcome another source of wine-quality ratings. Will we see the emergence of a newly created body with the goal of counteracting Robert Parker's influence? Only time will tell.

From the somewhat crude product in China more than 9,000 years ago to today's highly sophisticated beverage, wine has established itself as a perfect complement to many activities. In the interval since its discovery nine millennia ago, the quality of this beverage has changed dramatically. Today's wine consumer faces the choice between New World wines characterized by innovation and the more traditional wines of the Old World as both varieties fight for market share.

Throughout the ages, wine has been celebrated by poets and authors, used as medicine, enjoyed with meals, and utilized as a water-purifying agent. Today, it is recognized for its ability to prevent the onset of certain diseases. Although there is also a fair amount of criticism aimed at wine, its importance in the past and present cannot be denied.

> The current controversy between winemaking techniques of the past and of the future are exemplified in Jonathan Nossiter's 2004 documentary *Mondovino*. Although *Mondovino* is often considered quite long and lacking in humor, it epitomizes the ongoing battle between purists and traditionalists, and illustrates how corporate giants are preoccupied by market share and sales volume.

Figure 1.5.
Small vertical wine press located in Pfaffenheim, Alsace, France.

2.
Grape Growing

Jancis Robinson, MW defines viticulture as "the science and practice of grape culture." As discussed in Chapter 1, it is an art that has been practiced since ancient times. Its importance cannot be overstated, as there is no good wine without good-quality grapes. In fact, it is often said that great wine is made in the vineyard, rather than by the winemaker.

The steps performed by viticulturists are as follows: soil selection and preparation, selection of the most appropriate grapes, planting of *scions*—young vine shoots from the nursery, maturation of the plant, pruning, training, fertilization and/or irrigation, crop thinning, insect and fungal disease control, and harvesting. These steps can help ensure that the necessary quality of grapes required for the appropriate quality wine will be generated.

Consensus opinion is that grapes can only be transformed into wine when cultivated at certain latitudes. The map on page 16 shows how most of the world's wine-producing regions are located between 30° and 50° latitude in both the southern and northern hemispheres. Some countries outside this area, such as Peru, Mexico, Uruguay, Germany, Thailand, Vietnam, Laos, and the United Kingdom, are also home to wine production. Their inclusion may be due to the effects of global warming. Regardless of the reason, grape growers in regions outside these latitude lines are often faced with various obstacles. Those in tropical countries, for example, have two choices. They can accept two harvests per year and the resulting curtailed lives of their vines, or they can prune well and green harvest their vineyards, so that only one harvest becomes possible, and the vines do not become exhausted.

Selecting and Preparing The Soil

Not all soils are created equal, especially when they are being assessed for their ability to become fertile ground for a variety of grape. While the grape vine thrives in poor soil to produce quality grapes, it does require a minimum of nutrients. Moreover, the mineral and organic composition of soils and subsoil can vary enormously, even within a single plot of land.

Viticulture refers to any activity pertaining to the planting and growing of the vine until fresh grapes are harvested, while vinification is the transformation of grapes into wine.

Green harvest refers to the process whereby some or all of the bunches are cut off when the grapes are still green, either to simply avoid overproduction, or to cause nutrients coming up the trunk to be shared among fewer bunches—thus ensuring higher grape quality.

Figure 2.1. Perfectly matured grapes ready to be harvested.

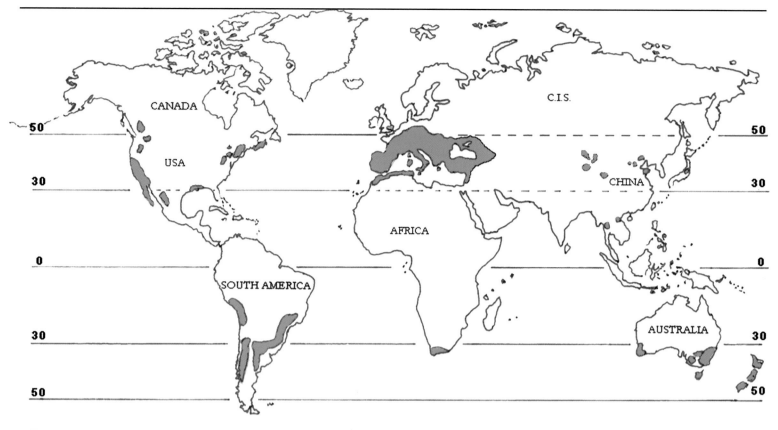

LOCATION OF VINEYARDS   )UCTION REGIONS IN THE WORLD

ALKALINITY AND ACIDITY

Basic soil chemical composition can range from alkaline to acidic. Soils with a pH below 5.5 are deemed too acidic to ensure sustained grape-growing activity. To make the soil more alkaline, lime (in the form of calcium hydroxide or calcium carbonate) can be added before vines are planted. At the other end of the acidity spectrum, alkaline soil with a pH above 10 is usually not considered for vine growing. This is especially true if it contains common salt (sodium chloride), which reduces the availability of potassium, an essential nutrient for vine-growth activity.

		Riesling	Chardonnay	Sauvignon Blanc	Semillon	Trebbiano	Muscat
TABLE 2.1 GROWING WHITE WINE GRAPES IN VARIOUS SOIL COMPOSITIONS							
	Sandy						
	Chalk			●	●		
SOIL (LIGHT TO HEAVY)	Limestone	●	●			●	●
	Marl		●				●
	Loam						●
	Gravel			●	●		
	Clay						
	Slate	●					
	Granite						

SOIL DRAINAGE

Most of the best wines available in the market come from grapes grown in well-drained soils. Such soils allow retention of only the necessary amount of water to sustain regular growth, and achieve good-quality grapes. This is important because excess water causes berries to swell, which then dilutes the must (unfermented grape juice) after harvest.

SOIL TEXTURE

It has been noted that very compact soils prevent vine roots from finding nutrients and water in the subsoil. Thus, prior to planting in a virgin field, soils—particularly those consisting of clay—have to be aerated. This is less applicable for loam soils, and not relevant for sandy soils.

SOIL COLOR

From the white albariza soils in southern Spain and the black volcanic ash of Pantelleria, Italy to the reddish-brown terra rossa found in Coonawarra, South Australia, the color of soil affects the temperature of the soil itself, as well as the air above it. This temperature variance affects the speed at which grapes can mature. In the northern limits of Europe, some vineyards can be exploited only because they sit on soils that can be warmed up by the sun during the day, and then reflect back that heat during the night when temperatures drop considerably.

Figure 2.2.
Iron rich terra rosa soil.
Magill Estate, Penfolds,
South Australia.

SOIL COMPOSITION

Usually, light soils are sandy, and heavy soils are clay. Rocky and stony soils that force grapes to search deeply for nutrients and moisture are particularly suitable to grapes such as Syrah.

Tables 2.1 and 2.2, below and on page 16, address which soils are best suited to the growing of specific grapes, with the aim of bringing

TABLE 2.2 GROWING RED WINE GRAPES IN VARIOUS SOIL COMPOSITIONS						
SOIL (LIGHT TO HEAVY)	**Cabernet Sauvignon**	**Syrah**	**Pinot Noir**	**Merlot**	**Grenache**	**Cabernet Franc**
Sandy						
Chalk			●			
Limestone	●	●	●			
Marl			●			
Loam			●		●	
Gravel	●			●	●	●
Clay				●		
Slate						
Granite		●			●	

Figure 2.3. Soya beans planted between rows of vines in fertile brown soil. Dynasty vineyards, Tianjin, China.

Figure 2.4. Pinot Noir during veraison, on a soil of marl, loess, and limestone. Pommard, Burgundy, France.

their best characters to the winery. The tables only represent obvious, vineyard-tested practices. Other soils may contain sand, marl (clay containing calcium carbonate), and loam, in varying proportions, all at the same time. A gravel soil with mixed minerals, for example, may be highly suitable for growing grapes that would not grow well in pure gravel.

When a wine grower selects the most appropriate plot of land on which to grow his grapes, he carefully studies the composition of not only the soil but also the subsoil. In some locations, the soil is relatively thin. This is known as *top soil*. Vine roots are extremely tenacious and can penetrate deep into the soil, down thirty feet (or six to seven meters), which is deeper than the top soil. Therefore, both soil and subsoil compositions directly influence the choice of grape variety.

SOILS AND WINE TYPES

In terms of both mineral composition and organic content, each soil type is different and yields different styles of wines. The organic content outlines the nutrients made available to the vine roots in ionic form, as individual charged atoms. (For example, calcium must be in the form of CA+ *cations*.) It is only through water that ions are transferred to the plants via root walls, to encourage vine growth.

In an experiment undertaken at Iron Horse Vineyards outside Sebastopol in California, two vineyards with different soil composition in terms of clay content were studied. One had 42-percent clay and the other 20-percent clay. They were planted with exactly the same Pinot Noir clone, yet yielded two different wines. The former yielded grapes with a deep-cherry color and deep berry and cherry-cola flavors, whereas the latter yielded grapes light cherry in color and light berry in taste. The second one also had softer tannins, a bigger *nose*—stronger aromatic components—and generally speaking more elegance than the first one (W. H. Terry Wright, 2001).

Vines growing in *calcareous*—containing lime and calcium carbonate—soils produce lemon- and citrus-flavored wines with a long acid finish. On the other hand, marl soils generate powerful and mildly peppery wines. Sandstone-based soils bring a nervy character to resulting wines, whereas clay soils emphasize any harsh or tannic characteristics. Schist-based soils outline the rangy and austere nature of a wine, and volcanic soils produce full-bodied wines with smoke-based aromas.

The effect of soil on wine quality contributes to the recognition of terroir. (As can be read in Chapter 1, terroir refers to a specific parcel of vineyard and its characteristics, which generate a particular style of wine.) The notion of terroir has long been recognized in Europe (particularly in France) but was somehow discarded in the New World at the onset of wine culture renewal.

However, American and Australian viticulturists and winemakers have begun to mark and delimit their vineyards according to both soil composition and the influence of particular microclimates. They now plant different grapes accordingly, and harvest their grapes with a view to different ripening periods, thus implicitly recognizing the importance of terroir in the elaboration of wines with unique characteristics. The terroir debate is not over, however. A study undertaken by Gergaud and Ginsburgh in 2005 counters the argument, by suggesting that winemaking technologies play a greater part than terroir in the production of great wines.

Different areas are suited for different grapes. The Pomerol region of Bordeaux, for example, is home to Château Petrus, producer of one of the best and most expensive wines in the world. Here, the soil is composed of clay, which suits Merlot extremely well, for this type of soil can retain the moisture and humidity needed by this grape to fully ripen and express its varietal characteristics.

Loam is a soil composed to varying degrees of clay, silt, and sand, and it is usually more fertile than sandy soil. Depending on the proportions of the three main components, loams are characterized as sandy, clay, or silt loams.

Veraison is the time when grape berries change color. Red wine grapes change from green to either blue or purple, while white wine grapes change from green to yellow.

Figure 2.5.
Excavated typical chalk soil, in which vine roots grow down to a depth of 16 to 20 feet (or 5 to 6 meters). Cumières, Champagne, France.

Figure 2.6.
Experimental Merlot plantings. Remich, Luxembourg.

The Vine and the Grape Berry

A vine consists of several parts: roots, trunk, spurs, canes, and shoots. The following outlines the characteristics of each part, the way they interact with each other, and their purpose as related to the plant as a whole, before exploring the importance of the grape berry.

THE ROOT

The *root* of a grape consists of the following three parts.

■ *Shallow roots* absorb water and nutrients from the top soil. Those roots are not particularly strong and usually disappear during the plowing process. They then grow back the next season.

■ *Subterranean roots* enable the vine to firmly anchor in the soil and resist strong winds, such as those found in maritime areas (like vineyards by the Mediterranean Sea, Atlantic Ocean, and Pacific Ocean).

■ *Main roots* can go as deep as thirty feet (or six to seven meters). With a storage area for water, minerals, and carbohydrates, they act as the reserve section of the vine.

> The canopy is the leafy structure that constitutes the top and sides of the plant. The leaves serve not only as a barrier for bunches against both excessive water and over-exposure to the strong midday sun but also to ensure the necessary photosynthesis.

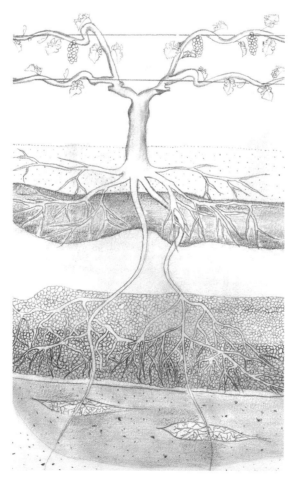

Figure 2.7.
Soil and subsoil.

THE TRUNK

Starting from the ground and going up to the first spurs, the *trunk* brings support to the vine and is the highway from the roots to the canopy for all nutrients needed for vine growth. Some trunks are kept deliberately short (such as in the Commonwealth of Independent States where the vines need to be buried in the soil during winter), while others are pruned and left to grow until they are as high as six-and-a-half feet (or two meters) in the style of a pergola (such as in Italy and Japan). The trunk supports the grape bunches, as well as the leaves and tendrils needed by the vine to attach itself to the wires of the optional training system. Training systems are described in detail on page 23.

THE SPURS AND CANES

The *spurs* and *canes* form the canopy, together with vine leaves. Spurs are shortened canes, while canes are shoots that have changed color (this usually happens in August in the northern hemisphere). Canes become spurs when less than five buds are left, yet remain canes if between five and sixteen buds are left on. The size and the number of canes determine the extent of pruning.

THE SHOOT

The *shoot* consists of the stem, the petiole (leaf stalk that links leaves to the trunk), the leaves, the tendrils (a thread-like growth used for climbing or support), the internode (the part of the stem between two nodes), the node (the part of the stem from which leaves or branches emerge), and the shoot tip at the end of the shoot itself.

THE GRAPE BERRY

The berry consists of several parts, as below:

■ The *pedicel* is the part of the stem that keeps the berry attached to the bunch. It carries the water and nutrients necessary for the ripening of the grape, and contains polyphenols (also called phenolic compounds) such as tannins.

■ The *brush* is the prolongation of the stem inside the berry. It keeps the seeds together.

■ The *pericarp* consists of the skin and pulp. The skin is also called the *exocarp*, and is composed of cuticle, epidermis, and hypodermis. It contains about fifteen percent of the polyphenols and anthocyan pigments, which give color to red or rosé wines. On the outside surface of the grape is a white pellicle called the *bloom*, which carries some of the yeast needed to start fermentation.

■ The *pulp* (also called flesh) contains 70 percent of the grape's sugar and half the acidity of the grape.

■ The *seeds* contain the embryo and endosperm, and are also the main source of bitter tannins. During maceration (a stage of the fermentation process), these seeds are released at high doses in red wine, but at minute doses in white wine.

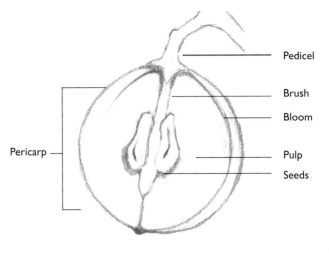

Figure 2.8. The grape berry.

Choosing a Grape to Grow

Most commercial grape vines (*Vitis vinifera*) are hermaphrodite plants, meaning they generate both male and female flowers for cross-pollination. When selecting the grape, the viticulturist will take the following factors into consideration.

■ Local practices and traditions.

■ Expected yield and character of the wine.

■ Quality expected from the harvest.

■ Resistance to disease and fungus.

■ Budding and ripening times.

■ Local rules and regulations, where applicable.

■ Recommendations for grapes in the region.

■ Local climatic conditions.

■ Location of the vineyard.

■ Marketability or popularity of particular grapes.

It is also extremely important to select disease-resistant rootstocks. In the 1990s, some Californian growers planted French clones, only to uproot them three years later when they realized these particular roots were prone to, and affected by, phylloxera. (See page 25 for more information on these insects.)

Plantation and Maturation of the Vine

Once the soil is appropriately prepared and fertilized, planting can take place. The first harvest does not take place until three or four years after the initial planting. During this period, the plants mature and develop sufficient vigor so as to be able to support bunch weight. Successive development steps of the vine and different training options are explored in the following pages.

Figure 2.9. Planting young vine scions in a nursery. Champagne, France.

Figure 2.10. Inflorescence of a Cabernet Sauvignon vine.

Figure 2.11. On a Chardonnay vine, the flower fades and berries appear. Jixian County, Tianjin, China.

VERAISON

Veraison is the stage in which grapes begin to ripen and acquire their final color. Black grapes change from green to black, and white grapes from green to yellow. Acidity levels decrease substantially, and sugar levels rise. Ripeness is achieved when desired sugar levels are reached, and the phenolic compounds (anthocyanins and tannins contained in the skin and seeds) have achieved maturity.

Figure 2.12. Pinot Gris grapes during veraison at the Paul Blanck vineyards. Schlossberg, Kientzheim, Alsace, France.

BUDBREAK

Around early April in the northern hemisphere and September in the southern hemisphere, a leaf bud grows from a node. This new bud opens up, exposing small bunches of flower buds.

FLOWERING

When flowers—also called *inflorescence*—appear, the next one hundred days will see further stages of development until the grapes reach maturity. Depending on pollination rates, between 10 percent and 50 percent of the flowers will yield grape berries.

HARVESTING

After considering grape variety, slope angle, and the location of the vineyard, grape growers decide between mechanical and hand harvesting. Chardonnay, for example, is better suited to mechanical harvesting than Pinot Noir. In Côtes du Rhône, the slopes are so steep that it would be impossible to machine harvest. In Champagne, where it is only permissible to harvest and press whole bunches, it is not possible to use a machine, as this process harvests individual grapes rather than whole bunches. However, harvesting by machine costs around one-third of doing the same job by hand.

Figure 2.13. Harvesting by hand. Vaud, Switzerland.

PRUNING

Pruning the vine refers to the process of cutting back spurs or canes. Whether or not to prune depends on the viticulturist's point of view, as well as the traditions and common practices of individual regions. Pruning begins after the leaves have fallen off, which usually occurs at the first frost. The objective of pruning is to guarantee a uniform shape of plants throughout the vineyard, and to increase the size and quality of berries by limiting the yield. Pruning is most often done by hand: it is only since the 1960s that mechanical pruning has appeared in large vineyards, particularly in Australia and the United States.

TRAINING SYSTEMS

Training systems consist of steel wires stretched between wooden or galvanized steel poles. Training the vine helps it to grow at a controlled pace and in a controlled direction. The vine uses its tendrils to attach itself to the wires. The training system chosen by the viticulturist depends on a number of factors such as the availability of qualified manpower, type of grape, prevailing climatic conditions, soil composition, cost, and whether the grapes will be harvested by hand or mechanically.

Guyot

Introduced in the nineteenth century by Dr. Jules Guyot, this training system relies on poles planted in the soil at the end of each row of vines. Wires are tied onto the poles at regular intervals, with the lowest one at sixteen inches (or forty centimeters) high. The vine relies on its tendrils to attach itself to these wires. Generally speaking, only one shoot is left to grow along the lowest wire. This shoot generates five to six nodes which then grow upwards. Two other spurs are trained upwards, and do not generate further shoots during the growing period.

This system is used all over Europe and found in some of the vineyards of Austria, Germany, Spain, Italy, Champagne, Loire Valley, Alsace, Burgundy, and the Rhône Valley. It allows an accurate control of yield.

Goblet

The oldest training system in the world, the goblet method keeps the trunk short, while the three

remaining spurs are trained low, creating a free-standing vine with low yields but good quality fruit. This system is also called the bush vine method, and is best suited to vines growing only limited foliage in drier climates.

The goblet system was used by the ancient Greeks and Romans. Its geographic spread includes Spain, Apulia, Sicily, Beaujolais, Côtes du Rhône, and the South of France.

Figure 2.14. Guyot training. Champagne, France.

Cordon

The favored method to train vines in the New World is cordon training. It is similar to Guyot in that it relies on wires, but instead of two spurs and one shoot being trained along the wires, only one spur emerges from the trunk. This system lends itself to mechanical pruning and harvesting.

This system is used extensively in South Africa, Australia, New Zealand, North and South America, and some parts of Europe (such as Burgundy). Some variations exist, such as cordon de Royat and the vertical cordon.

Pergola

Found in Japan and in some parts of Italy such as Abruzzo, Alto-Adige, Latium, Molise, Puglia, Trentino, and Valpolicella, the pergola system allows the vine to grow up to a certain height. It is then trained along a wire trellis. Harvest is less arduous because pickers do not have to bend their backs. In some regions, such as Abruzzo, the adoption of the pergola training system has resulted in greatly improved grape quality.

Trellis

Commonly found in Australia, the trellis training system relies on two horizontal cordons that take the shape of the letter "T." The system is convenient for mechanical pruning and harvesting, for the production of high-volume wines.

Pendelbogen

In this system, the vines are head-trained, or trained without the use of a trellis. They are cane-pruned on two trunks and vertically positioned in an arch, rather than being trained horizontally. The Pendelgoben system, also called the arch-cane system, is a variation of the Guyot system, and can be found in Germany and New Zealand.

Lyre

The Lyre system, also called the Geneva Double Curtain, is used in selected vineyards of Bordeaux, and enables a canopy that has been divided into two sections to receive more sunshine. It appears as a "Y" shape during the growing season. The Lyre system is now being introduced in the New World, and lends itself to mechanical pruning and harvesting.

Figure 2.15. Spraying vineyards with nutrients. Champagne, France.

Fertilization

To replace the nutrients and minerals absorbed by the vine during growth periods, fertilization is not only recommended but usually highly necessary. Commercial fertilizers with various compositions can be found readily, but organic fertilization is slowly becoming a trend, seeking as it does to replenish the soil with natural components, rather than adding chemical products.

Sustainable viticultural practices, to prevent soil erosion and degradation of the environment, are also becoming the norm. This can be achieved through the use of organic fertilizers, greatly reduced use of herbicides and fungicides, and the growth of secondary crops (such as mustard or simply grass) between the rows of vine to enhance soil fertility.

Irrigation

In some warm and dry countries, where rainfall occurs only during winter, irrigation is needed. Flood irrigation is used in Argentina, where water coming from the Andes mountain range literally floods the vineyards. In countries where water is precious, such as Israel and Australia, drip irrigation is used. The sprinkler method is efficient in California to counteract the effects of regularly occurring droughts. In Europe, irrigation is rarely necessary, and in any event is largely forbidden except around the Mediterranean Sea. The need for irrigation is largely dependent on the capacity of the soil to store water over a long period.

Crop Thinning

According to the desired quality and quantity of wine, crops may need to be thinned during veraison. This allows the remaining grapes to mature faster and better, and to achieve higher sugar content and optimal aromatic character.

Bordeaux viticulturists manage many châteaux estates in this way, since the chief objective is to obtain top-quality grapes with a maximum degree of ripeness, and thus the potential to yield expensive wines.

Insects, Pests, and Fungal Diseases

The grape vine, just like most other plants, is prone to be attacked by bacteria, fungi, and viruses, as well as by pests and insects. Only the most significant in terms of economic impact are described here.

PHYLLOXERA

Of all the disasters that can affect the vine, *phylloxera* is probably the most destructive. The *Phylloxera vastatrix*, as it is known in Latin, is an insect that attacks the roots of the vine and can completely destroy the plant within just three or four years. It is also commonly known as grape louse.

Although original American vine rootstock is resistant to this insect, the European *Vitis vinifera* is not. Almost every European vineyard was destroyed by phylloxera during the last quarter of the nineteenth century. The first infected vine was reported in 1866 in the South of France. It took ten years to find a remedy, which was to graft scions (vine shoots) onto imported American rootstocks. (Ironically, it is likely that the insect arrived from the United States.)

Although the disease has been studied for more than a century, plantings of Burgundian Chardonnay seedlings in California in the 1980s had to be uprooted a few years later after phylloxera began to attack them. A new emphasis has subsequently been placed on clonal selection, including the study of clonal resistance to various diseases and fungi. Chile, Argentina, Australia, and several other countries with strict quarantine laws are free of the insect.

DOWNY MILDEW

Downy mildew is a significant fungal disease introduced to Europe when phylloxera-resistant American rootstocks were imported at the end of the eighteenth century. It is prevalent in climates characterized by warm and humid summers. The fungus affects photosynthesis, hindering the ripening process by reducing the amount of carbohydrates reaching the grapes. Copper spraying can treat affected vines. Some areas are free of downy mildew, such as northern Chile and California, and German scientists are now introducing clones which are resistant to the fungus.

POWDERY MILDEW

Powdery mildew, also known as *oïdium*, was discovered during the first part of the nineteenth century in Europe. The name of this fungus reflects the fact that it appears in the form of powder. It spreads over buds, leaves, and berries. It is inhibited by sunlight, but the most effective method of control is the spraying of sulphur, either as powder or in liquid form. Another method is planting rose bushes at the beginning of the vine row to detect the appearance of the fungi, because it attacks rose plants before attacking the vines.

Figure 2.16.
Rose bushes planted to detect oïdium. Alsace, France.

PIERCE'S DISEASE

A bacteria mostly affecting vines in North and Central America, *Pierce's disease* spreads rapidly and is transmitted from vine to vine by an insect called the sharpshooter. When attacked by Pierce's disease, a vineyard can disappear in as little as one year.

BOTRYTIS

The *botrytis fungus* causes bunches to rot, but affects vines in two distinct ways. It can create *noble rot*, which leads to sumptuous sweet white wines such as Château d'Yquem and other botrytized wines, or it can develop into *grey rot*, which significantly reduces yield. It is know as *Botrytis cinerea* in Latin.

Other related diseases will be discussed in subsequent chapters. There are also some animals, as well as most birds, that can cause substantial damage to vines. In some countries, nets are spread over the vines close to the time of harvest to prevent birds from not only eating the grapes, but from damaging bunches and spreading rot and disease. Boars, rabbits, deer, kangaroos, squirrels, and various other rodents are also known to cause damage in the vineyard. Although some of the discussed problems can become unavoidable, it is important to be aware of all the possible disease and damage that can occur in the vineyard in order to protect the grapes.

Figure 2.17. Harvesting by hand. Champagne, France.

Harvesting

Harvest time is the pinnacle of the grape-growing season. It is the sum of a whole year's work, and is usually an occasion to celebrate. The folklore and traditions associated with harvest give rhythm to the life of many grape-growing villages.

THE TIME OF THE HARVEST

The point at which the harvest occurs is critical to the quality of the resulting wine. Ripeness of the grapes and must weight are balanced with acidity and tannins. Must weight is calculated with a *refractometer*, which measures the concentration of sugar in the unfermented grape juice. Depending on the region, it expresses the measurement in degrees Baumé, Brix, or Balling. The Baumé scale gives the easiest indication of potential resulting alcohol level, as one degree in the must usually yields one percent of alcohol in the wine after fermentation. Some grapes, such as Pinot Noir and Chardonnay, are harvested before full ripeness for the elaboration of Champagne and other sparkling wines, because the wines would taste dull and flat if not for a certain degree of acidity.

In the northern hemisphere, harvest time varies according to grape variety and growing location. Early ripening varieties harvest in July; late-ripening varieties grown in the extreme southern vineyards of Sicily harvest in November; and ice wine, called *eiswein* in

Figure 2.18. Checking grape ripeness with a refractometer.

HARVESTING
BY HAND OR MACHINE

Harvesting by hand is labor intensive and thus expensive. Yet it can be unavoidable in vineyards in which the terrain is unsuitable for the passage of machines. Two such areas are Côte Rôtie in France's Rhône Valley and the Mosel terraces in Germany. In addition, some vineyards do not harvest all the grapes at the same time. At Château d'Yquem, for example, pickers must go over the same area more than once because botrytis affects the ripening of the grapes in a very uneven way.

Mechanical harvesting speed is three to five times more efficient than hand-picking. However, it needs to be carried out carefully to prevent damaging the vines and ensure that too much of the canopy is not harvested along with the grapes. Too much canopy may give grassy overtones to a wine's flavor.

Germany and other German-speaking countries, harvests in January. In the southern hemisphere, harvest begins in January in the Canberra district of Australia, while starting as late as March in southern New Zealand.

Prevailing temperatures influence the harvest's time of day. In some warm-climate countries such as Australia, harvest takes place at night to prevent spontaneous fermentation before the grapes reach the winery. In countries where grapes are moved over long distances from vineyard to winery, they are transported in refrigerated trucks for the same reason.

Viticulture and Climate

In 1944, the University of California at Davis' Professors A. J. Winkler and M. Amerine devised a heat summation method that classifies the wine-growing sites in California. It divides the California vineyards into five regions that are based on climate, rather than specific geographic areas. This breakdown assumes a grape-growing season of seven months, and records the number

Figure 2.19.
Sorting of grapes during harvest by hand.

California Wine Regions

The wine-producing areas of California are broken into five different regions, as determined by University of California at Davis' Professors A. J. Winkler and M. Amerine. These regions were divided based on their numbers of heat degree days, an interval of twenty-four hours when the temperature rises above the lower threshold by one degree.

■ Region I has less than 2,500°F (or 1,372°C) heat degree days.

■ Region II has between 2,500°F and 3,000°F (or 1,372°C to 1,648°C) heat degree days.

■ Region III has between 3,000°F and 3,500°F (or 1,649°C to 1,926°C) heat degree days.

■ Region IV has between 3,500°F and 4,000°F (or 1,927°C to 2,205°C) heat degree days.

■ Region V has more than 4,000°F (or 2,205°C) heat degree days.

Australian Wine Regions

Australia is divided into five regions. Based on the areas climates, the regions are described by the type of wine for which their grapes are best suited. (The exception to this is Region V, which grows grapes that are usually reserved for raisins.)

■ Region I: sparkling, white, red.
■ Region II: white, red, brandy.
■ Region III: white, red, brandy, dessert wine.
■ Region IV: table wine.
■ Region V: raisins.

of heat degree days for each region. A *heat degree day* is an interval of twenty-four hours when the temperature rises above the lower threshold by one degree. For example, if the vine lower developmental threshold is 50°F (or 10°C) and the temperature remains at 51.8°F (or 11°C) for twenty-four hours, one heat degree day is recorded. It also takes into account average maximum temperature during each month, and classifies the regions from the coolest (Region I) to the warmest (Region V). See the inset above for a breakdown of heat degree days per region.

The method proposed is an extension and refinement of that introduced by France's Professor A. P. de Candolle in the middle of the nineteenth century. This was based on the identical assumption that the life cycle of a vine starts at 50°F (or 10°C). While the Winkler scale applies to California, and the Candolle scale to France, Drs. Smart, Dry, and Gladstone have further refined the concept and produced a method specific to Australia. It asserts that different regions are suitable for the production of different types of grapes and wines. See the inset above for a breakdown of this division.

Viticulture: Current and Future Practices

Every major wine-producing country boasts a leading university with a department dedicated to the study of viticulture and oenology. Among the most important are the University of California at Davis (United States), University of Bordeaux (France), Centre for Viticulture and Oenology at Lincoln University in Canterbury (New Zealand), University of Adelaide, Department of Horticulture, Viticulture & Oenology (Australia), University of Stellenbosch, Department of Viticulture and Oenology (South Africa), and Institut Jules Guyot, Université de Bourgogne (Dijon, France).

These universities compete through research for advancements in viticultural and vinification practices. Biodynamic, organic, and sustainable viticulture; the selection of suitable clones; and climatic impact on vineyards are the principal areas of research today.

BIODYNAMIC VITICULTURE

Biodynamic viticulture focuses on reconnecting the vine and the soil with the ecosystem, taking into account not only the intrinsic need of the soil for nutrients, but also the influence of the planets and the moon on bio-cycles. Demeter, an international bio-dynamics organization, has surfaced in the last few years and seems to be growing in terms of its influence on top producers worldwide.

ORGANIC VITICULTURE

Organic viticulture emphasizes the need to reduce dependency of the vineyard on chemical pesticides and fertilizers—with a goal of eventually eliminating their use. The use of natural fertilizers such as manure and compost for three to five years earns a vineyard and its resulting wine "organic" status. The other objective of organic viticulture is to achieve a balance between pests and predators, as mentioned earlier in this chapter.

SUSTAINABLE VITICULTURE

Sustainable viticultural practices are based on a sense of social responsibility. In effect, such practices replace the profit-at-all-costs race with objectives that embrace both the environment and a more hedonistic approach to business practice. Ultimately, sustainable practices, not only in the wine industry but in all business sectors, could provide proponents with a distinct competitive advantage in the future.

CLONAL SELECTION

Cloning and clonal selection have become critically important since the phylloxera disaster in California (at the end of the 1980s through to the mid-1990s). Based on advice from leading research institutes, Californian viticulturists planted French clones that were not grafted onto American rootstocks. The results were devastating: a quarter of Californian vineyards were attacked by phylloxera, and had to be uprooted and replanted. Millions of dollars were lost and wine production decreased, or stopped, for at least five years.

(There were two years of decreased production before the vineyards were replanted. Then, another three years passed before a harvest was possible again.)

Figure 2.20. Protecting vineyards from spring frosts by sprinklers. Champagne, France.

CLIMATIC IMPACT IN THE VINEYARD

Cold weather, such as spring frosts, may cause a substantial lowering of yields. The search of vine clones which show more resistance to such adverse weather conditions has been a leading source of inspiration for researchers in nurseries.

Summary

In recent years, much progress has been made in the vineyard. This is largely a result of intensive research and experimentation carried out at top research institutes. Particularly in the New World, soils and grape varieties are better matched, clonal selection is better adapted to local prevailing climatic conditions, and the pruning and training of vines is performed more professionally. Yields were brought down and quality was improved.

Many vineyards strive for more professionalism in their management, with an orientation towards organic and bio-dynamic viticulture. As of now, traditional viticulture practices cannot be entirely replaced by more environment-friendly ones, but they are slowly becoming more acceptable and even desirable. There are also major moves being made toward improved conditions at harvest—riper grapes and more careful sorting before fermentation. The delivery of riper grapes immediately after harvest goes a long way to ensuring that the next step—the winemaking—can be conducted with optimum raw material.

Figure 2.21. Furnaces prevent spring frosts from affecting vineyards.

3.
Wine Production

Vinification, or winemaking, is a term which refers to all the activities pertaining to the transformation of grapes into wine, from the moment the grapes are brought to the winery until the wine is bottled. Winemaking is different for each type and style of wine, and the vinification process for each is discussed below.

Fermentation

Fermentation is one of the most important steps of changing grape juice into wine. Missing it affects the whole harvest. On the other hand, controlling it and bringing it to a successful completion yields rewards of a wonderful nature: quality wine, ready to mature further and become iconic wines in some cases.

However, fermentation is both a simple yet complex process. Cheese, breads, and beers are results of fermentation. In the case of wine, several factors influence the conduct of the fermentation: yeasts, sugar content of must, temperature, vessel or container, and duration. Sometimes, the initial fermentation is followed by a second one—malolactic fermentation. This is discussed on page 32.

ALCOHOLIC FERMENTATION

Grapes are able to be transformed into wine because of a process called *alcoholic fermentation*. The sugars contained in grape juice react with

Figure 3.1. Winery built in a circular shape. Maison Louis Jadot, Beaune, Burgundy, France.

yeasts that are either naturally occurring on skins or added after pressing. The combination of sugar with yeast under carefully controlled conditions triggers a rise in temperature and an organic change that results in the production of alcohol and carbon dioxide (CO_2). French scientist and scholar Louis Pasteur discovered the mechanisms of alcoholic fermentation around 1863, although he was unable to fully explain the process.

The basic formula of alcoholic fermentation is: SUGAR + YEAST = ALCOHOL + CO_2. Gay-Lussac, a French scientist who lived across the eighteenth and nineteenth centuries, was the first to propose this chemical equation formula, although the process was well known by then.

During the fermentation process, yeasts—the most common being *Saccharomyces cerevisiae*—supply the necessary energy. The material is supplied by the sugars, which consist of fructose, glucose, pentose, and sucrose. The transformation of sugars into alcohol happens at a temperature between 50 °F and 90 °F (or

Figure 3.2. Typical stainless steel, thermo-regulated fermentation tank.

10°C to 32°C). Below 50°F (or 10°C), it is impossible for fermentation to begin. Above 100.4°F (or 38°C), the yeasts are destroyed.

Sugar

All grapes contain the natural sugars fructose and glucose. Total sugar content of the grape is called its *must weight*. The higher the must weight, the higher the potential final alcohol content of the wine.

Sugar content deficiency can result from insufficient sunshine exposure or excessive rain. *Chaptalisation*—the addition of sugar—may be permitted if this must weight is too low. The added sugar should be in the form of unfermented and concentrated grape juice, as opposed to raw sugar such as cane sugar. This practice is discouraged in Europe because chaptalisation often produces wines of a poor quality—which is unnecessary because of the area's huge wine-production surplus.

Yeast

Naturally present in small quantities in the ambient air around the vineyard and in the winery, wild yeasts in the form of grape *bloom* (the whitish covering on grape skin) cause alcoholic fermentation to begin. On the other hand, cultured yeast, also called wine yeast, is specially manufactured for a specific type of alcoholic fermentation, and enables the winemaker to have more control over the process.

Alcohol

Ethanol (commonly known as alcohol) is a by-product of alcoholic fermentation. It is an important element in finished wine, for it provides not only structure and *body*—weight—but also contributes to the dissemination of aromas in the air. In wine, alcoholic strength varies from 8 percent or 9 percent in very light white wines to 24 percent in some Oloroso sherries. Higher alcohol levels are the result of either *fortification*—addition of brandy to fermented grape juice in wines such as port; or *distillation*—extraction of alcohol obtained by heating the fermented grape juice.

Carbon Dioxide

Along with alcohol, carbon dioxide (CO_2) is a by-product of fermentation. Winery workers are urged to exercise caution while working above fermentation vessels, because excessive absorption of CO_2 can result in suffocation and asphyxia. Carbon dioxide can be seen as the small bubbles present in sparkling wine. CO_2 can also be used for a process called *carbonic maceration,* an alternate fermentation technique. In this process, red grapes are left for a period from one to three weeks in a container saturated with CO_2. This causes small-scale fermentation in each grape berry, which results in an excellent extraction of coloring agents and flavor compounds, as well as a substantial decrease of malic acid (a naturally occurring grape acid).

Heat

Another by-product of alcoholic fermentation is heat. It is not unusual to see some red wine alcoholic fermentation reach up to 96.8°F or (or 36°C). The fermenting liquid may even appear to be boiling.

MALOLACTIC FERMENTATION

Most wines also go through a second fermentation, called *malolactic fermentation* (also called *malo* or *MLF*). This occurs either after or at the same time as the alcoholic fermentation. Malolactic fermentation adds character and flavor and produces CO_2, which escapes into the air. It also decreases the amount of tart malic acid by converting it into the smoother-tasting lactic acid. The process occurs at temperatures of 86°F to 104°F (or 30°C to 40°C), and serves to both stabi-

Figure 3.3.
Red wine bubbling during alcoholic fermentation. Penfolds winery, Adelaide, South Australia.

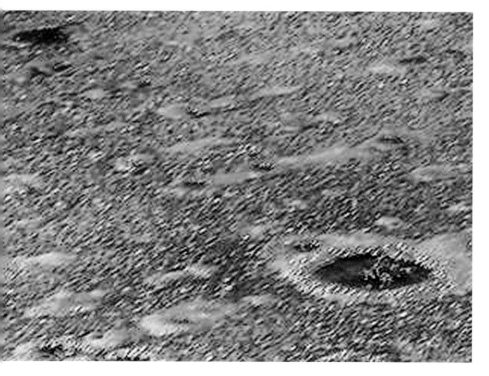

lize the wine and restrict malolactic fermentation inside the bottle at a later stage.

Malolactic fermentation is particularly recommended for both red and white wines in cold-climate countries because the cold allows only borderline maturity to be achieved by the grapes at harvest time. On the other hand, malo is sometimes avoided in warm and dry countries to conserve as much natural grape acidity as possible.

DRY WHITE WINES

Most white wines are made from white grapes. After the grapes are gathered, there are numerous steps to be taken before the wine is ready for sale. These steps are listed here. They are then explained in detail in the following sections.

1. White grapes arrive at the winery.

2. White grapes are crushed and de-stemmed in the same operation.

3. Sulphur dioxide (a preservative and disinfectant) and yeast (to start fermentation at the desired temperature) are added to the grapes.

4. Any juice that is running free of the grapes is separated. Then, the remaining grapes are pressed, generating the must (the liquid) and the pomace (the solid).

5. The free-run juice undergoes chilling, settling, racking, clarification, and yeast addition.

6. Alcoholic fermentation occurs.

7. Malolactic fermentation may occur.

8. The wine may be left in contact with the lees.

9. The wine is racked.

10. The wine is blended.

11. The wine is stabilized.

12. The wine is filtrated.

13. The wine is bottled and aged.

The Arrival of the Grapes

Grapes arrive at the winery in various containers, which are chosen based on the country, region, variety, and desired outcome of wine quality. Table-wine grapes are transported by the truckload, whereas fine-wine grapes are delicately laid down in small baskets. In warm-climate countries, grapes are harvested at night and transported to the winery in refrigerated trucks to prevent oxidation.

Figure 3.4.
Grapes are transported by truckload in Vaud wine region, Switzerland.

Crushing and De-Stemming the Grapes

In French, the process of crushing the grapes is referred to as *foulage*. It ensures a quick liberation of the juices contained in the grape, and a consequently rapid start to the fermentation process. *De-stemming* removes the stems from the grapes. In modern wineries, crushing and de-stemming are done simultaneously by the same machine, called a *crusher-de-stemmer*. Sometimes, though, the grapes are already de-stemmed by this point. If the vineyard is machine-harvested, for example, the stems stay on the vines, with only the berries finding their way to the winery.

Figure 3.5.
White grapes are crushed upon arrival at the winery. Vaud, Switzerland.

Adding Sulfur Dioxide

Sulfur dioxide is added to the grape juice to ensure a fast alcoholic fermentation. It kills bacteria, and also prevents spontaneous fermentation of residual sugars (in sweet wines) and oxidation.

About 1 percent of the general population and 5 percent of asthma sufferers are sulfite-sensitive. Therefore, most countries have specific rules regarding both the maximum amount of sulfur dioxide allowed per bottle and the declaration of its inclusion on the bottle's label. These regulations vary according to whether the wine is white, rosé, red, sparkling, or sweet. In the United States, most wine bottles contain sulfites, a fact that must be acknowledged on the label if the proportion is above ten parts per million (ppm).

The addition of sulfur dioxide can be avoided by heating the must to a temperature of 176 °F (80 °C). Some winemakers in the Rhône Valley, such as Château de Beaucastel, use this technique.

Pressing the Grapes

A machine called a *wine press* is used to crush the grapes, producing the must and pomace. The juice that runs freely from the crushed grapes (around 70 percent of the total juice) is called *free-run juice*. It is low in tannins and is the base for most wines. The additional juice obtained after pressing is called *press wine*. This juice has higher tannin content, and can be blended with the free-run juice to produce inexpensive wines. In top wine estates, however, the press wine is not used in the final product. Pressing can be done in horizontal and pneumatic (operated by compressed air) presses, as well as in more traditional vertical presses. In Champagne, France, the winemakers still use the traditional vertical basket press.

The Free-Run Juice

Winemakers then work with the free-run juice, which undergoes chilling, settling, racking, clarification, and yeast addition.

Chilling quickly lowers the temperature of the must to stabilize the liquid before fermentation begins. It also prevents spontaneous fermentation in hot winemaking regions, minimizes oxidation, and helps preserve the flavors and aroma compounds. *Settling* allows the sediment—particles suspended in the must that are also known as *colloidal elements*—to fall to the bottom of the tank. Only the top clear portion of the liquid is then transferred, by racking, to the fermentation vessel. *Racking* is the operation that drains the juice above the sediment level from a settling tank and transfers it to another tank, either for holding or processing. It is one of the grape must clarification processes. *Clarification* consists of separating solids from a particular liquid.

In years when the harvest produces a less than satisfactory must that lacks sugar concentration, it is possible to extract a certain amount of water from the must through reverse osmosis. This causes the must and sugars to become more concentrated, the color more enhanced, and the final wine more acceptable in terms of quality. The quantity, on the other hand, is somewhat reduced.

Alcoholic Fermentation

The alcoholic fermentation process (which was discussed in detail on page 31) of white wines usually takes place in stainless steel tanks, which keep oxygen at bay while preserving fruit aromas and natural acidity. These tanks are also used for

Before the invention of machines to both crush and de-stem the grapes, specialized personnel would tread on the grapes to crush them. This process is still seen in Douro, Portugal. Lagares—granite or concrete troughs—serve as containers where freshly harvested grapes are foot-trodden by teams of workers for up to twelve hours.

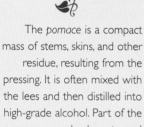

The *pomace* is a compact mass of stems, skins, and other residue, resulting from the pressing. It is often mixed with the lees and then distilled into high-grade alcohol. Part of the pomace may also be returned to the vineyard as fertilizer.

Figure 3.6.
Traditional vertical basket press in Champagne, France.

convenience, since stainless steel is much easier and more cost-effective to maintain than wooden barrels. There are, however, some countries and wine regions that use wooden barrels for the fermentation of their white wines.

Current trends dictate a cold fermentation for white wines to allow a slow transformation of the sugars and the maximization of fruit aromas. Cold fermentation is achieved by attaching chilling coils to the sides of stainless steel tanks.

Malolactic Fermentation

White wines produced in cold-climate regions are often put through malolactic fermentation. This process was discussed in detail on page 32.

Lees and Lees Stirring

Lees are the sediment present in wine after fermentation. They usually collect at the bottom of the barrel and are often made of dead yeast. Some winemakers choose to stir the lees approximately once a month to help develop and enhance flavor complexity. Stirring the lees also helps avoid a build-up of hydrogen sulfide, and limits the extraction of wood tannin and pigments.

Racking

Many producers consider *clarification*—the attempt to obtain a clear and transparent liquid by separating the liquid from the solid—a very important part of the winemaking process. The first step towards wine clarification is *racking*. During this process, the juice above the sediment that has settled at the bottom of the tank is removed and transferred to another tank.

Blending

Even single varietal wines are *blended* at some point. This encourages a quality consistency throughout a vintage, as the wines may come from different parcels and different tanks. On the other hand, several countries allow single varietal wines to have up to 15 percent of different grapes. In Bordeaux, most white wines are a classic blend of Sauvignon Blanc and Semillon. The New World, too, has experimented with all sorts of blends, such as the combination of Semillon and Chardonnay. The goal is a perfect balance of fruit, freshness, and crispness.

Stabilization and Fining

Winemakers stabilize wine to avoid structural and aromatic changes after bottling. Refrigeration and cold filtration are some of the methods used for this stabilization process, not only on a physical basis, but also microbiologically. Fining can also be considered as part of the stabilization process. Through this process, the wine is clarified through the addition of a coagulating agent. At the same time, particles are separated from and suspended in the wine. Fining agents are egg whites, bentonite clay, silica, kaolin, and charcoal. Charcoal is used in some purification processes, such as that leading to tasteless/odorless vodka. Some fine red wines, such as those from Bordeaux, undergo reduced stabilization and fining to retain the original structure and body envisioned by the winemaker—and, just as importantly, to maintain aging potential.

Filtering

To obtain perfectly clear wines, it may be necessary to filter them. This is done using machines equipped with membranes that retain impurities and other undesirable elements in the wine. Unfortunately, this action also removes some of the flavor compounds. As a result, filtered wines tend to be clean but lacking in aroma. Some winemakers choose not to filter at all, using only gravity and racking to eliminate the same suspended elements.

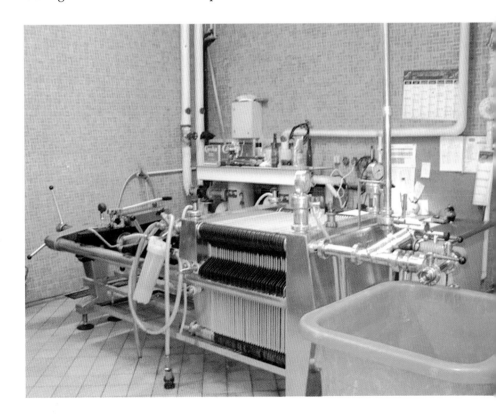

Figure 3.7.
A modern membrane wine-filtering machine mainly utilized for white wines. Cave Cooperative de Pfaffenheim, Alsace, France.

Figure 3.8. Quality control at the end of the bottling line. Dynasty Winery, Tianjin, China.

DRY RED WINES

Red wine is usually made from red or black grapes that retain their skins during the fermentation process. The length of time the skins are kept in contact with the grapes determines important qualities of the wine including color, flavor, and aroma. The steps taken to make dry red wines are listed here.

1. Grapes arrive at the winery.

2. At this point, the winemaker determines whether to de-stem the grapes or keep them as whole bunches. Steps 3 and 4 differ depending on which option is chosen.

If the winemaker proceeds by de-stemming the grapes, the following steps are then taken.

3. The grapes are crushed, and sulfur dioxide (SO_2) and yeast are added.

4. The grapes commence alcoholic fermentation. This stage usually occurs in closed barrels or tanks. Pumping-over is carried out to facilitate extraction of phenolic compounds and anthocyanins. At this point, the wine still contains the whole grapes.

If the winemaker is processing whole bunches of grapes, he proceeds with the following steps:

3. Without being crushed, the bunches undergo fermentation, with or without prior carbonic maceration. SO_2 and yeasts are added.

Bottling

The traditional bottling method relied on gravity and use of a flexible tube. Today's modern bottling plants use special equipment to guarantee a sterile and oxygen-free transfer of wine from barrel or maturation tank into the bottle. Although such equipment is rather costly, it guarantees nearly 100-percent absence of the defects that can occur due to the presence of oxygen or bacteria at the time of bottling.

Aging

The aging process occurs when the winemaker keeps the bottled wine at a controlled temperature for a certain period of time. During this process, the wine undergoes development before being released on the market. It loses a small proportion of its acidity and its tannins begin to soften. At the same time, its aromas continue to develop.

Using Black Grapes

The steps for making white wine from black grapes are the same as those explained for making white wine from white grapes, with one important difference: the process on arrival at the winery. With black grapes, the berries are rapidly processed and pressed without being crushed and de-stemmed, to ensure no coloration of the free-run juice by the anthocyanins. The best example of high-end white wine obtained from the vinification of black grapes is Champagne pressed from Pinot Noir (Blanc de Noirs).

Anthocyanins are antioxidant flavonoids found in grape skins. By leaving skins in contact with the juice for a prescribed length of time, red wines can achieve a deep color.

With the help of a pump, *pumping-over* moves the juice from the bottom of the fermentation tank to the top. This action ensures that grape skins are in constant contact with the juice, for maximum extraction of anthocyanins and other flavor compounds. Other means to achieve the same results are called *cap punching* or *cap immersion*: the cap, or the seeds and skin, must be constantly submerged in the fermenting juice.

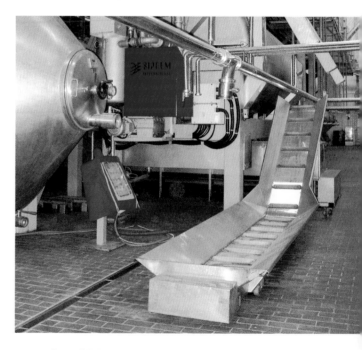

Figure 3.9. Pneumatic wine press at Dynasty Winery, Jixian County, China.

4. The bunches undergo alcoholic fermentation in open-top fermentation vessels. Juice is pumped over the stems and skins to increase extraction of phenolic compounds and anthocyanins. At this point, the wine contains not only the whole grapes, but also the stems.

Figure 3.10. Cabernet Sauvignon grapes and juice during alcoholic fermentation at Magill Estate, Penfolds Winery, Adelaide, South Australia.

The winemaker then moves onto the following steps, regardless of whether he chose the de-stemming or whole bunch option.

5. The grapes are pressed to separate the liquid and solid elements in the wine. The resulting grape residue is called *pomace*.

6. The juice is racked. Sediment contained in the wine forms a deposit at the bottom of the cask or barrel. Racking separates the clear wine from its lees (sediment). The lees become the basis for distillation of hard liquors, such as Marc de Bourgogne.

7. Malolactic fermentation is optional, but very suitable for overly acidic wines. The stronger malic acid is transformed into weaker lactic acid, and carbon dioxide is produced.

8. The winemaker decides whether or not to mature his product in wooden barrels (which are usually made of oak). This process is called *elevage*.

9. The wine is fined with either egg whites, bentonite (clay), activated carbon, copper, or iron to coagulate and precipitate the colloids (particles) in suspension in the wine.

10. If necessary, the wine is blended.

11. The last steps are clarification, bottling, and bottle aging.

Figure 3.12. A modern 10,000-bottle-per-hour bottling line in Dynasty Winery, Tianjin, China.

DRY ROSÉ WINES

Dry rosé wines, also called blush wines, are made in a very similar manner to dry red wines. The steps listed in the previous section remain the same, but the contact time between skins and juice is greatly reduced. This contact can be as short as one night for very pale pink wines (such as white Zinfandel), and up to three or four days for darker rosé wines such as Tavel, from Côtes du Rhône.

FORTIFIED AND NATURALLY SWEET WINES

For the vinification of fortified wines, the same procedures as listed for dry red wines are performed. At some point during the fermentation, however, a certain quantity of brandy at 77-per-

Figure 3.11. Two thousand French and Spanish oak barrels (59.44 gallons or 225 liters) in a cellar. Dynasty Winery, Tianjin, China.

Fortified wines show a higher sugar content because alcoholic fermentation is stopped before all the sugar has turned into alcohol. Sweetness of the final product may also result from the addition of sweetening agents such as mistella.

cent alcohol is added. This stops the alcoholic fermentation. As a result, some of the residual sugars are untransformed and serve as preservatives. At 17 to 22 percent, the alcohol content of the resulting beverage is higher. Port, vermouth, and sherry are fortified wines, as are Marsala, Malaga, and Madeira.

Naturally sweet wines (*vins doux naturels* or *VDN*) are vinified in the same way as fortified wines, except that the brandy added contains about 95-percent alcohol.

Figure 3.13. Sherry flor (film-forming yeast) at Magill, Penfolds Winery, Adelaide, South Australia.

SPARKLING WINES

To make sparkling wines, producers have the choice of four methods. The first and most expensive is known as the Traditional Method (called Méthode Champenoise in the Champagne region). It is expensive as well as time consuming because the second fermentation takes place within the bottles. The Transfer Method is more economical because wine is transferred to a tank after the second fermentation has taken place, prior to re-bottling. The Charmat Method costs even less because the second fermentation takes place in a tank rather than in the bottle. The fourth method is similar to the production of carbonated drinks. CO_2 (carbon dioxide) is simply injected into the base wine. This is the least expensive option. We will now explore these four methods in more detail.

For non-vintage Champagne (which reads NV its the label) or sparkling wine, base wines from the current vintage are blended with wines from other years. This helps to achieve a consistency of taste, acidity level, and olfactory characteristics, irrespective of the quality of a single vintage. This is called the *cuvée*.

Traditional Method

French law mandates that all sparkling wine from the region of Champagne (and, therefore, labeled "Champagne") be made using the Traditional Method. It is also used to produce sparkling wine in other regions. The first nine steps in the Traditional Method are the same as those undertaken in the elaboration of dry white wines. Once these first nine steps have been completed, winemakers proceed with the following to complete the production of sparkling wine or Champagne.

10. The sparkling wine is blended to establish the cuvée.

11. Yeast and sugar are added to the juice to provide material for the second fermentation.

12. Second fermentation takes place in the bottle.

13. Aging on lees, Champagne acquires its maturity and characteristic yeast-like smell. For this step, the lees are not stirred, allowing the wine to develop its flavoring compounds slowly and gently.

14. Yeasts and other sediments are brought to the neck by *riddling* the bottles either manually or by machine (called a gyro-palette). Riddling, known in French as *remuage*, consists of gently moving the bottle little by little until it is upside down. This causes all the sediment to gather in the neck of the bottle, rather than at its bottom.

Figure 3.14. A Champagne bottle held against a source of light, showing the accumulation of sediment in the neck of the bottle just before the operation of disgorgement.

15. The sediment is then frozen in the bottle's neck and disgorged, which means that the dead yeasts and other sediment in the neck of the bottle are removed. The wine then turns perfectly clear.

16. *Liqueur d'expédition,* or a dose of Champagne/sparkling wine liqueur, is added to the bottle. It determines the style of the wine, ranging from *extra-brut* (which contains less than 0.07 ounces, or 2 grams, of residual sugar per gallon, or liter) to *doux* (which contains around 1.76 ounces, or 50 grams, of residual sugar per gallon, or liter).

17. Lastly, the bottle is corked. The wine corks of sparkling wines are initially straight. They develop their mushroom shape over time, after being squeezed into the neck of the bottle.

Transfer Method

The process of making sparkling wines with the Transfer Method is very similar to the process for making Champagne or sparkling wine. It differs after the first twelve steps, as shown below.

13. After the second fermentation, the wine is transferred from the bottle to a tank for clarification, dosage, and re-bottling. This method avoids the cost-intensive method of riddling individual bottles.

Charmat Method

The Charmat Method for making sparkling wines is very similar to the Traditional Method. However, the second fermentation does not take place within the bottle, so only the first eleven steps of the Traditional Method are followed.

12. The wine is transferred to a pressure tank and undergoes second fermentation.

13. The wine is cooled down before being clarified. *Liqueur d'expédition* is added. The wine is then bottled.

Carbonated Wine

Inexpensive white, rosé, and red sparkling wines are produced using a different method. The carbon dioxide is injected into the drink, resulting in a simple, carbonated wine. Wine produced this way contains large bubbles (whereas small bubbles are deemed to reflect a higher-quality product) and does not contain yeast aromas.

Wine-Packing Methods

In France, each wine-producing region uses different types of bottles, from the long and narrow green or brown styles in Alsace to the shouldered shapes from Bordeaux. This system ensures immediate visual recognition of the wine. More importantly, the type of bottle found in each region is of the shape practical for the region's most popular wine.

There are three "classic" wine bottle shapes: the narrow Alsace or hock bottle, the Burgundy bottle which has sloped shoulders, and the Bordeaux or Claret bottle which has marked shoulders. The Bordeaux bottle's high shoulders are designed to partially retain the sediments traditionally found in aged wines from that region. On the other hand, Alsace wines are usually white and not aged long, so this type of shoulder is unnecessary. The standard bottle size adopted all over the world is 25.4 fluid ounces (or 75 centiliters).

The Australians have invested heavily in equipment to produce the "wine in the bag," a cardboard container lined with plastic and equipped with a spigot. Reserved for inexpensive wines and representing good value, this has become a hugely popular option for picnics and barbecues. Another advantage is that the collapse of the polymer bag inside the box, together with the spigot mechanism, prevents oxygen from entering the container even after it has been opened.

There are other new containers on the market as well. Some are made of aluminum and are similar to beer cans. Others are aluminum-lined Tetra Pak containers. These are commonly used for fruit juice and dairy products such as milk.

Corking and Other Wine Closure Systems

Traditional cork comes from the bark of specially raised oak trees. Until recently, this natural cork, mainly exported from Spain and Portugal, was

Disgorgement removes the dead yeasts and other sediments from the bottle's neck by first cooling down the wine to reduce pressure inside the bottle. Then, the neck of the bottle is plunged into a solution that freezes only the part of the liquid containing the sediments. The capsule is removed, and the frozen part ejects itself.

Liqueur d'expédition, also known as *liqueur de dosage* or *dosage,* is a small amount of sparkling wine mixed with sugar cane that is added to the wine to replace the small amount of wine lost from its disgorgement. It also helps determine whether the sparkling wine is dry or sweet.

the best material available for closing wine bottles. However, 2,4,6 trichloroanisole (TCA), a chemical compound found in traditional cork as well as a residue from the chlorine treatment that removes live material from inside the cork, can cause *cork taint*. Characterized by smells of decomposing wet cardboard, cork taint is the nightmare of sommeliers and wine stewards, and is estimated to occur in 5 to 7 percent of all wine bottles.

Another problem that can occur from the usage of natural corks is *cork shrinkage*. This generally occurs due to improper storage conditions, and can cause wine to either leak from the bottle or evaporate through the open space.

Because of cork taint and cork shrinkage, people have begun to look at other forms of bottle closures. There is the screwcap, which has eliminated the need for a corkscrew, as well as artificial corks made from silicone or other relatively supple plastics. Wine experts predict that the screwcap will take over from the cork. In New Zealand, for example, almost 95 percent of wines bottled are currently using screwcaps.

However, the Oeneo Group, a global supplier of barrels, natural cork, and cork-based wine closures, has built a plant in Spain that is equipped to remove certain chemical compounds from cork, particularly TCA. The plant became operational in 2005, and is the first battle in the cork war where leading suppliers fight for survival. This plant, and others like it, may encourage a return to the use of cork.

The art of winemaking is complex and requires specialized skills in the area of sensory evaluation, as well as knowledge of the intricacies of the chemical processes involved in the fermentation and maturation processes. Each wine, irrespective of its origin, represents hours of labor and monitoring in the winery, after which it can be bottled, labeled, and readied for shipment.

It is the responsibility of the winemaker to make the best use possible of the grapes when they arrive in the winery. To do so, he or she must balance knowledge accumulated possibly through generations with advantages of new technologies to produce a wine that will sell and satisfy the nose and palate of the consumer. In the wine market worldwide, there is a place for every type of wine, from those made in industrial quantity to those hand-crafted following traditional principles. However, what remains paramount to achieving the desired level of wine quality is the quality of the grapes, no matter which variety. Grape varieties are explored in the next section: their origins and history, as well as the best wines they are capable of generating.

There is a new product available on the market that claims to remove a great part (if not all) of cork taint from a corked wine. It is a plastic grape bunch that is placed directly in the wine. However, its efficiency has been demonstrated only on wines mildly affected by cork taint.

Figure 3.15. Bark of an oak tree from which oak corks have been carved. Museum of Wine, Macau, China.

PART 2

Grapes
of
The World

4.
Grape Classification

Famous French ampelographer Pierre Galet suggests that there are close to 10,000 grape varieties worldwide. This number is quite intimidating, and the overwhelming size of the topic as a whole can make it difficult to remember even a few. But the topic can be narrowed into the popular handful with which most wine consumers are familiar. The next two chapters will examine these varieties. First, you will read about the various ways these grapes are categorized and described in these later chapters.

Introduction

Each grape description in the following chapters begins with introductory information about the individual grape on which the section is based. This will include an explanation of the grape's importance, the regions in which the grape is most popular, significant wines in which the grape can be found, and any alternate names by which the grape is known, as well as other relevant information on the grape. Descriptions of the grape's clones will also be found in this section.

IDENTIFYING GRAPE CLONES

Some grape varieties have a tendency to mutate into a plant that is related to the original but has different characteristics. The resulting grapes are called *clones*. Usually, each clone of a grape is assigned a number by which to differentiate it from the grape's other clones.

An example is the Pinot Noir grape. According to Pierre Galet, author of *Dictionnaire Encyclopédique des Cépages* (*Encyclopaedic Dictionary of Wine Grapes*) and a well-known ampelographer, the Pinot Noir grape has about fifty clones which have received approval to be used for the production of wine in the Champagne region. One clone, number 115, covers 44 acres (or 18 hectares) in this region, and generates a medium-sized yield that results in wines of a very high quality. Other clones of Pinot Noir produce quantity over quality, thereby answering the needs of producers interested in a different, lesser type of wine.

Many clones are genetically reproduced in the nursery so as to generate uniformity across the vineyard in terms of plant characteristics. This process requires the hand of a specialist, who painstakingly reproduces the plant in terms of berry size, yield, color, and olfactory characteristics. On the other hand, some grapes naturally mutate in the vineyard. It is generally accepted that Pinot Gris is a natural mutation of Pinot Noir. In this case, the plant modifies its own genetic material. Pinot Noir produces only black grapes, whereas Pinot Gris yields bunches of grapes of both colors.

Clonal selection from among the many varieties is a very important topic for improvement in quality and productivity of vines. The variation of grape characteristics according to clonal selection includes a delay in the budding season to reduce exposure to spring frosts, a better *inflores-*

cence (or fruit set), and earlier ripening ability. Important work on grapes clones is taking place in research institutes and universities such as Cornell University, the University of California at Davis, and Australia's University of Adelaide. It is anticipated that the future holds great advances that will allow grape growers and winemakers across the world to select the most appropriate clones for their own soil, weather, and desired quality outcome.

RECOGNIZING DIFFERENT GRAPE NAMES

Many grapes that originated in a specific region or part of the world are now grown with much success in many more locations. Other grapes have been harvested in several areas for many thousands of years. As a result of the varied locations in which they can be found, most grapes are known by more than one name. Even within a single country, a grape may be known by different names from region to region—or within the same region. The most common names by which a grape is known are given in the introductory section.

Grape identification can be difficult because certain grape species can be quite similar to another. However, DNA fingerprinting (which is discussed below) often allows researchers to conclusively determine which grape names refer to the same grapes.

History

Some grapes have been around for thousands of years. Others were created more recently through cross pollination between two older grapes. There are also grapes of as-of-yet unknown origin. This section of the chart will include the available information on the history of the grape species.

Ampelography

Ampelography is the study and classification of wine-grape varieties. The word "ampelography" dates back thousands of years. It is a complex field, due to both grape cloning and the mutation of grapes in a natural, unsolicited manner. This ancient science of identifying grapevines by their physical characteristics is based on detailed hand drawings, and a comprehensive description of each grape and its foliage. More recently, DNA analysis, or genetic fingerprinting, has enhanced this science for the twenty-first century.

IDENTIFYING GRAPE SPECIES

Wine grapes almost all belong to one of two distinct groups: *Vitis vinifera* or *Vitis labrusca*. *Vitis vinifera* represents the largest group, and is used for the production of wine originating from Europe and the Middle East. The origin of *Vitis labrusca* grapes is the North American continent. During the period when Europe was experiencing devastation by phylloxera, disease-resistant *labrusca* rootstocks were grafted with *vinifera* species to replant vineyards.

Today, about 90 percent of grape plantings across the world are from the *Vitis vinifera* species, of which two distinct groups are found: *Vitis vinifera Linné*, which includes well-known grapes such as Chardonnay and Pinot Noir, and *Vitis silvestris Gmelin*, which groups together all the wild vines of Europe and Asia.

In this *Vitis vinifera Linné* species, the most popular grapes from which white wine is made are Chardonnay, Sauvignon Blanc, Riesling, Semillon, Pinot Gris, Pinot Blanc, Gewürztraminer, Melon de Bourgogne, Airén, Muscat Blanc, Muscat d'Alexandrie, and Ugni Blanc.

Among the *Vitis vinifera Linné* grapes that yield red wine, Cabernet Sauvignon, Merlot, Pinot Noir, Syrah, Carignan, Cinsaut, Sangiovese, Barbera, Malbec, Montepulciano, Grenache, Gamay, Cabernet Franc, and Tannat are the most popular. Each of these grapes has a good reputation across vineyards in both the Old and New Worlds.

GENETIC FINGERPRINTING

Today's ampelography is significantly enhanced by DNA fingerprinting. The University of California at Davis is credited with bringing these techniques to the wine world. The official recognition and categorization of most grapes is now determined on a proven scientific basis, as well as according to their adaptability and suitability to various climates, soils, and geographic locations. Consequently, viticulturists planting a vineyard today face a task that is far less a matter of trial and error than it was fifty years ago.

As the prices of certain wines skyrocketed in the last decade of the twentieth century, counterfeiters tried their hand at selling fake *grand crus* of Bordeaux. They also forged high-tier wines from Burgundy and Alsace. To combat this problem, the auction houses of Christie's and Sotheby's recognized a need to assess the contents of each bottle. Genetic fingerprinting, which allowed them to separate genuine wines from counterfeits, was the perfect solution. There are other techniques which can correctly identify grapes, but none that can do so with the accuracy of DNA fingerprinting.

Ideal Soil

There are nearly as many different types of soils as there are varieties of grapes. The most common differences between soils are related to their composition, mineral content, pH levels, and ability to drain.

Most grapes have a particular type of soil in which they are best suited to be grown. Others are more resilient to change and can be planted in a variety of soil types. Yet the type of soil in which a grape is grown can have a large effect on the characteristics of the grape and resulting wine. Soil type is part of an area's terroir, and is the reason why a grape grown in two different locations can produce two very different wines.

Climatic Conditions

An area's climatic conditions are another part of its terroir and an important consideration when local growers choose which grapes to grow. There are many factors that come into play: length of summer, arrival of spring frost, hours of daily sunlight, direct or indirect sunlight, and humidity are just a few. These factors influence the grapes that are grown in each area because each grape has specific requirements for proper growth.

Olfactory Characteristics

Wine enthusiasts consider a wine's olfactory characteristics, or smell, to be as important as the drink's taste. Its aromas offer insight into the wine itself, including its production and the grape varietals utilized. Therefore, wine growers and producers must consider the olfactory char-

acteristics of the grapes they are growing in order to produce a quality product.

The smells produced in a wine by a specific grape can vary depending on how the grape was grown, vinified, and aged. This section of the table will provide the most common olfactory characteristics of each grape.

Geographic Spread

Some grapes are cultivated in many regions around the world, while others tend to be grown in one or two countries. Information is given regarding those areas that have the most plantings of each grape. The importance of the grape to the country, the most popular types of wines produced from that varietal, and the specific regions in which the most important vineyards can be found are all explored in this section.

Conclusion

Grape variety is determined using the methods and observations explained in this chapter. In the next chapter, the most popular white wine grape varieties are examined in terms of their history, the best soils in which to grow them, their ampelography, and the best regions in which to grow them. These white wine grapes are Chardonnay, Sauvignon Blanc, Riesling, Semillon, Pinot Gris, Gewürztraminer, Ugni Blance, Sylvaner, Viognier, Chenin Blance, Muscat, Rkatsiteli, Marsanne, Roussanne, Malvasia, and Pinot Blanc.

The subject of the subsequent chapter is red wine grapes, also called black grapes. The red wine grapes presented are Pinot Noir, Cabernet Sauvignon, Merlot, Syrah, Sangiovese, Grenache, Tempranillo, Malbec, Carignan, Primitivo, Cabernet Franc, Petit Verdot, Nebbiolo, Pinotage, Cinsaut, Mourvèdre, Camenère, Tannat, and Touriga Nacional. Thorough study of Chapters 4 and 5 will allow your knowledge of wine grapes to expand exponentially as you read about each wine grape.

There are many different types of soil, including Sandy, chalk, limestone, marl, loam, gravel, clay, slate, and granite. A grape's characteristics are often dependent on the type of soil in which it is planted.

5.
White Wine Grapes

Starting dinner with a cool glass of white wine can be a serene experience. Yet there are as many types of wine to choose among as there are choices of dinner entrees. Should you serve glasses of Chablis, made from Chardonnay grapes, or pop open a bottle of Sancerre, made from Sauvignon Blanc? Both are white wines produced in France, but the two varieties are completely dissimilar in both aromatic characteristics and taste.

This chapter will introduce you to many of the most popular white grape varieties. The history and origin of each grape are explored, as well the region in which it thrives, its aromatic profile, and the best and most popular wines in which it can be found. Grape varieties are presented in order of recognized importance in the worldwide markets. Therefore, the most popular grapes that produce the most respected wines are described first. These are followed by grapes that are important in the wine market, but are either less well-known or less widely utilized in most common wines.

In some countries, notably areas of cooler climes such as Germany, Austria, Switzerland, and Canada, white represents the bulk of wine production. While the prevailing argument is that red wine is best when being utilized for good health, white wine has a well-deserved place in the taste spectrum. As a wine lover, it is important that you familiarize yourself with the following varieties.

Figure 5.1. Grand Cru Furtenstum vineyards, above Kientzheim, Alsace, France.

Chardonnay

Chardonnay is a white grape variety with compact clusters comprising small, spherical berries. When the berries mature, they turn yellow-amber in color. Chardonnay is a fine variety capable of producing very high-quality wines. It is also relatively delicate and, because of its thin-skinned berries, has a tendency to easily *oxidize*—combine with oxygen and lose its freshness.

The planted surface of each wine grape is recorded and ranked. Although it is ranked only forty-first and is found behind other white grape varieties such as Airen, Ugni Blanc, Chenin Blanc, and Riesling, Chardonnay has increased in popularity and availability to the point where it is almost generic. The grape can yield up to a very generous 5.93 tons per acre (or 80 hectoliters per hectare)—or even more when grown along a training method. (See Chapter 2 for more information on training systems.) At the same time, higher quality vines such as those from Burgundy, and its subregion Chablis, usually generate less than 2.6 tons per acre (or 35 hectoliters per hectare) when vines are trained low.

Chardonnay is grown on every continent and is considered, along with Pinot Noir, (a red grape variety described on page 85,) the best grape to reflect a wine's origin and that area's terroir. One of the three grapes used in Champagne produc-

Figure 5.2.
Chardonnay

tion (the others being Pinot Noir and Pinot Meunier), it also delivers extremely sophisticated and elegant Burgundy wines such as those from Meursault and Puligny-Montrachet.

The grape's popularity has grown since the 1970s, when Californian growers first managed to produce Chardonnay-based wines of consistently high quality year after year. Plantings of California Chardonnay had reached 56,600 acres (or 22,640 hectares) in 1991, up from 18,000 acres (or 7,200 hectares) in 1980. However, there is strong competition from other grapes, as evidenced by the later decrease of Chardonnay-based wines. In 1992, the grape variety represented 40 percent of top-selling wines in American restaurants—a figure reduced to just 20 percent by 2002.

Each of the thirty-four official French clones of Chardonnay produces its own distinctive set of aromas and flavors, which vary greatly according to account yield and quality expectations. Common Chardonnay clone varieties are 76, 95 (which is generally appreciated for its ability to produce on a consistent basis, richness in sugars, and excellent aromatic development), 96, and 277. In New Zealand, grape growers use the heavy-cropping clones 4 and 5, while Mendoza in Argentina prefers 6 for the generation of heavier fruit. Growers in the Russian River region of California use Hyde, Wente, and Sees clones, which all produce good yields while preserving their attractive fruit aromas.

> Terroir is a French word referring to a wine-growing area and its attributes which affect the resulting wine's quality. Although the precise importance of terroir has long been debated, there is growing recognition that certain combinations of these attributes can create an exceptional setting for the growing of extraordinary grapes.
>
> Sometimes a clone is given the name of the person who propagated it. In 1912, a member of the Wente family brought grape cuttings from France to plant in California. The use of that cutting spread far and wide, and the clone was later given the name Wente.

History

There seems to be a consensus of opinion that the name Chardonnay originated from either the Macon region in eastern France or from Lebanon, where the variety is often called Meroué or Obaideh. A village named Chardonnay is located at the heart of the Macon region, which is just below Burgundy in France, and supports the first assertion. However, some researchers claim that the name of the village appeared after that of the grape.

Historically, the name Chardonnay was first associated with grapes in 1330, when Cistercian monks cultivated this variety in Clos de Vougeot, a walled vineyard in Burgundy, France. The name "Chardonnay" can be found thereafter throughout historical literature.

Several researchers have associated the names Morillon and Feinburgunder with Chardonnay production in the Chablis region, as well as with the Chardonnay of Styria, a wine-producing region in the south of Austria. In France, particularly Burgundy, the same grape has been called Aubaine, Arnoison, Auvernat Blanc, Beaunois, Chardenet, Chaudenet, Epinette Blanche, Melon Blanc, Petite Sainte-Marie, Pineau Blanc, Pinot Blanc, and Weisser Clevner.

Ampelography

Described by many producers and winemakers as the "king" of white wine grapes, Chardonnay has long been thought to be a mutation of the Pinot grape, and is sometimes still called Pinot Chardonnay. In 1999, however, the University of California at Davis used DNA profiles to show that

Anything But Chardonnay

"ABC" stands for "Anything But Chardonnay," a dismissive statement often heard at cocktail parties, at banquets, and in restaurants. It illustrates the remarkable rise and fall of the most popular white grape in the world. In the 1980s and 1990s, many producers switched their white-grape production from more obscure varieties to Chardonnay in anticipation of a surge in demand. Yet they managed to not only satisfy the market, but

saturate it. Consumers became tired of being offered only Chardonnay and began asking for other varieties. Wine experts believe that the popularity of wine varieties are like those of other consumer products, in that they tend to rise upon discovery and promotion, and fade away when new wines surface. This is exemplified by the recent growth in popularity of white wines such as Pino Grigio, Viognier, and Sauvignon Blanc.

Chardonnay is in fact a cross between Gouais Blanc and a member of the Pinot family, most likely Pinot Noir. Gouais Blanc originates from Croatia, and was most probably imported by the Romans.

Ideal Soil

There are a myriad of soil types. The most common are alluvial, chalk, clay, granite, gravel, limestone, loess, marl, quartz, sand, schist, terra rossa, tuffeau, and volcanic. There are also many variations on these. For example, there are two types of limestone soils: white ones with a high chalk content that are found in Burgundy, and red ones with a high iron content that are found in Coonawarra. (This red soil is called terra rossa in South Australia.) Limestone soils, both white and red, assist in the production of elegant Chardonnay wines but only in cool climate areas. These soils are made of a harder material than chalk, and force the roots of the vines to go deeper to find water and nutrients. Which soil produces the best Chardonnay? In the case of the best Chardonnay in the world, Le Montrachet from the Côte de Beaune in Burgundy, France, soils show a predominantly limestone and chalk mineral content. Limestone soil drains better and is less fertile than the richer soils of marl and clay.

Climatic Conditions

Generally speaking, Chardonnay thrives in Regions I and II (region types were explained on page 28), because cool climates are more effective for the production of high-quality Chardonnay wines than warmer ones. Yet the grape ripens mid-season (from late September to early October) and can readily adapt to many different regions and soils. It is, however, susceptible to bunch rot.

Olfactory Characteristics

Primary aromas of the Chardonnay grape are easy to recognize, but less easy to characterize. They are first and foremost fruity, often bringing to mind apple (from green to Golden Delicious), melon, pineapple, pear, peach, apricot, and lemon and other citrus fruits. In some countries and terroirs, tropical fruits such as banana, mango, and kiwi may emerge. Depending on the extent of oak-barrel treatment, secondary aromas and flavors such as vanilla, caramel, toast, honey, cream-butter, and hazelnut are also found.

Wines from different regions exhibit different olfactory characters. Also, specific country styles such as crisp and flinty Chablis from France, or rich and buttery Chardonnay from California, tend to be subject to fashion. In 2006, global trends suggested a rediscovery of strong fruit aromas and varietal characteristics, as opposed to an emphasis on the influence of the winemaker during vinification. Sadly, the legacy of new oak and its vanilla overtones does remain popular, leading numerous winemakers to abandon wines which express terroir in favor of the fashion-driven product.

Geographic Spread

Total worldwide plantings of the Chardonnay grape were around 367,000 acres (or 149,550 hectares) in 2006. It can be found in Argentina, Australia, Austria, Bulgaria, Canada, Chile, England, France (Alsace, Ardèche, Burgundy, Chablis, Jura, Languedoc, Loire, Savoie, and Roussillon), Germany, Hungary, Italy, Lebanon, New Zealand, Portugal, Romania, Slovenia, South Africa, Spain, Switzerland, and the United States.

FRANCE

French Chardonnay plantings have grown from 17,950 acres (or 7,325 hectares) in 1958 to 86,050 acres (or 35,123 hectares) in 1999. Chardonnay from the Chablis region tends to be more acidic and crisp than when produced elsewhere. At the same time, Burgundy *premier crus,* or "first growths," generate outstanding wines that are capable of aging in years of good vintages. Some Burgundy *grand crus* ("great growths"), too, are extremely complex and sophisticated, reflecting the long-established mastering of Chardonnay growing and winemaking at its best. Some wines from exceptional vintages are known to keep their olfactory qualities for as long as thirty years after harvest. The best Burgundy wines based on the Chardonnay grape include the likes of Corton Charlemagne, Meursault, and the grand crus of Chablis. A breakdown of the French wine regions and their sizes in 2006 can be found in Table 5.1 on page 53.

Figure 5.3.
Vineyards in the village of Hautvillers, the final resting place of Dom Pérignon, the monk credited with inventing the second fermentation in the bottle. Champagne, France.

Champagne

In Champagne, Chardonnay vineyards are spread over 73,500 acres (or 30,000 hectares) between the cities of Reims and Épernay. The region consists of five subregions: Montagne de Reims, Vallée de la Marne, Côte des Blancs, Côte de Sézanne, and Aube. Around 250 million bottles are produced annually in these five subregions. A list of selected Champagne producers can be found in the inset below. The houses are classified according to Champagne's own system of grape production, buying, and blending. This information can be found on the labels of every Champagne bottle, and is explained further in Chapter 10.

This area is particularly famous for its sparkling wines, commonly called Champagne. But it was only in the second half of the seventeenth century that Dom Pérignon introduced the new vinification methods, particularly the blending process, that led to these drinks. Appropriate bottle thickness to allow the wine to be shipped effectively needed to be determined. Similarly, a new closure system needed to be worked out to replace the wood and oil-soaked hemp-wrapped stoppers. A cork was developed that spread into a mushroom shape after being inserted, and secured with a twisted wire basket. These developments allowed the sale of Champagne to begin to flourish.

Champagne subsoils are composed of chalk, and can have a depth of 590 feet (or 180 meters). Chalk can hold up to 40 percent of its weight in water, so this depth creates a natural water reserve needed to assemble the cuvée for non-vintage wines. The town of Épernay also has 177 miles of surrounding caves, which are used for wine storage. In fact, most of these underground alleys bear the name of the street located above to avoid confusion among their many travelers.

While most Champagne wines are a blend of Chardonnay, Pinot Noir, and Pinot Meunier, there are a few types—called blanc de blancs—produced exclusively from Chardonnay. It is more unusual to find blanc de noirs, which is Champagne made from only red wine grapes Pinot Noir and Pinot Meunier.

*F*amous Champagne Producers

The following list includes some of the most famous Champagne producers. Each owns only small parcels of land, and buys most grapes directly from grape growers. Houses that produce particularly prestigious cuvee—a special blend of wine—are followed by the name of this wine in parenthesis. You should also note that René Geoffroy, H. Billiot Fils, Fleury Père et Fils, and A. Margaine are Champagne houses which are less prominent but also produce excellent wines.

- Billecart-Salmon
- Bollinger
- de Castellane
- Charles Heidsieck
- Deutz
- Gosset (Grande Réserve)
- Henriot
- Jacquart

- Krug (Grande Cuvée)
- Lanson
- Laurent-Perrier
- Mailly
- Mercier
- Moët et Chandon (Dom Perignon)
- Mumm (Cuvée René Lalou)
- Nicolas Feuillatte (Palmes d'Or)

- Perrier Jouët (Belle Epoque)
- Piper Heidsieck
- Pol Roger
- Pommery (Cuvée Louise)
- Roederer (Cristal)
- Ruinart (Dom Ruinart)
- Taittinger
- Veuve Clicquot (La Grande Dame).

Chablis

Chablis, or the Yonne region, covers around 7,500 acres (or 3,000 hectares). It is located northwest of Burgundy and produces dry and steely white wines made exclusively from Chardonnay grapes. In descending order of quality, the best wines from this region are Grand Cru Chablis, Premier Cru Chablis, Chablis, and Petit Chablis. The seven grands crus are Blanchots, Bougros, Grenouilles, Les Clos, Les Preuses, Vaudésir, and Valmur.

Planted on top of a mixture of clay and limestone (part of the Kimmeridgean plateau that dives under the Paris basin to resurface in Dorset, England), Chablis vines need to be protected from spring frosts. Viticulturalists use heaters or smudge pots alternating with sprinkler systems to coat the buds with a protective layer of ice.

Figure 5.4. Champagne bottles stored inside caves dug in the chalk soil underneath the Moët et Chandon winery at Épernay.

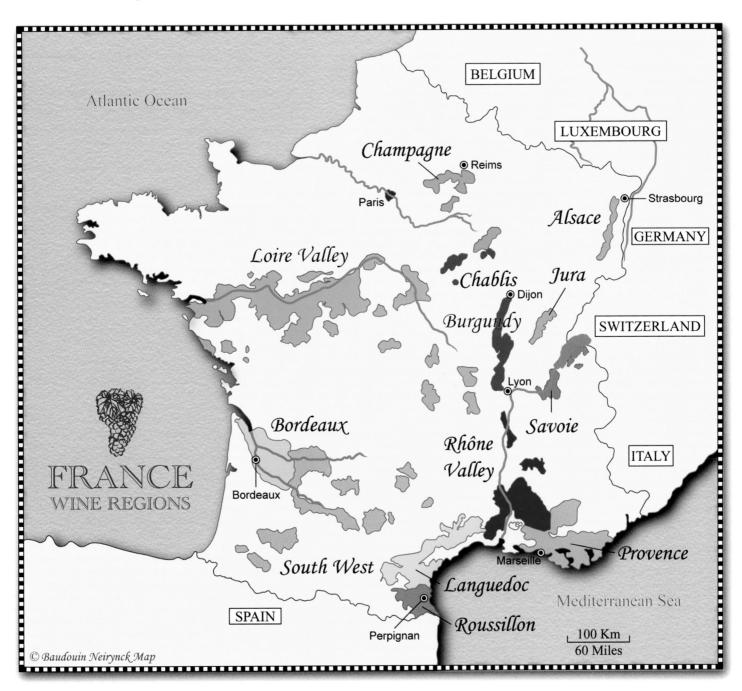

Burgundy

Burgundy is a region surrounded by controversy as to its geographical delimitations. Purists argue that Burgundy is strictly limited to the vineyards between the cities of Dijon and Cheilly Les Maranges. On the other hand, a true *Bourguignon* (inhabitant of Burgundy) would likely include Beaujolais, Chablis, Maconnais, and Côte Chalonnaise as part of the region. This book accepts the latter spread.

Burgundy is divided into the Côte de Nuits and the Côte de Beaune. The entire region is called the Côte d'Or, which means the Gold Coast. This name has two accepted explanations: It evokes the golden color that some white wines of the Côte de Beaune acquire after vinification and maturation in oak barrels, and it underlines the effective "golden" revenues derived from Burgundian vineyards. There are 20,880 acres (or 8,450 hectares) of vineyards in Burgundy, and they produce some of the most magnificent Chardonnays in the world. However, the vineyards, which were once painstakingly assembled by monks, are now extremely fragmented as a result of both the inheritance laws implemented in the Napoleonic era (which demanded equal sharing of wealth among siblings) and the French Revolution.

There are many applications, particularly concentrated in southern Côte de Beaune. There are also smaller *climats*—a terroir which can consist of a whole commune or a tiny vineyard. Aloxe-Corton is a climat composed of the vineyard commune; within that larger area, Le Corton is a smaller climat. Other appellations and some of their popular climats are Ladoix-Serrigny and its Corton-Charlemagne; Puligny-Montrachet and its Chevalier-Montrachet and Bienvenues-Bâtard-Montrachet; and Chassagne-Montrachet and its Le Montrachet, Bâtard-Montrachet, and Criots-Bâtard-Montrachet.

Reputable Burgundy houses specializing in white wines include Bonneau du Martray, Bouchard Père et Fils, Chanson, Chapuis, Coche-Dury, Faiveley, Hospices de Beaune, Joseph Drouhin, Louis Jadot, Louis Latour (which also commercializes Chardonnay wines from Ardèche), Olivier Leflaive, Rollin, and Roumier.

Planted in limestone soil and benefiting from a continental climate, the vineyards of Burgundy are subject to spring frosts in some years, and usually suffer from rain in May and June. These rains can cause fungal diseases such as mildew and grey or black rot. Although vines can be treated against those fungal diseases, such actions require additional chemicals in the vineyards, which can also be harmful to the vines. Another devastating problem grape growers in this area face are hailstorms.

Côte Chalonnaise and Mâconnais are located in southern Côte d'Or. Spread over 26,950 acres (or 11,000 hectares), these regions are home to Rully, Montagny, Givry, Pouilly-Fuissé, Pouilly-Vinzelles, and the various appellations of Mâcon Villages. The white wines are made from Chardonnay. In the Mâconnais, permitted yields are up to 4 tons per acre (or 55 hectoliters per hectare), which is far above those of other parts of Burgundy vineyards. Mercurey, a village located in the same region, stands apart, for it produces mainly red wines from Pinot Noir, and its permitted yields are in line with those of the rest of Burgundy.

Ardèche

Varietal wines, quite a rarity in France outside of the Alsace region, are one of the assets of the Ardèche region. (Its other main contribution to the wine world is produced from a second white grape variety, Viognier.) The Louis Latour house of Burgundy also produces wine in this region, and has done much to promote its varietal Burgundian Chardonnay around the world.

Blanc de blancs Champagne is made from only Chardonnay grapes. Popular bottles include Deutz, Pol Roger, and Taittinger.

La Moutonne has been awarded grand cru status by the Bureau Interprofessionnel des Vins de Bourgogne, the Burgundy wine authority, but, controversially, has been denied the same status by the Institut des Appellations d'Origine Contrôlée (INAO), a branch of the French Ministry.

A smudge pot is an oil burner designed to heat up the air in orchards or vineyards, with the aim of limiting or preventing frost damage to fruit trees.

Figure 5.5. Maison Louis Jadot, an important Burgundy wine producer and merchant. Beaune, France.

TABLE 5.1　FRENCH WINE REGIONS AND THEIR RECENT SIZES

Region	Acres	Hectares
Languedoc-Roussillon	741,000	300,000
Bordeaux	282,500	113,000
Charente and Charente Maritime	191,538	78,179
Rhône Valley	185,710	75,800
Champagne	85,750	35,000
Loire Valley	85,750	35,000
Burgundy	58,163	23,740
Jura	49,000	20,000
Provence	49,000	20,000
South West	39,200	16,000
Ardèche	17,150	7,000
Corsica	17,150	7,000
Savoie	4,900	2,000

The Loire Valley

The Loire Valley is considered to grow a melting pot of grape varieties. Some small areas, mainly around the Haut-Poitou area, are planted with Chardonnay. Other grapes, however, dominate the region. Melon de Bourgogne and Folle Blanche are the widespread grapes in the west, Cabernet Franc and Chenin Blanc in the middle Loire, and Sauvignon Blanc in the east.

UNITED STATES

With close to 117,000 acres (or 47,755 hectares) planted with Chardonnay, the United States is the world's largest grower of this grape, far ahead of France's plantings of 88,000 acres (or 35,918 hectares). Most of the US plantings are found in California. California Chardonnay has a cult following among those who enjoy luscious, buttery, oak-flavored wines.

California

California vineyards tally more Chardonnay plantings than all the vineyards in France put together. For the past twenty years, grape growers and winemakers have experimented with all manners of style, from wines overexposed to oak-barrel fermentation and maturation, to overly acidic and fruit-driven Chablis-style wines. The American consumer bought Chardonnay according to both fashion and the whims of winemakers.

Today, however, the range of wines produced in California reflects the varying soils and climatic conditions across the region in a far superior manner. In collaboration with the University of California at Davis, researchers have proven that matching grapes with soils and microclimates leads to greatly enhanced wine quality.

The wine-producing regions of California are North Coast, Sierra Foothills, Central Valley, Central Coast, and South Coast. The best subregions for growing grapes are those with cooler climates, such as Los Carneros and Sonoma Valley. Depending on the type of oak used, some Californian Chardonnays exhibit similar characteristics to those emanating from Burgundy.

In Napa Valley, Chardonnay was for a long time the most widely planted grape with around 9,065 acres (or 3,700 hectares). Influenced by fogs rising from the Pablo Bay along the valley, Napa

Oak-barrel fermentation and maturation creates wines with specific characteristics and added complexity. The oak imparts a wine with flavors such as vanilla, smoke, and toasted bread.

Some well-known French Champagne houses, such as Mumm, Roederer, and Moët et Chandon (also known as Domaine Chandon), have set up shop in California, taking advantage of attractive soils and climatic conditions to produce sparkling wine.

TABLE 5.2　RECENT CHARDONNAY PLANTINGS

Country	Acres	Hectares	% of Worldwide Plantings
United States	116,865	47,700	31.6
France	88,200	36,000	24
Australia	41,650	17,000	11.3
Italy	32,340	13,200	8.8
Moldavia	26,950	11,000	7.3
Chile	18,620	7,600	5
South Africa	15,190	6,200	3.7
Bulgaria	9,800	4,000	3
Austria	5,390	2,200	1.5
Spain	4,900	2,000	1.5
Argentina	3,675	1,500	1
New Zealand	3,300	1,350	1

OREGON

NEVADA

Mendocino
Sonoma Valley
Napa Valley
North Coast
El Dorado

Sierra Foothills

Napa

San Francisco
Livermore Valley
San Jose
Santa Clara
Central Valley

Monterey

Central Coast

Pacific
Ocean

Paso Robles

San Luis Obispo

Las Vegas

ARIZONA

Santa Maria Valley
Santa Ynes Valley

Los Angeles

South Coast

CALIFORNIA
WINE REGIONS

MEXICO

© Baudouin Neirynck Map

Valley consists of three different regions. These regions are labeled types I, II, and III according to the Winkler scale (described on page 27). These extraordinary climatic conditions allow for a wide variety of styles, depending on ripeness of the grapes and extent of sun exposure.

Famous producers in California include Arrowood in Sonoma Valley, Beringer in Napa Valley, Ferrari-Carano Reserve from Napa/Carneros and Alexander Valley, and Cuvaison in Carneros. Reputable makers on the North Coast include Saintsbury in Carneros, Chateau St. Jean in Kenwood, Laurel Glen at Glen Ellen, Marcassin in Calistoga, and Hanzell in Sonoma.

In the Central Coast of California, a recognized American Viticultural Area (AVA), the vineyards are located along the Pacific Ocean coast from Santa Barbara to San Francisco. There are close to twenty-five appellations, the largest being Livermore Valley, Santa Ynes, Santa Maria, Santa Cruz Mountains, Santa Clara Valley, Monterey, San Benito, and Paso Robles. Among the largest winemakers are Wente Vineyards in Livermore Valley and Edna Valley Vineyards located in San Luis Obispo. Small producers include Au Bon Climat, an estate in Santa Maria with just 45 acres (or 18 hectares) under vine, and Ridge Vineyards in Cupertino. Several wineries buy grapes from outside sources, and place their personal mark on the wine during vinification.

Among the best Californian Chardonnays are those produced by Ramey Wine Cellars Hyde Vineyards, Mount Eden Wolff Vineyard, Baileyana Grand Firepeak Cuvée, Stag's Leap Wine Cellars Arcadia Vineyard, Beringer Vineyard, Cakebread Cellars, Grgich Hills, Chateau Montelena, Chalk Hill Estate, Clos La Chance, Fess Parker Ashley's Vineyard, Franciscan Cuvée Sauvage, Geyser Peak Winery, J. Lohr Vineyards Vista, Landmark Wines Damaris Reserve, and Marimar Torres Estate "Dobles Lias."

Oregon

Although Oregon is best known for the quality of its Pinot Noir, there are significant plantings of Chardonnay in this state because the climate is well suited to the grape. Veronique Drouhin, a descendant of the Drouhin house in Burgundy, has been very active in the region since her father bought some land there in the 1980s. She produces Chardonnay of excellent quality alongside the prerequisite Pinot Noir. Chehalem and Adelsheim Wineries, both from Newberg, also deliver quality Chardonnay-based wines.

Washington

In Washington State, the vineyards of Columbia, Walla Walla, and Yakima Valleys are located inland, far away from the fogs and breezes of the Pacific Ocean apart from the Puget Sound region. This is contrary to the situation in Oregon where the wine regions are located close to the coastline. Washington's climatic conditions are also more extreme. Nevertheless, there are many Chardonnay producers here. The largest are Columbia Crest, which plants on 2,220 acres (or 900 hectares), and Château Sainte Michelle, which plants on 1,240 acres (or 500 hectares). Most of the smaller wineries buy their grapes from growers.

Idaho

The high-altitude vineyards of Idaho are suited to grapes, like Chardonnay, that rely on high acidity to exacerbate their character. The wine industry in this state dates back to 1863, and the vineyards can be found in the southwest corner, near Snake River. Most of the sixty wineries plant a substantial portion of their vineyards with Chardonnay.

Texas

Excellent Chardonnay is produced in the hot and dry Texas climate. Throughout the state, there are more than one hundred wineries. Llano Estacado, Fall Creek, Sainte Genevieve, and Pheasant Ridge are among those that produce Chardonnay.

Virginia

Despite its uncompromisingly hot climate, some excellent wines are made in Virginia. Sometimes, locally produced Chardonnays even rival those from California.

New York State

The Finger Lakes and Long Island regions are particularly suitable for Chardonnay grapes. The most famous Chardonnay-producing NY estates are Bedell Cellars and Hargrave on Long Island, Four Chimneys Farm and Glenora in the Finger Lakes, and Rivendell and Benmarl on the Hudson River. Many native American grapes continue to be cultivated here as well.

AUSTRALIA

Chardonnay was first imported to Australia in the collection of James Busby in 1832, but gained its notoriety after its re-introduction in the 1950s. There are areas of both warm and cool weather, resulting in a variety of Chardonnay produced in different parts of the country.

South Australia

The major Australian wine region of Barossa Valley is located in South Australia. Barossa Valley's warm, dry weather and limestone soils allow Chardonnay grapes to attain levels of ripeness rarely achieved in Europe. Because of the resulting high residual sugar combined with low acidity levels, Australian winemakers tend to produce very rich wines that are highly palatable, though somewhat short-lived in the mouth. These luscious wines, conceived with extensive use of new oak, have served to alter the taste preferences of consumers, particularly in the United Kingdom and the United States. Some outstanding Chardonnay wines, such as M3 from Shaw & Smith, are produced in the cooler climate of Adelaide Hills, which is at a higher altitude than the rest of the South Australian wine-growing areas.

Victoria

Chardonnay is produced very successfully in the state of Victoria. Particularly sophisticated and complex Chardonnay wines can be found on the Mornington Peninsula, one of the coolest areas of Victoria. In the relatively high altitude of the Macedon Ranges, producers such as Virgin Hills grow Chardonnay to make sparkling wine.

ITALY

Italian winemakers have come to appreciate the virtues of the Chardonnay grape and have managed to satisfy a growing demand, both domestically and internationally, for wines made with this grape. Not all Italian regions are suitable for the production of such wines, but Franciacorta in Lombardy, Veneto in the Breganze and Soave, Tuscany in the Vin Santo, and Molise all produce *vino da tavola* Chardonnay.

NEW ZEALAND

New Zealand represents only 0.2 percent of annual global wine production. In 2003, however, its international wine trade generated a surplus of NZ$100 million (or US$74 million). In the same year, Chardonnay plantings represented 8,600 acres (or 3,500 hectares)—approximately a quarter of the total vineyards area of New Zealand—and were used to produce both dry and sparkling wines. Exports of New Zealand wines that, in 2001, stood just below 5.3 million gallons (or 20 million liters) are expected to be three times as successful in 2007. The main grape-producing areas are Marlborough (40 percent of total production), Hawke's Bay (28 percent), Gisborne (15 percent), and Auckland (just under 4 percent). Prominent Chardonnay producers in New Zealand include Babich, Dry River, Palliser Estate, and Villa Maria Estate.

SOUTH AFRICA

With a total 2006 wine production of 1.25 million tons (or 1.1 million liters), South Africa has established a name for itself on the world's Chardonnay map. Asara Wine Estate and Radford Dale in Stellenbosch, Hamilton Russell in Walker Bay, Paul Cluver in Elgin, and Count Agusta in Franschoek represent some of the country's most prestigious Chardonnays.

Vino da Tavola is the lowest-quality wine category in Italy, bearing no indication of region of origin or vintage. For IGT (Indicazione Geografica Tipica), the next level, region of origin and vintage are stated. DOC (Denominazione di Origine Controllata) and DOCG (Denominazione di Origine Controllata e Garantita) are the highest-quality levels.

Sauvignon Blanc

The main competitor to Chardonnay in terms of popularity, Sauvignon Blanc has experienced something of a revolution over the last twenty years. This has been in large part due to New Zealand grape growers and winemakers from the Marlborough region. Producers like Cloudy Bay, Babich, and Kim Crawford all deliver wines with a crisp finish and sensational tropical fruit aromas and flavors. The Sancerre, Pouilly-Fumé, and Bordeaux dry whites that have been based on the Sauvignon Blanc grape for centuries, on the other hand, predominantly produce flavors and aromas of gooseberry, with herbaceous or vegetal compounds.

Overproduction of this wine in Bordeaux led to huge quantities of unsold bottles. This dictated a decrease in Sauvignon Blanc plantings: more than 6,125 acres (or 2,500 hectares) were uprooted between 1968 and 1979. However, more recent developments have seen the same grape plantings exceed 24,500 acres (or 10,000 hectares). This means that close to 47 percent of the total vineyard plantings in Bordeaux are Sauvignon Blanc.

Changes in clonal choices and vinification methods have together generated wines throughout the world with a wide range of characteristics and styles. Sauvignon Blanc is naturally high in both alcohol and acidity, and is present on every continent, as shown in Table 5.3 on page 61. Also called Fumé Blanc—a name created by Robert Mondavi in the 1970s—in California, this grape has caught up with Chardonnay in price terms, and is a model of well-planned production levels causing offer to equal demand.

The enviable reputation established by New Zealand Sauvignon Blanc has spawned competition from the country's immediate neighbor. Australian viticulturists, growers, and winemakers located in the regions of Adelaide Hills, Coonawarra, and Western Australia—namely Frankland, Margaret River, and Pemberton—have begun to experiment with the grape. They have also started to master the Bordeaux blanc blend, blending Sauvignon Blanc with a little Semillon, in the same style as labels such as Château Pape Clément, which is located in Pessac Léognan.

In a botrytized (noble rot) form, the grape, when blended with Semillon and sometimes Muscadelle, forms the basis of some of the world's most reputed sweet wines, such as Château d'Yquem from Sauternes, Bordeaux. *Botrytis cinerea* is a mold that pierces the skin of the grapes, causing a slow evaporation of the juice inside the berry. This process concentrates the grape juice and, by extension, flavors and aromas, to produce a highly aromatic, golden-amber sweet wine. *Botrytis cinerea* affects a vineyard unevenly, necessitating a number of harvests at different times. Since its presence is beyond the control of grape growers, some Sauternes wines are produced only in certain years.

Mutations of the main variety include Cabernet Sauvignon (a red wine variety), Sauvignon Noir, Sauvignon Jaune, Sauvignon Rosé, and Sauvignon Gris. Other similar grapes have sometimes been mistaken for Sauvignon Blanc, including Sauvignon Vert (which is also called Sauvignonasse). Until recently, Sauvignon Vert represented a majority of the varietal plantings in Chile.

Figure 5.6.
Sauvignon Blanc.

History

Sauvignon Blanc viticulture started around the year 380 AD along the banks of the Loire River in France. In 582, medieval historian St. Gregory of Tours lauded the quality of Sancerre wines made from Sauvignon Blanc. Monks, particularly those belonging to St. Augustin's order, perfected the viticulture and vinification of the grape through the years. Blended with varying amounts of Semillon, the grape has been glorified in the Bordeaux region, in both dry and sweet styles.

Ampelography

Sauvignon Blanc is a descendant of the ancient Fié variety once prolific along the Loire River. The grape was crossed in the eighteenth century with Cabernet Franc to produce the red grape variety Cabernet Sauvignon.

Ideal Soil

Lighter limestone soils, such as those occurring in the central Loire Valley of France, are ideal for wines representing the true olfactory characteristics of Sauvignon Blanc. Heavy soils usually encourage leaf growth, resulting in vineyards where canopies—the green leafy part of the vine—become too intrusive, and inhibit swelling of the grapes by shielding them from the sun.

Climatic Conditions

According to the Winkler scale, the growing of Sauvignon Blanc is suitable in Regions I and II, with the best results obtained in Region I. When cultivated in warmer climate, Sauvignon Blanc tends to develop an oily quality reminiscent of certain wines produced around the Mediterranean basin, in Israel, and in Lebanon.

Olfactory Characteristics

For the Sauvignon Blanc grape, aromas and flavors vary according to climate. However, professional wine tasters emphasize a gooseberry character detectable in all clonal variations. In warmer climes, the grape develops citrus-like flavors and aromas such as grapefruit and pear; in New Zealand, for example, the grape tends to have distinct passion fruit characteristics. In cooler climates, herbaceous and grassy tones dominate; at the extreme end it can be reminiscent of "cat's pee," in areas such as Bué in Sancerre.

By circumventing the grassy and herbaceous flavors and aromas while emphasizing gooseberry and tropical fruit aromas, the New Zealand region of Marlborough is renowned for the quality of its Sauvignon Blanc more than any of its other grapes.

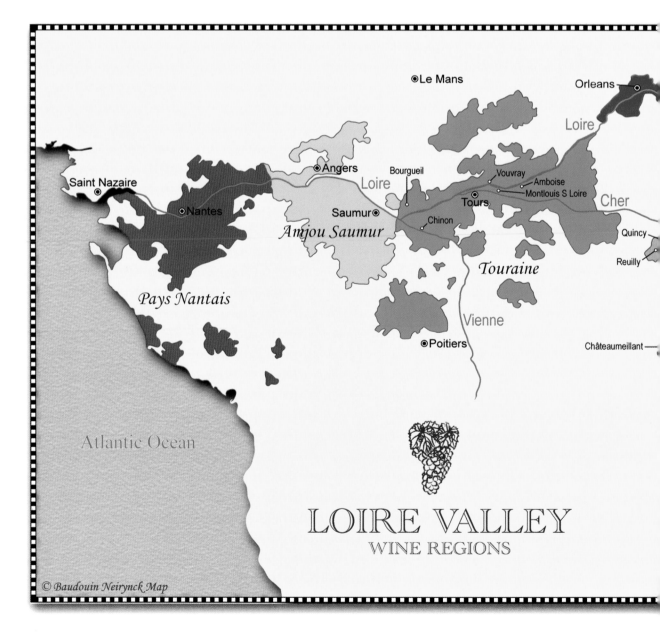

LOIRE VALLEY
WINE REGIONS

© Baudouin Neirynck Map

Geographic Spread

A recent survey put the total worldwide plantings of Sauvignon Blanc at around 112,700 acres (or 46,000 hectares). This wine grape is extremely popular in France, but it can also be found in many other countries throughout the world.

FRANCE

Sauvignon Blanc is responsible for the outstanding reputation of the white wines from the Loire Valley. Planted on some of the best terroirs, the grapes result in both dry and botrytized styles from Bordeaux. Sauvignon Blanc from the Loire Valley has structured minerality and sustained gooseberry aromas. In Bordeaux, the grape is usually blended. There are also plantings of Sauvignon Blanc in Languedoc-Roussillon.

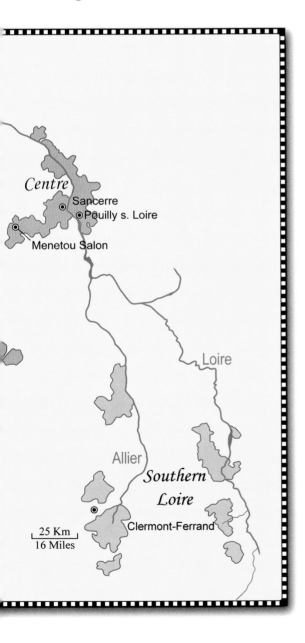

Bordeaux

In Bordeaux, dry white wines based on Sauvignon Blanc are produced in many subregions. The Entre-Deux-Mers region (literally translated as "in between two seas") is located between the Garonne and Dordogne rivers, and only a small portion of the region is planted with white wine grapes such as Sauvignon Blanc, Semillon, and Muscadelle. In the Graves region, Sémillon, the dominant grape, is blended with smaller amounts of Sauvignon Blanc. In the Pessac Léognan region, the blending proportions of Sauvignon Blanc and Semillon vary from estate to estate. Pessac Léognan is the home of great dry whites such as Château Haut-Brion, Domaine de Chevalier, Château Laville-Haut-Brion, and Château La Mission-Haut-Brion. Among lesser-known but equally compelling estates stand the likes of de Fieuzal, La Louvière, Malartic-Lagravière, Haut-Bailly, and Pape-Clément.

In 2002, a ruling authorized the new appellation of Saint-Bris, which was formally known as Sauvignon de Saint-Bris VDQS. It became the one-hundredth appellation of Burgundy, and the only non-Chardonnay grape area in the region. Here, Sauvignon Blanc covers around 250 acres (or 103 hectares).

Loire Valley

Located along the Loire River, the Loire Valley is the largest white wine region in France. It stretches from the Atlantic Ocean to the regions of Menetou-Salon, Pouilly-sur-Loire, and Sancerre. Also known as the land of castles, the Loire Valley does indeed boast one of the highest concentrations of castles in the world, all built during the last millennium. Close to Paris, the Loire River was a major wine transportation route from the centre of the country to the Atlantic Ocean.

This wine region is the main territory for high-quality Sauvignon Blanc. It produces wines such as Sancerre, Pouilly-Fumé, Menetou-Salon, and Touraine. A number of outstanding producers, such as Ladoucette at Château du Nozet and Sancerre Comte Lafon, have sealed the region's reputation. Other outstanding Sauvignon Blanc wines can be found in Sancerre at the Domaine Alphonse Mellot and Saint-Andelan at the Domaine Didier Daguenau. Thanks to the discovery of cold fermentation in stainless steel tanks, those wines have enjoyed a resurgence of consumer interest.

The popular Loire Valley wine Pouilly-sur-Loire does not contain Sauvignon Blanc. Instead, it uses Chasselas grapes.

The Loire Valley is divided into four main subregions, namely Pays Nantais, Anjou-Saumur, Touraine, and the Upper Loire Valley. The Upper Loire is a Sauvignon Blanc paradise, producing wines such as Sancerre and Pouilly-Fumé. Here, the herbaceous and grassy characteristics of the grape are ever-present, and sometimes even exaggerated. Reuilly and Quincy also fall within the Loire River wine region. Coteaux du Loir and Jasnières are the last of the nine districts, located on the Loire River, north of the city of Tours.

NEW ZEALAND

The majority of producers from the Marlborough region on the South Island of New Zealand have established their vineyards as hotbeds for Sauvignon Blanc. The success story began in 1973, when Yugoslavian immigrant Ivan Yukich of Montana Wines decided to invest in plantings of Sauvignon Blanc in this particular region. The resulting wines not only displayed anticipated olfactory characteristics, but also tropical fruit

© Baudouin Neirynck Map

aromas such as lime, mango, and passion fruit that beautifully complemented the herbaceous and grassy distinctiveness of Sauvignon Blanc.

UNITED STATES

In the United States, Sauvignon Blanc has been heralded as a savior in a market hitherto saturated with Chardonnay. Here, Sauvignon Blanc wines are sometimes called Fumé Blanc. Some of the best examples are found in California, Oregon, and Washington State. Top wines include Cakebread, Chalk Hill, Clos La Chance, Dry Creek Vineyard Fumé Blanc, Geyser Peak Winery Block Collection, St. Supery, and Trinchero Family Estates' Mary's Vineyard.

SOUTH AFRICA

The Elgin and Walker Bay regions located at the western tip of South Africa, between the cities of Hermanus and Kleinmond, provide ideal Sauvignon Blanc growing zones. They are influenced by gentle maritime air streams, yet are also protected from harsh Atlantic Ocean winds by the Cape of Good Hope peninsula. Here, the likes of Hamilton Russell, Bouchard-Finlayson, Paul

TABLE 5.3 RECENT SAUVIGNON BLANC PLANTINGS			
Country	Acres	Hectares	% of Worldwide Plantings
France	49,000	20,000	43
Chile	18,130	7,400	16
United States	14,580	5,800	13
South Africa	9,555	3,900	8.5
Italy	7,500	3,000	6.5
New Zealand	3,500	1,400	3
Australia	4,215	1,720	3
Others: Argentina, Austria, Canada, Croatia, Hungary, Portugal, Russia, Serbia, Slovakia, Spain, and Switzerland.	8,575	3,500	7

Cluver, Beaumont, and Newton-Johnson cultivate the art of transforming Sauvignon Blanc grapes into the best-possible wines.

Riesling

Known by different names in different countries (Rhine Riesling in Australia, Riesling Renano in Italy, Rheinriesling in Austria, and Johannisberg in Switzerland), Riesling is a grape that always surprises first-time tasters. It shows distinct floral, steely, and honeyed smells and aromas, particularly in the highly reputable German wines that became popular around the world in the late nineteenth and early twentieth centuries. Its ability to age in the bottle while still maintaining its olfactory characteristics is legendary, and made German white wines the rival of reds from Bordeaux and Burgundy on royal tables across Europe. It is also the perfect grape with which to make wines of varying degrees of sweetness, from bone-dry to very sweet ice wine.

Figure 5.7. Riesling.

There are several clones of this grape. Numbers 90, 198, 239, and 356 are those most commonly planted by grape growers.

In 2006, Riesling plantings represented about a quarter of German vineyards. Depending on the planting density, yields can attain 5.2 tons per acre (or 70 hectoliters per hectare) without substantially affecting the quality of the resulting must. Because the variety is a late budding one, it rarely suffers from spring frosts. Yet Riesling is not an early ripener. It requires a long growing season to deliver a balance of acidity and optimal flavor. Harvest in the northern hemisphere usually takes place between mid-October and early November (or much later in the case of *eiswein*, when grapes are picked only when heavy frosts occur). Grapes affected by botrytis are known in Germany as *trockenbeerenauslese* or *TBA*. Yielding 3 to 6 tons per acre (or 7 to 14.7 tons per hectare), Riesling is not a highly productive grape. When ripe, it has small, round, soft berries with tender, greenish-yellow skins.

History

Riesling probably originated in Germany. The first mention of Riesling in German literature, albeit under a different spelling, is in the middle of the fifteenth century. In her *Oxford Companion to Wine*, Jancis Robinson mentions several German books and texts from this time that include mention of Riesling. The German wine industry was already in full swing before the fifteenth century, but favored the grape varieties Elbling and Silvaner over Riesling.

There is a good chance that the history of this grape extends further back in time. In his grape dictionary, Pierre Galet associates Riesling with the *Argitis minor* mentioned in Roman texts, which was first cultivated in Alsace around the ninth century AD.

Ampelography

Along with Elbling and Silvaner, the Riesling grape may be derived from ancient crossings of the even more ancient Heunisch (or Weiss) and Fränkisch grape varieties. These are now considered the progenitors of all modern wine grapes. The original grape is called Weisser Riesling, Rielsinger, and Riesler in Luxemburg, while in Germany it is called Rheingauer, Johannisberg, Pfefferl, and Hocheimer.

Ideal Soil

The most suitable soils for cultivating Riesling are those made of schist (crystalline rock) and slate. In cool climatic conditions, ideal planting locations are not-too-fertile soils on steep slopes. Steep angles promote maximum exposure to sunshine, from both the sun itself and its reflection in the bordering river. The slope also allows for proper drainage, to avoid excessive moisture absorption by the roots.

Climatic Conditions

Because of its hard wood—its spurs, cane, and trunk are hard to cut and prune—the Riesling grape can sustain harsh climatic conditions and is suitable Region I on the Winkler scale. There have been attempts to cultivate the grape in warmer climates, such as in the Barossa Valley in South Australia, but cooler climates such as the Clare Valley usually produce better results.

Olfactory Characteristics

Riesling has a high content of *monoterpenes*—flavor compounds—and is often described as one of the most aromatic white wine grapes. Its aroma often portrays floral, mineral, and honey characteristics. Of the floral notes, the most predominant are rose petal, woodruff, other white flowers such as lily and jasmine, and violet. Apple, pear, peach, and apricot are its most dominating fruit aromas. A mineral taste such as flint, steel, or gunmetal sometimes appears, usually as a reflection of the schist subsoils in German vineyards.

Geographic Spread

Total worldwide Riesling plantings were around 147,000 acres (or 60,000 hectares) in 2006. The highest concentration of Riesling grapes occurs along Germany's Rhine River and its tributaries—the regions of Rheingau, Mosel, Rheinhessen, and Nahe—and in Alsace, France.

FRANCE

The Vosges mountain range shields the Alsace vineyards from cold and northerly winds. As a result, these vineyards benefit from relatively good climatic conditions. The particularly dry weather prevailing here, the driest region of France, enables quality white wines to be produced year after year. Alsace, a territory that formerly belonged to Germany but is now French, is home to some of the best Rieslings in the world, along with wines made from Pinot Blanc, Gewürztraminer, Pinot Noir, and Tokay Pinot Gris.

Some of the most reputable names in Alsace include large houses such as Hugel, Léon Beyer, Zind Humbrecht, Pierre Sparr, and Dopff & Irion as well as smaller producers such as Paul Blank and Domaine Weinbach.

UNITED STATES

Riesling is quite successful in the Finger Lakes region of New York State (as well as in Canada). Local wine growers favor Mosel-style wines, with a certain degree of acidity balanced with fruity characteristics. It is also grown in California (Santa Barbara, Monterey, Santa Cruz, and Mendocino), Washington State, and Oregon.

GERMANY

German vineyards produce mainly (80-percent) white wines, because it is difficult to turn out great red wines in the mostly northern wine districts. The Romans were the first to plant German vines. These were found along the Rhine and Mosel Rivers. After the barbarian invasions, these vineyards became the property of the church. The drive toward quality took place during the eighteenth century, a time when German wines were highly regarded in royal courts throughout Europe. However, application of the Napoleon code of law deeply fragmented the large wine estates, which were sold at auction, as was also being done in France

Many acres of vineyards are planted throughout Germany. However, unlike the situation in France, where most winemakers are occupied full-time in their trade, German grape growers

TABLE 5.4 RECENT RIESLING PLANTINGS			
Country	**Acres**	**Hectares**	**% of Worldwide Plantings**
Germany	56,350	23,000	38
South Africa	10,050	4,100	7
Australia	9,550	3,900	6.5
France	8,575	3,700	6
United States	7,235	2,950	5.5
Bulgaria	3,675	1,500	2.5
Slovakia	3,675	1,500	2.5
Austria	3,200	1,300	2
New Zealand	735	300	0.5
Italy	675	275	0.5
Others: Argentina, Brazil, Canada, Chile, China, Cyprus, Czechoslovakia, Greece, Hungary, Macedonia, Mexico, Portugal, Romania, Serbia, Slovenia, South Korea, and Spain.	41,650	17,000	29

are more likely to treat the vineyard as a weekend hobby. Most of these grapes are delivered to cooperatives, and the lion's share of annual production is for domestic consumption. *Chaptalization*—adding sugar to the wine during fermentation to increase the product's alcohol content—is not permitted for quality wines of the *Qualitätswein mit Prädikat* classification. More information on German wine classification can be found in Chapter 11.

A Breakdown of German Wine-Growing Regions

In Germany, most vineyards are located near a major river: the Rhine, the Mosel, the Nektar, or the Main. These rivers help to create ideal conditions for viticulture in such a cold climate. The vineyards are usually located on south-facing slopes, which allows the sun to beat directly down as well as reflect off the nearby river.

A variety of soils are found across the different German regions. These soils range from clay and slate in Mittelrhein, and sand and slate in Nahe, to flint and slate in Mosel-Saar-Ruwer. In the Rheinpfalz—also called the Pfalz—the clay soils generate excellent Rieslings. In Baden, soils range from shell-lime and volcanic stone to clay, limestone, and gravel. The different wine regions, as well as more information about each, are found in the following list.

■ Rheinhessen produces mainly white wines from Müller-Thurgau, Silvaner, and Scheurebe grapes. Comprised of 61,250 acres (or 25,000 hectares), this is the largest wine region in Germany.

■ Rheinpfalz is the second-largest wine production district. It contains close to 56,350 acres (or 23,000 hectares). Riesling, Müller-Thurgau, and Kerner are the dominant grapes for most white wines from this region.

■ Baden is a long and narrow vineyard between the cities of Freiburg and Baden Baden. Because of its southern location, red wines can be produced (from the grape Pinot Noir, known as Spätburgunder in Germany). White wines are made from Müller-Thurgau, Rülander (Pinot Gris or Pinot Grigio), and Gewürztraminer.

■ Mosel-Saar-Ruwer, located along the river of the same name, is the most western point among German vineyards. Exclusively white wines are made from Müller-Thurgau, Riesling, and Elbling.

■ Württemberg, located in a square-shaped territory between the cities of Stuttgart, Karlsruhe, Heidelberg, and Heilbronn, is crossed by the Nektar River. Half of this area's wine production is red. The white wines are made from Riesling, Trollinger, and Müllerrebe (which is called Pinot Meunier in France).

■ Franken, also called Franconia, is in the northeast of the country along the Main River, and produces mainly white wines from Müller-Thurgau, Bacchus, and Silvaner. Bottles from this region are squat and green, and called bocksbeutel.

■ Nahe borders the Rheinhessen region and the Nahe River. It is a bastion for white wines from Müller-Thurgau, Riesling, and Silvaner.

■ Rheingau is situated between the Mittelrhein and the Rheinhessen. This region yields a majority of white wines from grape varieties Müller-Thurgau and Riesling. It also produces some red wines from the Spätburgunder grape.

■ Mittelrhein, Ahr, and Bergstrasse are smaller wine districts with a dominant white wine production from Riesling and Müller-Thurgau. Ahr's production also yields around 30-percent red wines, made with Spätburgunder and Portugieser.

Semillon

Semillon is one of the classic wine grapes of the Bordeaux region. Today, however, it is also grown with much success in many other parts of the world, including California and Australia. The grape has a very distinctive set of aromas and flavors that are reminiscent of figs. Seven clones of the Semillon grape have been certified. Among the most popular are 173, 299, 315, and 380.

Although overall worldwide plantings are in decline, this grape, particularly when blended with Sauvignon Blanc and Muscadelle, produces some of the most reputable unfortified sweet wines in the world. The wines of Sauternes and Barsac can age for up to one hundred years—possibly even longer—due to the noble rot *botrytis cinerea* which attacks the grapes' thin skins.

Far easier to cultivate than Riesling and Chardonnay, Semillon generates good yields. It is usually blended with Sauvignon Blanc to compensate for its over-herbaceous character. However, the Hunter Valley in Australia produces reputable unblended Semillon wines, rarely oaked and with good aging potential. Semillon is widely planted in Australia, and ranks second behind Chardonnay in terms of tons crushed. It is an early ripening grape, so is rarely adversely affected by rain or frost. Semillon is also fairly resistant to the common vine diseases. It is in second position behind Ugni Blanc in terms of plantings in France.

In Australia, the grape is referred to as Hunter (River) Riesling, Barnawartha Pinot, and Sercial. In Turkey, it is called Semmilon. In France, it is known by the names Chevrier, Columbier, Malaga, and Blanc Doux. In South Africa, where the grape has been grown for some time, the names Green Grape and Semillion are used. The grape is known as Semilhão in most parts of Portugal and used in the production of vinho verde. On the island of Madeira it is called Boal and Bual, while in the Douro region it is called Boal. Around the world, other variations of its name include Chevier, Crucillant, St-Emilion, Semijon, Semillon Muscat, and Semillon Roux.

Figure 5.8.
Semillon.

History

Semillon originated from the Gironde region of Bordeaux in France, but little is known of its history. Its name first appeared in the eighteenth century. It was exported to the rest of the world in the nineteenth century, and there are traces of Semillon plantings in Australia's Hunter Valley dating to 1840.

Ampelography

Although there is no precise documentation, it is believed that Semillon's origins go back to the sixteenth or seventeenth century. Pierre Galet believes this variety appeared naturally in the vineyard as a result of genetic mutation. However, the name itself seems to originate from the contraction of St. Emilion, highlighting a possible connection with the famous city of the Bordeaux region.

Ideal Soil

The Semillon grape variety generates its best wines in the Graves and Entre-deux-Mers regions of Bordeaux, where the soil consists of alluvial deposits—material deposited by a stream—and gravel.

Climatic Conditions

Best cultivated in Regions II and III on the Winkler scale, the Semillon grape also grows well in regions of type I. Although quite sensitive to botrytis, the grape is fairly resistant to oïdium and mildew.

Olfactory Characteristics

Often described as "waxy" due to its marked flavor of lanolin, fully mature French Semillon grapes can produce exceptional wines which are fruit-driven in their youth, but develop intense butterscotch and honey flavors later. There are spice notes of saffron, as well as herbal aromas such as grass and weeds. When the grape is affected by *botrytis cinerea*, extraordinary fruit flavors emerge such as apricot, quince, peach, honey, pineapple, vanilla, and candy. A light oak treatment generates more vanilla and sweet wood, whereas lengthy exposure to oak imparts smoky, burnt toast, and oak flavors. In Australia's Hunter Valley, winemakers produce bottle-aged Semillon wines of a deep golden color. These wines have flavors of honey and toast in a full-bodied, long-lasting palate.

Geographic Spread

Total worldwide plantings of Semillon consists of 83,300 acres (or 34,000 hectares). As of 2005, there were 19,600 acres (or 8,000 hectares) of Semillon

TABLE 5.5 RECENT SEMILLON PLANTINGS			
Country	Acres	Hectares	% of Worldwide Plantings
France	34,790	14,200	42
Australia	7,600	3,100	22
Chile	4,460	1,821	9
Argentina	3,200	1,300	4
South Africa	2,450	1,000	3
United States	1,840	770	2
Others: Croatia, Cyprus, Hungary, Japan, New Zealand, Portugal, Serbia, Slovenia, and Russia.	14,700	6,000	18

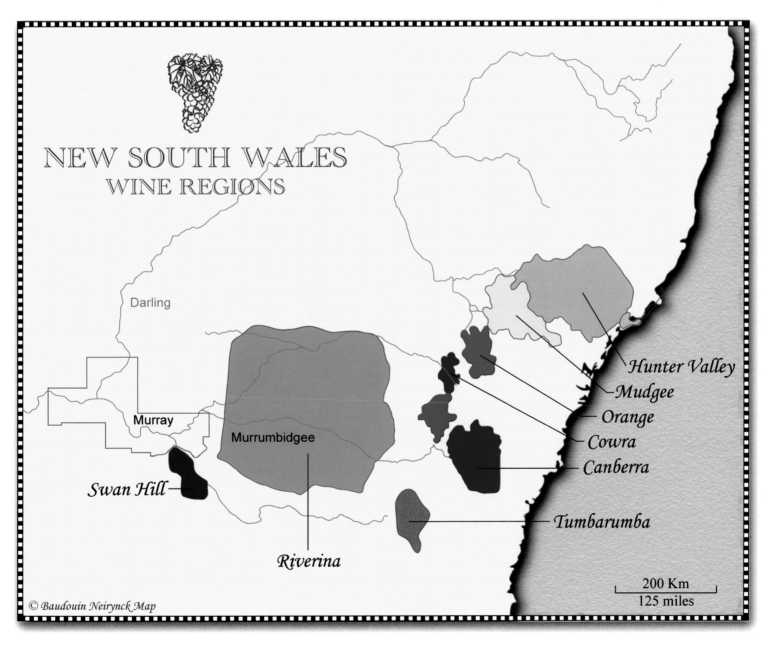

NEW SOUTH WALES
WINE REGIONS

Darling

Murray

Murrumbidgee

Swan Hill

Riverina

Hunter Valley
Mudgee
Orange
Cowra
Canberra

Tumbarumba

200 Km
125 miles

© *Baudouin Neirynck Map*

Australia and New South Wales

Australia is relatively new to the global wine trade, but has already become a very powerful player which has taken markets by storm in the past three decades. However, its wine industry actually dates back to 1788, and the most important year in the diary of its wine industry was 1824. That year, young Scotsman James Busby landed in Sydney, Australia. Eight years later, he introduced a collection of the best vine varieties he had found in Europe. To this day, these grapes remain the most widely planted.

The country's main wine regions are located in four states, namely South Australia, Victoria, Western Australia, and New South Wales. While the first three states are under the influence of a range of climatic conditions and are quite suitable for the production of quality wines, New South Wales (NSW) is characterized by humid weather conditions.

Nevertheless, since NSW was the first landing place of immigrants, it was an obvious choice for the planting of vines,

and the Hunter Valley, along its namesake river, remains the best-known production region in the state. The other regions are the Murrumbidgee Irrigation Area, Mudgee, Forbes, and Cowra. The Hunter Valley is also renowned for the quality of its Semillon wines and Semillon-based blends, with the leading producers being Lindemans, Rothbury Estate, Tyrrell's, and McWilliam's.

Rosemount Estate is another Australian marketer of Semillon wines. The majority of these wines are produced from grapes of the Hunter Valley, but a significant amount of the grapes also emanate from the cool-climate areas of Western Australia. This practice of blending grapes from different regions is prevalent in Australia, where winemakers traditionally label their bottles by grape variety. On the contrary, European quality standards are predominantly based on the origin of the grapes, and recognition of the notion of terroir.

in Bordeaux, in the vineyards of Graves and Sauternes. Two of the most illustrious white wines from here are Château d'Yquem (which is sweet) and Château Haut-Brion (which is dry). In California, the total Semillon plantings in 2006 represented 1,538 acres (or 600 hectares), about a

tenth of the amount of Sauvignon Blanc plantings in the same area. The Californian Livermore Valley Semillons made by Wente at El Mocho's vineyard, from old vines supplied by the owner of Chateau d'Yquem in 1880, are highly reputable. In Australia, Hunter Valley is referred to as the "home" of Semillon, but the grape has also been planted in Western Australia. Here, Cape Mentelle's Semillon-Sauvignon Blanc blend illustrates the potential of this grape. In New Zealand, recent plantings of Semillon have produced good wines in Hawke's Bay and Marlborough. South Africa has also shown good results in the production of full-bodied Semillons with attractive, creamy characteristics.

Pinot Gris

Originally a variant or mutation of Pinot Noir, the grape Pinot Gris—which is also commonly called Pinot Grigio—and its resulting wines have recently begun to acquire cult status among wine enthusiasts. This is because this grape yields soft and gently perfumed wines, but with a rich texture and dry character. It is easily mistaken for Pinot Noir when the two are planted side by side, as the leaves are almost identical. The occasional Pinot Gris vine can be found in the vineyards of Burgundy, where it is harvested at the same time as Pinot Noir. Its hand in the production of wines that have light floral notes and a delicate fragrance, such as Pinot Grigio, has resulted in a substantial increase of its plantings in the last few years. It is one of the few vines which can bear grapes of different colors, which range from white to pink and even black.

Great Pinot Gris wines can be found in several reputable wine houses in Alsace, including Léon Beyer, Zind-Humbrecht, Dopff & Irion, Hugel, Schlumberger, Pierre Sparr, and Domaine Weinbach. In Germany, several winemakers, such as Bercher, Dr. Heger, and Fürst, have achieved remarkable recognition for their wines. In Italy, the best Pinot Grigio wines are from Esperto in Veneto, Kris and Maso Canali in Trentino-Alto-Adige, and Pighin in Collio. In California, Swanson and Long Vineyards "Laird Vineyard" in Napa Valley, as well as MacMurray Ranch in Russian River, are outstanding. King Estate Winery from Oregon is also highly regarded.

The most common synonyms of Pinot Gris are Auvernat Gris, Auxerrois Gris, Auxois, Fauvet, Fromentot, Grauerburgunder, Grauklevner, Grey Friar, Grey Pinot, Rülander, Rulonski Szurkebarat, Tokay d'Alsace, and Tokay-Pinot Gris. It is also called Malvoisie in the Loire Valley and Switzerland, and Pinot Beurot in Burgundy.

History

The Pinot Gris grape originated in either France or Germany, and was disseminated across Europe by European nobility. In his *Encyclopaedic Dictionary of Grape Varieties*, Pierre Galet notes that the French Emperor Charles IV of Luxemburg took some Pinot Gris shoots to Hungarian monks in 1375. They then planted them on the shores of Lake Balaton. General Lazerus von Schwendi first planted Pinot Gris in Alsace in 1568, following his victory over the Turks in the region of Tokay. Soon, the grape was thriving in many European countries. Today, Pinot Gris is planted on 36,750 acres (or 15,000 hectares) worldwide.

Ampelography

Pinot Gris is surely a genetic mutation of Pinot Noir and many of its vines can be found in the Burgundy vineyards alongside those of Pinot Noir. Yet the two cousins can be nearly undistinguishable. The leaf shape of both grapes are identical. The identity of Pinot Gris can only be determined after veraison, when the berries take on their final color. Pinot Gris grapes are usually lighter and bluer than the darker and blacker Pinot Noir.

Figure 5.9.
Pinot Gris.

Ideal Soil

Pinot Gris is suited to most soil types, as exemplified in the Alsace region. The higher slopes of the Vosges Mountains consist of granite, sandstone, schist, and volcanic sediments. The lower slopes, on the other hand, are of clay, marl, limestone, and sandstone. Pinot Gris wines with more elegance come from grapes grown in lighter soils, while full-bodied versions usually reflect heavier soils. This grape is quite capable of growing in both environments.

Climatic Conditions

Regions I and II on the Winkler scale are particularly suitable for the cultivation of Pinot Gris. However, a long summer season, such as that experienced in Alsace, enables the grape to develop particularly exotic aromas redolent of honeysuckle and spice.

TABLE 5.6 RECENT PINOT GRIS PLANTINGS			
Country	Acres	Hectares	% of Worldwide Plantings
Italy	8,575	3,500	23
Romania	7,350	3,000	20
Germany	6,125	2,500	17
France	4,900	2,000	13
California	1,600	650	4
Hungary	1,225	500	4
Oregon	1,270	520	4
Austria	1,000	400	3
Others: Canada, Czechoslovakia, Luxemburg, Moravia, Netherlands, New Zealand, Portugal, Russia, Slovenia, South Africa, and Switzerland.	4,655	1,900	12

Olfactory Characteristics

The main characteristic of Pinot Gris is its ability to develop honey-like flavors and aromas. Whereas Alsace Pinot Gris outlines spices and musk, the Italian wines come in a lighter and more mineral-based form. On the other hand, New World wines like those from New Zealand and Oregon show tropical fruits aromas such as mango. Pinot Gris is quite susceptible to *botrytis cinerea*, leading to naturally sweet wines in a style similar to Sauternes. Styles, therefore, range from dry to sweet.

Geographic Spread

The star of Veneto, Lombardy, Emilia Romagna, and Trentino, Pinot Grigio produces very aromatic wines with a true character in northern Italy. However, it is a grape variety that thrives in cool climate wine regions, as exemplified by its spread in countries where such conditions are usually found. These countries include Germany, Hungary, Oregon, Romania, and parts of France.

Gewürztraminer

Gewürztraminer is easily the most aromatic grape variety as well as the easiest grape to recognize by smell alone. Because of this, it is the delight of beginners to the art of wine tasting. However, because of this, the relationship between Gewürztraminer and more experienced wine drinkers is usually that of "love or hate." The wine is slightly cloying, rich, and powerful. It is seductive to a small proportion of the wine lover population.

According to Pierre Galet, Gewürztraminer assumes a host of other names including Savagnin Rose Aromatique and Gentil Rose Aromatique in Alsace; Gewuerztraminer in Austria; Roter Traminer, Fleischweiner, Fleischroth, Dreimänner, Kleinbraun, and Roter Nürnberger in Germany; Traminer Aromatico and Termeno Aromatico in Italy; Traminer Perfume in Luxemburg; and Mala Dinka in Bulgaria.

History

The Gewürztraminer grape is known to have been planted around the year 1000 AD in a village of the Alto-Adige region in the north of Italy under the name Traminer. It was also found in the sixteenth century in regions of Alsace and Germany. In the eighteenth century, the grape spread to the Palatinate region in Germany.

Ampelography

According to Pierre Galet, Gewürztraminer is actually a variation of the aromatic Savagnin Rose grape. Gewürztraminer grapes are relatively small and have thick skins and a musky, perfumed juice. Sensitive to oïdium (a fungal disease), spring frosts, and coulure (not fully developing because of cold weather), the grape requires great care and protection.

Ideal Soil

The type of soil in which Gewürztraminer is grown is directly related to the desired quality and style of the resulting wine. The best combination seems to be a rich soil of limestone and clay found in Alsace.

Climatic Conditions

Gewürztraminer grapes develop superb wines when grown in the following conditions: dry but cool weather and plenty of light and sunshine. These conditions are found in the Alsace region of France, where the most spectacular Gewürztraminer wines are generated. Where humidity prevails, vines tend to become infected with diseases. Warm climates result in Gewürztraminer wines with lost freshness and olfactory appeal.

Olfactory Characteristics

A distinction needs to be made between the dry, off-dry, and sweet wines obtained from the Gewürztraminer grape, as the olfactory characteristics vary according to style. The unmistakable aromas of rose, lychee, and spice are dominant in dry styles. These same characteristics are displayed in off-dry wines. (Off-dry wines contain higher residual sugars and

Figure 5.10.
Gewürztraminer.

TABLE 5.7 RECENT GEWÜRZTRAMINER PLANTINGS			
Country	Acres	Hectares	% of Worldwide Plantings
France	7,350	3,000	37.5
Germany	2,200	900	11
United States	2,060	840	10.5
Austria	1,715	700	9
Australia	1,470	600	7.5
Italy	1,225	500	6
South Africa	860	350	4.5
Others: Brazil, Canada, Chile, Croatia, Luxemburg, Moldavia, New Zealand, Portugal, Romania, Sardinia, Spain, and Switzerland.	2,695	1,100	14

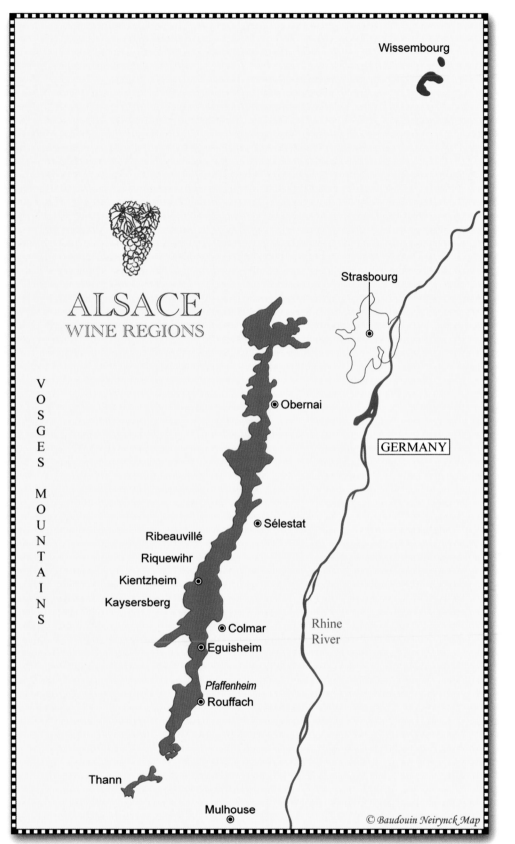

ALSACE
WINE REGIONS

V O S G E S   M O U N T A I N S

Wissembourg

Strasbourg

GERMANY

Obernai

Sélestat

Ribeauvillé
Riquewihr
Kientzheim
Kaysersberg

Colmar
Eguisheim

Rhine
River

Pfaffenheim
Rouffach

Thann

Mulhouse

© *Baudouin Neirynck Map*

peel, honey, and gingerbread. These wines also have a high degree of alcohol—up to 16 percent.

Oz Clarke, a former actor who appeared in the 1978 movie *Superman* and a prolific wine writer since 1984, likens the multi-faceted aromas of the grape with that of the global moisturizing cream called Nivea, to which he adds notes of cinnamon, orange blossom, tea, and bergamot (found also in Earl Grey tea). Botrytized Gewürztraminer wines show a much-reduced rose and lychee smell, but are marvelously rich and sophisticated.

Geographic Spread

Compared with the likes of Chardonnay or Sauvignon Blanc, Gewürztraminer is a grape with a relatively small worldwide diffusion. Its biggest followings are in France and Germany. In most other countries, Gewürztraminer is more a curiosity than anything else. It is planted on 19,600 acres or 8,000 hectares worldwide.

FRANCE

Gewürztraminer is among the group of noble grapes. It is seldom blended, except in Alsace, France. Here, the wines Zwicker and Edelzwicker are blends of noble grapes—Edelzwicker is made by mixing Gewürztraminer, Riesling, Pinot Gris, and Muscat, while the inferior Zwicker adds Chasselas to the similar blend. For more information on the regions of Alsace, see the inset on pages 73 to 74.

The best Riesling plantings can be found around the German towns of Riquewihr, Kellenberg, Ribeauvillé, and Dambach. The *Comité Régional d'Experts des Vins d'Alsace* (CREVA) is a committee of experts that determine each year's acreage and the varieties to be planted, to preserve and enhance the reputation of the region.

lower alcohol levels than dry wines.) Sweet or semi-sweet late-harvest wines, otherwise known as *vendanges tardives,* highlight citrus

The Regions of Alsace

Located in the northeastern corner of France, the region of Alsace contains vineyards that stretch from the Rhine River to the Vosges Mountains, and from the city of Strasbourg to Colmar and Mulhouse. Throughout history, Alsace has alternated between being under the rule of France and Germany. From 1648 to 1871, Alsace was French; from 1871 to 1918, it was German; and in 1918, it returned definitively to France.

These changes of governance were detrimental to the area's wine industry, due mainly to the different markets served by the region. When under German domination, Alsace produced low-quality wines en masse. Under French governance, on the other hand, the focus was on quality—as it is to this day.

Varietal wines—wines produced mainly from one grape and labeled according to the grape used—are the norm in Alsace, the only French region to have adopted this practice. The South of France is also slowly adopting this practice, although the grape information is usually provided in addition to the appellation of origin.

The French Revolution of 1789 triggered a fragmentation of large wine estates, by virtue of inheritance laws put in place by Napoleon. However, with time, some estates consolidated small terroirs, and today's marketplace is shared between cooperatives, small producers, and large companies such as Hugel, Beyer, Dopff & Irion, Lorentz, and Willm. In 1983, the best terroirs in Alsace were given official recognition, through the awarding of Grand Cru (and Premier Cru) status. This ruling was followed by two amendments in 1992 and 2001, outlining authorized and recommended grape varieties and yields that would qualify a vineyard for Grand Cru status. The following list contains the names of all the Grand Crus as well as the recommended grape varieties for those sites.

■ Altenberg de Bergbieten (Riesling, Gewürztraminer, and Muscat)

■ Altenberg de Bergheim (Riesling, Gewürz-traminer, Assemblage, and Pinot Gris)

■ Altenberg de Wolxheim (Riesling and Gewürztraminer)

■ Brand in Turckheim (Riesling, Pinot Gris, and Pinot Noir)

■ Bruderthal in Molsheim (Riesling, Gewürztraminer, and Pinot Gris)

■ Eichberg in Eguisheim (Riesling, Gewürztraminer, and Pinot Gris)

■ Engelberg in Dahlenheim and Scharrachbergheim (Riesling and Gewürztraminer)

■ Florimont in Ingersheim and Katzenhal (Riesling, Gewürztraminer and Pinot Gris)

■ Frankstein in Dambach-la-Ville (Riesling, Gewürztraminer, and Pinot Gris)

■ Froehm in Zellenberg (Riesling, Gewürztraminer, Pinot Gris, and Muscat)

■ Furstentum in Kientzheim and Sigolsheim (Riesling, Gewürztraminer, Pinot Gris, and Pinot Noir)

■ Geisberg in Ribeauvillé (Riesling)

■ Gloeckelberg in Rodern and Saint-Hippolyte (Riesling, Pinot Gris, and Pinot Noir)

■ Goldert in Gueberschwihr (Riesling, Gewürztraminer, Muscat, and Pinot Gris)

■ Hatschbourg in Hattstatt and Voegtlinshoffen (Riesling, Gewürztraminer, Pinot Gris, and Muscat)

■ Hengst in Wintzenheim (Riesling, Gewürztraminer, Pinot Gris, Pinot Blanc, and Pinot Noir)

■ Kanzlerberg in Bergheim (Riesling, Gewürztraminer, and Pinot Gris)—the smallest of all Grand Crus with only around 8 acres (or 3.23 hectares) of vineyards planted

■ Kastelberg in Andlau (Riesling)

■ Kessler in Guebwiller (Riesling and Gewürztraminer)

■ Kirchberg de Barr (Riesling, Gewürztraminer, Pinot Gris, and Assemblage)

■ Kirchberg de Ribeauvillé (Riesling and Pinot Gris)

■ Kitterlé in Guebwiller (Riesling, Gewürztraminer, and Pinot Gris)

■ Mambourg in Sigolsheim (Riesling, Gewürztraminer, and Pinot Gris)

■ Mandelberg in Mittelwihr and Beblenheim (Riesling, Gewürztraminer, and Pinot Gris)

■ Marckrain in Bennwihr and Sigolsheim (Pinot Gris, Gewürztraminer, and Pinot Noir)

■ Moenchberg in Eichhoffen and Andlau (Riesling, Gewürztraminer, and Pinot Gris)

■ Muenchberg in Nothalten (Riesling and Pinot Gris)

■ Ollwiller in Wuenheim (Riesling, Gewürztraminer, and Pinot Gris)

■ Osterberg in Ribeauvillé (Riesling, Gewürztraminer, Pinot Gris, and Assemblage)

■ Pfersigberg in Eguisheim and Wettolsheim (Riesling and Gewürztraminer)

■ Pfingstberg in Orschwihr (Riesling, Gewürztraminer, and Pinot Gris)

■ Praelatenberg in Kintzheim (Riesling, Gewürztraminer, and Pinot Gris)

■ Rangen in Thann (Riesling, Gewürz-traminer, Pinot Gris, and Assemblage)

- Rosacker in Hunawihr (Riesling and Gewürztraminer)

- Saering in Guebwiller (Riesling and Gewürztraminer)

- Schlossberg in Kientzheim (Riesling, Gewürztraminer, and Pinot Gris)—the largest of the Grand Crus covering around 198 acres (or 80 hectares)

- Schoenenbourg in Riquewihr and Zellenberg (Riesling, Gewürztraminer, and Pinot Gris)

- Sommerberg in Niedermorschwihr and Katzenthal (Riesling and Pinot Gris)

- Sonnenglanz in Beblenheim (Gewürztraminer, Pinot Gris, and Assemblage)

- Spiegel in Bergholtz and Guebwiller (Riesling, Gewürztraminer, and Pinot Gris)

- Sporen in Riquewihr (Riesling, Gewürztraminer, and Assemblage)

- Steinert in Pfaffenheim and Westhalten (Riesling, Gewürztraminer, Pinot Gris, and Muscat)

- Steingrubler in Wettolsheim (Riesling and Gewürztraminer)

- Steinklotz in Marlenheim (Riesling, Gewürztraminer, Pinot Gris, and Pinot Noir)

- Vorbourg in Rouffach and Westhalten (Riesling, Gewürztraminer, Pinot Gris, Pinot Noir, Assemblage, and Sylvaner)

- Wiebelsberg in Andlau (Riesling)

- Wineck Scholssberg in Katzenthal and Ammerschwihr (Riesling and Gewürztraminer)

- Winzenberg in Blienschwiller (Riesling, Gewürztraminer, and Pinot Gris)

- Zinnkoepflé in Soultzmatt and Westhalten (Riesling, Gewürztraminer, Pinot Gris, and Assemblage)

- Zotzenberg in Mittelbergheim (Riesling, Gewürztraminer, and Sylvaner)

Figure 5.11.
Entrance to the fortified village of Kientzheim, Alsace, France.

Ugni Blanc (Trebbiano)

Although the grape varietal Ugni Blanc is almost never marked on a wine label, it is the most planted white wine grape variety in France. In fact, its French production is about five times that of Chardonnay. This is in many ways due to the production of Cognac and Armagnac, both of which utilize Ugni Blanc. Total worldwide plantings of Ugni Blanc cover 561,000 acres (or 229,000 hectares).

Ugni Blanc produces very different wines under different climates. In the Cognac region, the cold northern limit for viticulture, grapes are harvested before reaching full maturity, resulting in must that is relatively acidic. This is a necessity for elaborating this world-famous brandy, because this wine is destined to be distilled.

On the other hand, its growth in warmer regions produces wines with lower acidity but higher alcohol content. In the regions of Corsica, Provence, and Languedoc, Ugni Blanc is often vinified into dry white wine with these characteristics. The grape variety is a very late budder, which protects it from spring frosts, and is a heavy producer with common yields of up to 11.1 tons per acre (or 150 hectoliters per hectare).

In Italy, most regions produce their own version of Ugni Blanc, which is called Trebbiano throughout this country. The exceptions are in the far north, where climatic conditions are too cold for this grape. It was used as part of the blend for wines such as Soave, Orvieto, Lugana, Verdicchio, and Frascati for a good part of the twentieth century, and was even used in Chianti wine production (although as a diluting agent more than anything else).

Ugni Blanc is known by many names. It is called Trebbiano and Tribbiano in Italy; Talia, Branquinha, and Douradinha in Portugal; Clairette à Grains Ronds, Chatar, Cadillac and Muscadet in France. This grape has been the subject of intensive and successful cloning. Clones 284, 479, 482, 483, and 485 are the most widely planted. In Italy, almost every region has developed its own clone or variety under the name of Trebbiano followed by the name of the region such as Trebbiano Romagnolo, Trebbiano Modense, Trebbiano di Soave, and Trebbiano d'Abruzzo.

History

Roman scientist and ampelographer Pliny described a *"vinum trebulanum"* in Campania that may well have been our present-day Ugni Blanc, but the origins of this grape can definitely be traced back to Italy as early as third century AD. The first formal recognition of this grape came in 1303 from the Bolognese agronomist Petrus De Crescentiis. It was probably imported to France around 600 years ago. Jancis Robinson, MW, mentions the establishment of the Papal court in Avignon as the triggering event for the arrival of Ugni Blanc in France.

Ampelography

Characterized by a large leaf, long bunch, and small berries, Ugni Blanc's presence in the vineyards of Europe dates back to pre-Roman times and has given birth through genetic mutations to numerous sub-varieties under different names.

Ideal Soil

Depending on the soil composition in which Ugni Blanc is planted, its natural ability to resist certain pests and diseases may be adversely affected. Sandy soils trigger the appearance of mildew and eutypa dieback, a fungal disease. Therefore, clay, limestone, and well-drained rocky soils are preferable for the viticulture of Ugni Blanc.

Climatic Conditions

It is a generally accepted fact that Ugni Blanc cannot produce drinkable wines above 47° north longitude, due to its susceptibility to winter frosts and downy mildew. Therefore, warmer climates enable the production of dry wines with this grape, whereas cooler climates tend to dictate distillation rather than vinification.

Figure 5.12.
Ugni Blanc,
Trebbiano, Italy.

TABLE 5.8 RECENT UGNI BLANC PLANTINGS			
Country	**Acres**	**Hectares**	**% of Worldwide Plantings**
France	236,140	96,370	41.9
Italy	237,650	97,000	42.3
Bulgaria	61,250	25,000	11
Argentina	9,800	4,000	1.7
Mexico	4,900	2,000	0.8
Brazil	4,165	1,700	0.7
Greece	2,450	1,000	0.3
Others: Australia, California, Portugal, Romania, Russia, South Africa, and Uruguay.	7,460	3,046	1.3

Olfactory Characteristics

Ugni Blanc is not a particularly aromatic grape. It is far more memorable for its tartness, waxy character, and acidity than for its smell. However, this grape is favored by producers of balsamic vinegar in the region of Modena in Italy.

Geographic Spread

With a very neutral olfactory output, Ugni Blanc is the basic wine widely cultivated in Europe, mainly France, Italy, and Bulgaria. Unless it provides the base wine for popular spirits and hard liquors such as Cognac in France, its plantings will probably decrease in the future as wine markets seek more aromatic and characteristic wines. The size of plantings in France and Italy are explained by long history and tradition. However, outside of Europe, this grape has little appeal to winemakers.

Sylvaner

Sylvaner is the main variety grown in the German wine-producing regions of Rheinhessen, Pfalz, and Franken. It is also grown in Alsace, France. Wines made from the Sylvaner grape are generally considered light and pleasant to drink. They usually contain a good dose of acidity, but are generally unsuitable for aging.

Sylvaner ripens earlier than Riesling and produces medium-sized berries with an excellent, slightly acidulated juice. Yielding between 4.4 to 5.9 tons per acre (or 60 to 80 hectoliters per hectare) on the slopes of Alsace, it can produce up to 11.1 tons per acre (or 150 hectoliters per hectare) in plains where drainage is less efficient. Sylvaner is susceptible to fungi and diseases such as oïdium, mildew, and grey rot.

Around the world, Sylvaner is known by many names. It is called Grüner Sylvaner in Austria; Gros Rhin, Gros Plant du Rhin, Gros Riesling, Plant du Rhin, and Johannisberg in Germany; Grande Arvine in Switzerland; Silvaner Bianco and Silvania in Italy; Zelena Sedmogradka and Silvanai Zeleni in Croatia; and Franken Riesling, Monterey Riesling, and Sonoma Riesling in California.

History

This grape is from Austria, but its name suggests it may have actually originated in Transylvania. Oz Clarke wrote that the first written plantation records to include Sylvaner were those in 1659 in Franken, a wine region in Germany.

Ampelography

With cylindrical and compact bunches, Sylvaner leaves are slightly yellow and relatively round in shape. Its berries are average in size, spherical or slightly conical, and bunches appear compact.

Ideal Soil

Judging by the areas where Sylvaner is planted, it is suitable for any soil apart from sandy ones. In Franconia (Germany), where Sylvaner dominates, a variety of soils such as red sandstone, clay, loess, and shelly limestone seem to suit the grape variety equally. In other regions where plantings occur along rivers, soils such as schist and slate produce grapes with good to excellent results.

Climatic Conditions

Regions I and II on the Winkler scale are better suited for the maturation of this grape than warm-weather regions. This is because retention of the crispiness which is the attractiveness of this grape requires that a minimum acidity level must be maintained—which is only possible in cool-weather regions.

Olfactory Characteristics

The Sylvaner grape produces wines with little ambition besides being light, medium-bodied, fresh, and crisp. Earthy tones and vanilla are characteristics found in particularly good bottles from good locations and vintages.

Geographic Spread

Although its origins can be traced back to Austria, Sylvaner is seldom cultivated in that country. Instead, it migrated to the west during a major replanting exercise in the area in 1659, according to Jancis Robinson, MW. Sylvaner traveled particularly to the German region of Franken. Worldwide, Sylvaner is grown on 29,400 acres (or 12,000 hectares).

Figure 5.13.
Sylvaner.

TABLE 5.9 RECENT SYLVANER PLANTINGS			
Country	Acres	Hectares	% of Worldwide Plantings
Germany	18,375	7,500	62.5
France	4,900	2,000	17
Switzerland	735	300	2.5
Hungary	610	250	2
United States	490	200	1.5
Italy	490	200	1.5
Others: Argentina, Australia, Austria, Croatia, New Zealand, Russia, and South Africa.	3,800	1,550	13

Viognier

For a grape that was almost extinct around forty years ago, Viognier has made a remarkable comeback. From its presence in Condrieu—a little-known wine of extreme quality—viticulturists have rediscovered the beauty and intrinsic qualities of this grape. A difficult vine to grow, Viognier is prone to several fungi and vine diseases such as mildew. In addition, yields are unpredictable and often very low. Wines made from Viognier show only a limited aging potential. A maximum of five to six years may bring out additional flavors and bouquet in certain bottles, but young wines are perfectly drinkable, and have usually already reached their full aromatic spectrum. Higher alcohol content, at around 13 percent, is the norm.

According to Pierre Galet, the name and spelling of the Viognier grape includes all the following French alternatives: Vionnier, Petit Vionnier, Viogné, and Galopine à La Tronche. It is also called Vugava Bijela on the island of Vis in Croatia. Oz Clarke mentions a mutation that may have been planted in countries other than France but which does not yield wines of a similar taste and aroma to the original grape.

Figure 5.14.
Viognier.

History

The origin of Viognier is the Dalmatian mountains of Croatia, where it is still today cultivated under the name Vugava Bijela. It was imported to France by the Romans, who planted it in the region of the Rhône Valley in Condrieu, just south of Côte Rôtie. Although it has grown in the Rhône Valley for millennia, this low-yield grape was undesirable during times when quality was less important than quantity. However, it has always been vinified with Syrah in some of the best appellations in the same region.

Ampelography

With a sinus in a "U" shape, Viognier leaves are of average size. Its berries are small.

Ideal Soil

Viognier's best results are grown in stony soils such as granite where roots need to dig very deep to find the necessary moisture. This is the type of soil found in the grape's original home of Condrieu in the Rhône Valley. Other Viognier plantings around the world cannot reproduce the aromatic results found there.

Climatic Conditions

Viognier grows extremely well in warm climatic conditions, especially in cases of drought. This is due to its ability to dig very deep in the soil, and explains the low yields but very seductive aromatic spectrum of the grape.

Olfactory Characteristics

The Viognier variety has often been cited as a cross between Chardonnay and Gewürztraminer. A heavily perfumed grape with unmistakable apricot, orange blossom, and acacia smells, Viognier produces wine with aromas reminiscent of honeysuckle and peaches. It also has an impressive spicy and musky finish. Smells of candied peel, jasmine, mint, primrose, and tobacco can be found in some of the top Rhône versions, such as Château Grillet.

TABLE 5.10 RECENT VIOGNIER PLANTINGS			
Country	Acres	Hectares	% of Worldwide Plantings
France	5,733	2,340	58.5
United States	2,205	900	22.5
Australia	612	250	6.25
Others: Argentina, Brazil, Canada, Chile, Japan, Mexico, New Zealand, South Africa, and Uruguay.	1,250	510	12.75

Geographic Spread

Total worldwide plantings of Viognier cover 9,800 acres (or 4,000 hectares). A large majority of these plants are in either France or the United States.

A few wineries in traditionally non-Viognier producing countries have recently started planting and harvesting the grape. One of the most notable examples which has seen very good results is Quinta do Monte d'Oiro in Estremadura, Portugal. Its Madrigal Viognier is very aromatic yet true in terms of varietal smells and flavors.

Chenin Blanc

The most planted grape in South Africa, Chenin Blanc is a versatile variety. It originated in France's Loire Valley, and the best-known Chenin Blanc wines are probably the ones from this same area. A medium-sized grape berry that displays itself in a compact bunch, Chenin Blanc can yield between 1.5 and 2.2 tons per acre (or between 20 and 30 hectoliters per hectare) in vineyards in which crops are thinned and quality is the objective. In fertile soils, the total can reach as high as 7.4 tons per acre (or 100 hectoliters per hectare).

Known as Plant d'Anjou, Blanc d'Anjou, Pinet d'Anjou, Pineau de Vouvray, Pineau Nantais, Pinot de la Loire, Gros Chenin, and Plant de Brézé in various regions of France, Chenin Blanc is also known by Pinot Blanco in Argentina and Chile, and Vaalbaar Stein (or Steen) in South Africa.

Figure 5.15.
Chenin Blanc

History

Chenin's existence is well documented. In 845 AD, it appeared in Anjou in the Loire Valley of France. According to Oz Clarke, the grape's name comes from the village of Mont-Chenin located in the South of Touraine. Exported in the seventeenth century to South Africa, it became the most widely planted grape in this region due to its ability to conserve acidity even in warm to hot climatic conditions.

Gaston Huet (1910 to 2002) was a formidable winemaker, a World War II POW, a pioneer of biodynamic viticulture, and a mayor of the village of Vouvray. The wines produced by his estate earned an excellent reputation in three styles: dry, semi-dry, and moelleux—wines with around 21 ounces per 34 fluid ounces (or 60 grams per liter) residual sugar.

Ampelography

The Chenin bunch shows at maturity oval shape berries of a golden yellow color. It is of average size. Yields vary from 1.5 tons per acre to 7.5 tons (from 20 to 100 hectoliters per hectare).

Ideal Soil

The ideal soil for Chenin Blanc grapes is found in the Loire Valley, which is famous for its *tuffeau*, or light chalk soils. The best Chenin Blanc wines, both dry and sweet, are produced in this region.

Climatic Conditions

Chenin Blanc is particularly important to the vineyards of the New World. Here, climatic conditions are usually warm and dry, and this is a grape that manages to retain a certain degree of acidity even in very hot, dry weather. The grape can generate wines that age with grace, and can be vinified into both dry and sweet wines. It can even be used to produce sparkling wine (such as AOCs Saumur, Vouvray, Montlouis, and Touraine in France). However, the best expression of the grape is in wines from the Loire Valley, where summers tend to be hot but short.

Olfactory Characteristics

A whole spectrum of flavors is displayed according to how the Chenin Blanc grapes are vinified. The wines Anjou and Vouvray are simple and dry, while Savennières is complex and luscious. In their 2001 book *Grapes and Wines*, Oz Clarke and Margaret Rand highlight the olfactory characteristics of young Chenin Blanc, which is acidic and resembles crisp green apples mixed with greengage and angelica. Interestingly, as Clarke also mentions, malolactic fermentation may render some other very young wines much less acidic. Aged wines, on the other hand, bring other flavors such as acacia, honey, and brioche, combined with quince. When affected by noble rot, Chenin Blanc wines display aromas highlighting peaches, pineapple, barley sugar, cream and marzipan. New World versions outline tropical flavors such as banana, guava, and pineapple.

Geographic Spread

Chenin Blanc was known and documented as early as 845 AD under the name of *plant d'anjou* in Anjou. The grape was exported to the neighboring region of Touraine in the 1400s, according to ampelographer Pierre Galet.

Today, Chenin Blanc is planted on 129,850 acres (or 53,000 hectares). With more than 66,000 acres, South Africa is really the home of Chenin Blanc. This grape was the backbone of this country's wine industry for centuries. Chenin Blanc also maintains a strong presence in France, its country of origin.

FRANCE

Chenin Blanc is responsible for some of the most elegant and durable wines produced in France. It is largely produced in the Loire Valley and its neighboring *departments,* or geographical districts. These include Vouvray, Bonnezeaux, Coteaux de l'Aubance, Coteaux du Layon, Jasnières, Anjou, Saumur, and Savennières. Domaine Huet (managed by Noël Pinguet, the son-in-law of Gaston Huet, and famed for its Le Haut Lieu Vouvray), Domaine du Clos Naudin in Vouvray, Domaine de La Taille-aux-Loups in Montlouis-sur-Loire, and Domaine des Aubusières, also in Vouvray, are some of the top producers of this wine.

Nicolas Joly is a leading advocate of biodynamic viticulture. His French domain, Château La Roche-aux-Moines, produced the great wine Coulée de Serrant. Pierre Aguilas, in the village of Chaudefonds-sur-Layon, also produces a fantastic Chenin Blanc: Coteaux du Layon Les Varennes.

SOUTH AFRICA

Chenin Blanc is a very important grape in South Africa. It occupies around a quarter of all planted vineyards, and is known here as *steen,* the Afrikaaner word for stone. Jan van Riebeeck, a Dutch trader who established one of the first wine estates in South Africa in the middle of the seventeenth century, imported the grape from France. Grown mainly in the regions of Paarl and Worcester, the grapes are usually bought by cooperatives and utilized either as distillation material or to make inexpensive white wines.

© *Baudouin Neirynck Map*

TABLE 5.11 RECENT CHENIN BLANC PLANTINGS			
Country	Acres	Hectares	% of Worldwide Plantings
South Africa	66,150	27,000	51
France	22,050	9,000	17
United States	21,560	8,800	16.5
Argentina	10,500	4,300	8
Australia	2,100	850	2
Mexico	1,225	500	1
New Zealand	490	200	0.5
Others: Brazil, Canada, Chili, Spain, and Uruguay.	5,190	2,100	4

Nevertheless, some small producers, such as those from Forrester-Meinert in Helderberg, Stellenbosch, are successful in creating quality wines. Here, the grape is limited to a low yield—3.3 tons per acre (or 45 hectolitres per hectare)—and is cultivated on a topsoil of sandy loam on top of clay. Brothers Bruwer and Jasper Raats, both Chenin Blanc enthusiasts, cultivate an old-vines vineyard, owned by a family friend, and make terrific wines.

NEW ZEALAND

This country has shown a lot of promise in the form of exceptionally generous Chenin Blanc plantations, but it may take some time before these receive the recognition currently afforded to the area's Sauvignon Blanc.

A WHITE WINE GRAPE LESS TRAVELED

The following white wine grapes are not as well known as the grapes previously described in this chapter. Some of them are not found throughout the world wine market with the same frequency as the other grapes, but many extraordinary wines are produced from their juices. Others are found in substantial quantities in many different wines, but these wines are of a lesser quality than those produced from the other grapes. However, they are all significant in the world of wine, and most wine lovers find knowledge of them to be a necessary part of their wine education.

Muscat

Muscat is found across the world in many guises and names. As indicated by its full name, Muscat of Alexandria originated in Alexandria, Egypt. The Romans propagated it around the Mediterranean Sea, but the grape was seldom used for the production of wine. In Italy, the Muscat grape is known as Moscato, while it is called Moscatel in Spain and Portugal. It can also be found under other names such as Muskateller in German-speaking countries, Muskadel in South Africa, and Malvasia in Greece.

Muscat produces both white and red wines, depending on vinification. It has one particular advantage over most other wine grapes. Besides its potential to be used in wine, this grape is also usually very suitable for the production of both table grapes and raisins. Muscat of Alexandrie and Muscat of Hamburg are best suited as table grapes or raisins whereas Muscat à Petits Grains gives the best wines.

Muscat is found across the world in many guises and names. A staggering 150 Muscat grapes are registered by Pierre Galet. They cover every country where there is the potential to cultivate grapes. In the New World, it is best expressed in Australia and California's San Joaquin Valley, San Luis Obispo, and Central Valley.

The three most widely planted varieties are Muscat of Alexandria, Muscat Blanc à Petits Grains, and Muscat Ottonel. In Italy, Muscat Blanc à Petits Grains is used in the production of the famous sparkling white wine Asti Spumante, as well as for liquor wines in the south of the country. Muscat d'Ottonel is a more recent development, and was bred in France's Loire Valley in the middle of the nineteenth century. It was created, according to Pierre Galet, by crossing Chasselas with Muscat of Saumur.

Airén (Lairen)

With plantings close to 980,000 acres (or 400,000 hectares), this is the most widely planted white grape in the world. It is found primarily in Spain, where it (blended with Cencibel, a dark black grape) provides the base material for light red wines, as well as a range of light, unassuming white wines for everyday consumption. Airén is also used in the production of Spanish brandy.

Low-density, bush-style plantings are utilized for this grape.

As a result, although the plantations are the largest of any grape variety, the yield is not correspondingly significant.

Rkatsiteli

By far the most widely cultivated white wine grape in the Commonwealth of Independent States, Rkatsiteli's origins can be traced back to Georgia. Its high acid and sugar content render it an ideal grape for a wide range of wine styles, from dry to off-dry and dessert wines. It is even utilized for brandy.

The names under which this grape can be found are numerous: Rkatsiteli in Romania; Kakoura in Georgia; Korolek, Tapolek, and Koroliok in Russia; Baiyu in China; and Rkaciteli in Yugoslavia. It is also planted in Armenia, Azerbaidjan, China, Georgia, Kazakhstan, Moldavia, Ouzbekistan, Tadjikistan, and Turkmenistan. Estimates of the number of hectares planted show substantial variations. This is due to both unreliable statistics and frequent uprooting of Rkatsiteli in favor of better quality varieties. Figures range from 117,600 acres (or 48,000 hectares) in 1990 according to Pierre Galet, down to only 49,000 acres (or 20,000 hectares) in 2006 according to the *Office International du Vin* (OIV). In 1992, on the other hand, Jancis Robinson, MW, estimated 637,000 acres (or 260,000 hectares) of Rkatsiteli plantings in her *Oxford Companion to Wine*.

Marsanne

Often blended with Roussanne, this white wine grape variety has contributed to the reputation of white Rhône wines around the world. Grown on terraces in the Rhône Valley, it produces wines with low levels of acidity at the rate of around 4.4 tons per acre (or 60 hectoliters per hectare). Only about 4,900 acres (or 2,000 hectares) of Marsanne are planted in the world. These are mainly located in the countries of France, Switzerland, Italy, and Australia. The best wines produced from the grape are in the French appellations of Hermitage, St. Joseph, Crozes-Hermitage, and St. Péray. Here, Marsanne is also an authorized grape in red wines to the tune of up to 15 percent. In Australia, the grape is grown in Victoria and New South Wales, and, in Italy, is produced in Piacenza.

Roussanne

A white wine grape grown predominately in the Rhône Valley, Roussanne is also produced in small quantities in Australia, Italy, and the United States. Although able to be produced in both warm and cool climates, it is notoriously difficult to grow. This grape generates small yields, but the resulting wines are usually very elegant, with aromas of apricot, honey, and hawthorne.

The Roussanne grape, which is also known as Bergeron, is very often blended with white wine grapes Marsanne and Grenache Blanc. Unlike most wines produced from white wine grapes, Roussanne wines are usually able to continue maturing in the bottle for up to ten years.

Malvasia

Malvasia is a white grape of Greek origin. It is a versatile grape which has variously mutated into Istriana, cultivated in the Friuli-Venezia region; Malvasia del Lazio, found in the Latium region; and Malvasia Bianca del Chianti, which is blended with Sangiovese and Canaiolo Nero to add softness to the sometimes austere wines of Chianti. In Piedmont, it has its own recognition as a DOC in Casorzo and Castelnuovo, as well as in the regions of Alto Adige and Puglia.

Pinot Blanc

In terms of olfactory characteristics, Pinot Blanc wines outline smooth, fruity, nutty, and buttery notes. Pinot Blanc is a cousin, or mutation, of Pinot Gris, and can be found in Alsace, Germany, Austria, and Italy. In Alsace, it is sometimes vinified on its own, but is more often blended with Chardonnay to produce Crémant d'Alsace, the local sparkling wine.

In Italy, this grape is called Pinot Bianco. It gives light, crisp, and relatively tart wines, and is used extensively in the blending of spumante (sparkling wines). In the New World, Pinot Blanc can be found in Argentina and Uruguay, in simple un-wooded form, whereas in California it is vinified using oak barrels and malolactic fermentation.

6.
Red Wine Grapes

Figure 6.1.
Pinot Noir.

You are now familiar with many important white wine grapes. There are also a variety of red wine grapes with which every student of wine should be aware. The red wine grapes discussed in this chapter are among the most well known and widely used. As in the last chapter, each grape will be discussed in terms of its history, origin, main planting regions, and aromatic profile. For most grapes, information will also be provided regarding the best and most popular wines in which they can be found. The grapes that are most important in the global wine market are presented first.

PINOT NOIR

The red wine grape Pinot Noir belongs to the Pinot family, which includes Pinot Meunier, Pinot Gris, Pinot Blanc, Pinot Gris, and Auxerrois. Alternate names for this grape include Auvernat Noir, Pinot Droit, Blauer Klevner, Cortaillod, Noirien, Schwartz Klevner, Vert Doré, Spätburgunder, Blauburgunder, and Pinot Nero.

Pinot Noir grapes strongly reflect their *terroir*—the combination of soil and climatic conditions associated with a particular piece of land where wine grapes are grown. Having found a home on every continent, this grape generates some of the best and richest red wines in the world, including Burgundy's Domaine Romanée Conti. Yet Pinot Noir is a difficult grape to grow.

It buds early, resulting in a vine that is prone to damage by spring frosts, coulure, mildew, and rot, as well as viruses such as leaf-roll and fan-leaf.

There are currently more than 200 different Pinot Noir clones planted around the world, resulting in a wide variety of wines of differing quality, alcoholic content, aging potential, and style. France recognizes forty-six Pinot Noir clones. In Burgundy, varieties 114 and 115 are the most widely planted, while the varieties numbered 667, 777, and 828 continue to gain in reputation. Since Pinot Noir is usually regarded as a delicate grape with a relatively thin skin, clonal selection has been used to reduce the size of its berries and increase its skin thickness. The resulting grapes are called Pinot Fin, Pinot Tordu, and Pinot Classique.

Some mutant varieties of Pinot Noir have resulted in the popular Pinot Meunier and Pinot Gouges. Pinot Musigny is a mutant that changed grape color from the original black to white, and is produced in Burgundy on a 6.2-acre (or 2.5-hectare) parcel.

Wines made from Pinot Noir grapes are lighter in color than those made from Cabernet Sauvignon or Syrah, and show lower tannin levels because Pinot Noir grape skin is relatively thin. Its wines are usually enjoyed young, but some are capable of aging for decades.

> There are eight noble grapes that are generally acknowledged to produce wine of the highest quality. Chardonnay, Riesling, Sauvignon Blanc, and Chenin Blanc are the white grape varieties; Cabernet Sauvignon, Pinot Noir, Syrah/Shiraz, and Merlot are the red.

History

Pierre Galet claims that Columella, one of the first ampelographers, very accurately described the grape variety Pinot Noir and its leaf. Therefore, it is generally accepted that Pinot Noir was present in the vineyards of the Roman Empire. Written evidence surfaced in fourteenth century Burgundian writings, when the grape was referenced by the names Pynoz, Pinot Fin, and Plant Fin.

Ampelography

As Jancis Robinson MW wrote in the *Oxford Companion to Wine*, "There is some evidence that Pinot existed in Burgundy in the fourth century AD. Although Morillon Noir was the common name for early Pinot, a vine called Pinot was already described in records of Burgundy in the fourteenth century and its fortunes were inextricably linked with those of the powerful medieval monasteries of eastern France and Germany." Indeed, a 1999 study reported in *Science Magazine* determined that Chardonnay, Gamay Noir, and many of the other varieties responsible for the stellar reputation of Burgundy wines can be traced back to a cross that occurred between a certain ancient Pinot variety and Gouais Blanc.

Ideal Soil

Pinot Noir grows best in well-drained, somewhat infertile, limestone soils. Rich and fertile soils are avoided because of the excessive vegetal growth in these areas, which blocks sun exposure from getting to the bunches. In addition, herbaceous or vegetal aromas and flavors are likely to characterize the resulting wine.

Climatic Conditions

Pinot Noir gives its best results under cool climatic conditions. It grows well in fog. Excessive sunshine is not beneficial for this grape. Although a warmer climate can deliver a grape that produces wines with a much higher degree of alcohol than a cooler climate, this comes at the expense of the grape's aromas. The degree of alcohol is also affected by the size of the grape's yield: the higher the yield, the lower the alcohol level.

Olfactory Characteristics

The primary aromas of Pinot Noir are associated with red fruits such as cherries, strawberries, raspberries, and ripe tomatoes; floral notes of violet and rose petals; and spices such as peppermint, rosemary, caraway, and cinnamon. In some wines, herbaceous smells such as rhubarb, beet, green tomato, green tea, and oregano are also present.

Depending on the oak-barrel aging and/or fermentation processes, Pinot Noir can develop gamey aromas, as well as mushroom, barnyard, truffle, leather, and earthy flavors. These scents are essential in the identification of the wine's origin and the vinification processes it has seen. A light oak-barrel exposure of six months to one year generates aromas of sweet wood, coconut, and vanilla, while a longer exposure imparts flavors of oak, smoke, burnt toast, and tar. Pinot Noir wine that is aged inside the bottle may develop cedarwood flavors.

Geographic Spread

The total worldwide plantings of Pinot Noir consist of 163,225 acres (or 66,200 hectares). A majority of these are found in Burgundy, some parts of South Africa, and Oregon. For the best aromatic results, Pinot Noir should be produced in Region I or II.

FRANCE

Pinot Noir was originally cultivated in France, throughout Burgundy, Loire, Mâconnais, Languedoc, Côte Chalonnaise, and Champagne. It is also grown in smaller quantities in Jura, Rhône, Savoie, and Midi. In 2006, Pinot Noir plantings covered 63,700 acres (or 26,000 hectares) in France.

Burgundy

Nearly all red wines from Burgundy contain Pinot Noir. The exceptions to this are those wines from the Beaujolais region which are based on the Gamay grape (which is discussed on page 120).

Coulure (which is also called shatter) adversely affects the vine by restricting the development of its fruit and causing it to bear either small grapes or none at all during the growing season.

Several types of grapes have the word "Pinot" in their name. This comes from the resemblance of the grape bunch to that of a pine cone.

The release of the film *Sideways* in 2005 substantially boosted the status of Pinot Noir versus Merlot. From a purist's point of view as well as that expressed in the movie, the latter grape is less interesting.

The Great Winemakers and Merchants of Burgundy

Many different brands of wine are produced in Burgundy, France, which has long been famous for its magnificent wines. The region is divided into extremely fragmented vineyards, due in large part to Napoleon's law of equal inheritance among siblings in Burgundy, France. As a result of this law, there are a myriad of producers, each of whom owns small parcels of land. Further, different generations of the same family sometimes vinify under different first names, introducing a host of wines with many different names.

Viticulturists plant predominantly Chardonnay and Pinot Noir. They are also allowed to cultivate several other grapes, including white wine grapes Aligoté, Pinot Blanc, Sacy, and Melon de Bourgogne, and red wine grapes Pinot Liebault, Gamay, and Pinot Gris, throughout the region.

Covering about 98,000 acres (or 40,000 hectares), the vineyards of Burgundy show predominantly limestone and Kimmeridgian clay soils. Limestone, in particular, is well suited to the region's two prized grapes, Chardonnay and Pinot Noir. As a result, Burgundian winemakers produce wines that are among the most elegant expressions of these grapes in the world. However, the climate is somewhat capricious and can adversely affect the ripening of the grapes. In less than favorable years, this can necessitate chaptalization—the pre-fermentation addition of sugar, in the form of unfermented concentrated grape juice, in order to obtain the desired level of alcohol in the finished wine.

The following is a list of producers, growers, and merchants who have achieved international reputation because of the quality of their wines. They are arranged by subregion. Burgundy, as well as the following list, is divided into two subregions: Côte de Nuits and Côte de Beaune.

Côte de Nuits

GEVREY CHAMBERTIN & CHAMBERTIN

Bachelet, L. Boillot, Burguet, Charlopin, Damoy, Drouhin, Dugat-Py, Faiveley, Jadot, Leroy, Denis Mortet, Ponsot, Rossignol-Trapet, and Trapet.

MOREY SAINT-DENIS

Amiot, Dujac, H. Lignier, Moillard-Grivot, Mommessin, Ponsot, Rousseau, and Serveau.

CHAMBOLLE-MUSIGNY

Barthod, de Vogue, Drouhin, Faiveley, Groffier, Jadot, Mugneret, Rion, Roumier, and Serveau.

VOUGEOT AND CLOS DE VOUGEOT

Drouhin, Engel, Faiveley, Grivot, Hudelot-Noellat, Jadot, Chateau De La Tour, Leroy, Chantal Lescure, Méo-Camuzet, and Mugneret.

VOSNE ROMANÉE

Arnoux, Cathiard, Confuron-Cotétidot, Domaine de la Romanée Conti (DRC), René Engel, Jean Grivot, Anne Gros, Jayer, Lamarche, Latour, Leroy, Méo-Camuzet, Mongeard-Mugneret, Mugneret, and Rion.

NUITS-SAINT-GEORGES

Ambroise, Jean Chauvenet, Robert Chevillon, Confuron, Faiveley, Grivot, Lechéneaut, Leroy, Machard de Gramont, Rion, and Thomas-Moillard.

Côte de Beaune

PERNAND-VERGELESSES

Bonneau Du Martray, Chandon de Briailles, Chanson, Delarche, Jadot, Latour, and Rollin.

SAVIGNY-LÈS-BEAUNE

Chandon de Briailles and Guyon.

CHOREY-LÈS-BEAUNE

Tollot-Beaut and Germain Père et Fils.

ALOXE CORTON

Louis Latour.

BEAUNE

Bouchard Père et Fils (Beaune du Château) and Drouhin (Clos des Mouches).

POMMARD

Billard-Gonnet, Comte Armand, De Courcel, De Montille, Gaunoux, Jean Marc Boillot, Leroy, Machard de Gramont, and Pothier-Rieusset.

VOLNAY

Hospices de Beaune, Jean Marc Boillot, Lafarge, Lafon, De Montille, Marquis D'Angerville, and Pousse D'Or.

Loire

Pinot Noir is found in the upper Loire region. It is used to make Sancerre, Menetou-Salon, Touraine, Rosé de Loire, and Crémant de Loire.

Alsace

Pinot Noir wines are the only red or rosé wines produced in Alsace. Labeled under the varietal name, they are light in color.

Champagne

There are substantial plantings of Pinot Noir—more than 24,500 acres (or 10,000 hectares)—in the Champagne region. Here, this grape is blended with Pinot Meunier and Chardonnay.

GERMANY

Occupying around 9 percent of the total acreage of Germany, Pinot Noir is known throughout this country as Spätburgunder. The best German wines produced from this grape come from the regions of the Ahr and the Rheingau. The Ahr has many small producers. Among them, Meyer-Näkel and Nelles have achieved excellent reputations. Meyer-Näkel is known for its natural approach to viticulture, while Nelles is known for its long tradition, which dates back to 1479.

In the Rheingau, estates are relatively larger than those in the Ahr. The best-known names are Schloss Schönborn in Hattenheim, Schloss Reinhartshausen in Erbach, and the state-owned Staatsweingüter Kloster Eberbach in Eltville and Assmanshausen. Yields are the main determinant of quality in these wines, which are made from grapes that are usually cultivated at the northernmost limit for viticulture (50° N).

AUSTRALIA

Australian Pinot Noir is found principally in areas with cool climates. It is grown in Geelong, Yarra Valley, and Mornington Peninsula in the state of Victoria; in Tasmania; and around the Adelaide Hills in South Australia. These plantings yield interesting wines with good structure and olfactory characteristics appreciably different from those of the country's other leading varieties (Cabernet Sauvignon and Shiraz). Some of the best Australian producers of Pinot Noir wines are Yarra Yering and Mount Mary in the Yarra Valley and Bannockburn in Geelong.

SWITZERLAND

Mainly cultivated in the German part of Switzerland in the cantons (divisions) of Zürich (principally Schaffhausen, Graubünden, Thurgau, and Sankt Gallen), the Pinot Noir grape is also found in the French-speaking cantons of Neuchatel and Valais. It is the second-most important

Tonnerrois

Chablis

Châtillonais

Auxerrois

Jrancy

Vézelay

◉Dijon

Côte de Nuits

Hautes Côtes de Nuits

Côte de Beaune

Côte d'Or

◉Beaune

Hautes Côtes de Beaune

◉Chalon-sur-Saône

Côte Chalonnaise

Côte Maconnaise

St. Véran

◉Mâcon

Pouilly Fuissé

BURGUNDY
WINE REGIONS

25 Km
16 Miles

© *Baudouin Neirynck Map*

grape after Chasselas, accounting for 27 percent of total plantings in Switzerland. Every year, an annual Pinot Noir competition is held in this country. Domestically produced wines compete against a range of other Pinot Noir wines from around the world. Wine produced by Martha and Daniel Gantenbein of Flach, Graubünden has recently been voted the best Pinot Noir from Switzerland.

SOUTH AFRICA

South Africa is home to Stellenbosch, a historical wine region located at the western tip of the coastal waters around the city of Cape Town. Two other main regions are located on the Northern Cape—Douglas and Lower Orange River. As only 8,575 acres (or 3,500 hectares) of this grape are grown here, the area's Pinot Noir plantings are relatively minor. However, if one recognizes Pinotage (a cross between Cinsaut and Pinot Noir) as a true Pinot Noir planting, the figure increases to around 39,200 acres (or 16,000 hectares).

Most South African Pinot Noir grapes were originally planted with a Swiss clone. However, a Burgundian clone is gradually replacing it in most areas. Hamilton Russell from Walker Bay has achieved a great reputation for its Pinot Noir. Its wines show excellent structure, good aging potential, and a varietal character very similar to that of Burgundian wines.

UNITED STATES

Pinot Noir has become the king of grapes in Oregon. The state's Pinot Noir wines have achieved cult status among wine drinkers. Harvested in the three American Viticultural Area (AVA) regions of Rogue Valley, Umpqua Valley, and Willamette Valley, Pinot Noir grown in Oregon develops a character so true to its name that it has attracted the house of Joseph Drouhin, a well-known Burgundy merchant, to produce wine here.

TABLE 5.10 RECENT PINOT NOIR PLANTINGS			
Country	Acres	Hectares	% of Worldwide Plantings
France	63,700	26,000	39
Germany	18,620	7,600	11.5
United States	14,000	5,700	8.7
Switzerland	10,290	4,200	6.4
Italy	8,820	3,600	5.4
South Africa	8,575	3,500	5.3
New Zealand	8,575	3,500	5.3
Australia	4,900	2,000	3
Chile	3,920	1,600	2.5
Romania	3,675	1,500	2.4
Hungary	1,225	500	0.7
Others: Argentina, Austria, Azerbaidjian, Bulgaria, China, Croatia, Czechoslovakia, Georgia, Hungary, Russia, Serbia, Slovenia, and Uruguay.	15,925	6,500	9.8

NEW ZEALAND

Pinot Noir is grown in several regions of New Zealand, from the coolest areas of Central Otago and Canterbury to sunny Marlborough (an area most famous for its Sauvignon Blanc). Although plantings of Pinot Noir across New Zealand double every five years, the quality is also continually on the rise. Its excellent products include Felton Road from Central Otago, and Seresin and Highfield from Marlborough.

CABERNET SAUVIGNON

Cabernet Sauvignon is one of the most popular grapes in the world. It has the ability to generate truly great wines full of complexity and sophistication. They not only age gracefully, but also need cellaring for at least five to ten years before they can begin to be appreciated. The reputation of this grape is owed to the quality of Bordeaux wines, as well as the newer varietals from California and Australia. Cabernet Sauvignon is likely the most recognizable grape variety in the world.

In Bordeaux, Cabernet Sauvignon is usually blended with Cabernet Franc (a cousin of sorts), Merlot, Petit Verdot, and Malbec. Australian winemakers, on the other hand, primarily blend this grape with Shiraz and Merlot. The wines of the Médoc, such as Margaux, St-Julien, Pauillac, and St-Estèphe, are predominantly based on Cabernet Sauvignon, since this grape pairs well with the region's gravelly soils. However, the similarly reputable vineyards of St-Emilion and Pomerol rely far more on Merlot. Chateau Petrus, for example, is made with up to 95-percent Merlot.

Cabernet Sauvignon grapes contain high levels of tannin, yield interesting astringency, and show the aromas of wild fruit, all for a comparatively low-volume harvest. Old vines yield 1.1 to 1.85 tons per acre (15 to 25 hectoliters per hectare). Young vines can produce up to 7.4 tons per acre (100 hectoliters per hectare), but the quality level is lower than that of older vines.

The biggest enemy of Cabernet Sauvignon in the vineyard is oïdium, which is also called powdery mildew. This is a fungus that attacks the green parts of the vine and causes grey-white, ash-like spores. Oïdium is easily treatable with the application of sulfur.

In a 1997 study published in *Nature Genetics Journal*, Meredith and Bowers discovered that Cabernet Sauvignon's ancestors were Sauvignon Blanc and Cabernet Franc—which explains the derivation of its name. Galet provides numerous names for Cabernet Sauvignon such as Bidure (hard wood in local dialect of Brodeaux), Vidure Sauvignonne, Bouchet Sauvignon in Bordeaux, Petit Cabernet in Morocco, Burdeos Tinto in Spain, Kaberne-Sovinjon in CIS, and Lafite in Bulgaria.

History

Although Roman authors such as Pliny and Columella did not mention grapes by name, it is thought that Cabernet Sauvignon already existed in the first century. The first official recognition was in the seventeenth century. The grape was then exported to other continents in the nineteenth century. Today, the Médoc and Graves regions in Bordeaux are the cradle of Cabernet Sauvignon.

Ampelography

Usually described as a small bunch and containing small- to medium-sized berries almost blue in color, Cabernet Sauvignon is a late budder with thick skin and compact, crunchy flesh.

Ideal Soil

Cabernet Sauvignon tends to grow best when planted in well-drained soils such as the gravelly ones in Médoc or the sandier ones along the banks of the Gironde River. It also generates decent wines in soils such as clay and those consisting of alluvial deposits. However, the subsoil is also important: that consisting of clay tends to yield heavier but less fine wines, while a chalky one results in lighter but finer wines.

In recent years, public reaction against a marketing (and consumer) trend that saw Cabernet-based wines becoming dominant on restaurant wine lists and in private cellars, at the expense of other red wine grapes, resulted in a growing movement towards wines made from Syrah, Pinot Noir, and Grenache.

Climatic Conditions

The Cabernet Sauvignon grape is suitable for the fairly cool Regions I and II, although in dry climates the resulting wines can be quite herbaceous. On the other hand, flood irrigation, such as that in Argentina and Chile, adversely affects quality, producing wines with good fruit but a short finish.

Olfactory Characteristics

Cabernet Sauvignon-based wines exhibit a heady, multi-berry fruit spectrum of aromas such as blackcurrant, redcurrant, and other berries combined with bell pepper. They also contain strong tannins, and are almost undrinkable during the first year after harvest. These wines exhibit a dark, intense color immediately after production. After a few years of aging and maturation in the bottle, the bouquet shows hints of violets, dark berries, and cedarwood.

Geographic Spread

Cabernet Sauvignon is grown in abundance in many countries. Worldwide, the grape is planted on 595,450 acres (or 243,110 hectares). It is known by different names in certain countries. For example, this popular grape is known as Bouchet, Petit Cabernet, Petite Vidure, and Vidure Sauvignonne in the Bordeaux region of France and Uva Francese in Italy.

FRANCE

The Cabernet Sauvignon grape can be found in the Loire Valley region of France, where it is used to produce Rosé d'Anjou. Its most popular wines, however, are from the region of Bordeaux, where the grape is widely planted and to great success.

Cabernet Sauvignon is part of the hugely successful "Bordeaux Blend"—a mix of four grapes that has proved to be a winning combination for winemakers around the world. Cabernet

Cabernet Sauvignon and the Vineyards of Bordeaux

The Romans were the first to establish vineyards in Bordeaux. Agronomist Pliny in the first century BC, writer Ausone in the first century AD, and ampelographer Columella in the fourth century AD mention Burdigala—which is Latin for Bordeaux—in their writings. Today, the region's vineyards cover around 282,500 acres (or 113,000 hectares) and surround the cities of Bordeaux and Libourne. The various regions are Médoc (which produces mainly red wines), which stretches up to the Atlantic Ocean; Haut-Médoc (red wines), which includes the appellations of St.-Estèphe, Pauillac, St.-Julien, Margaux, Listrac, and Moulis; Graves (red and white wines); St-Emilion and Pomerol (red wines); and Sauternes and Barsac (sweet white wines).

In Bordeaux, a lot of vineyards are divided into individual estates where viticulture, vinification, bottling, and aging are still taking place on a scale that could never compare with the huge wine estates found in the New World. While this fragmentation is not necessarily synonymous with quality, it goes a long way to ensure that the top 5 percent of these estates

are build on tradition, brand recognition, and loyalty. In addition, nowhere else in the world is the soil composition so important. Two wines from a pair of contiguous estates that have different soil composition may be quite different from each other and command vastly different prices when put on the market. In Graves, Médoc, and Haut-Médoc, the soils contain alluvial deposits (sand and gravel), whereas in Pomerol and St-Emilion, clay creates a far heavier base—resulting in a need for a greater mix of grapes if wines are to reach their ultimate potential.

Most Bordeaux wines, both red and white, are the result of blending: red wines are produced from Cabernet Sauvignon, Merlot, Cabernet Franc, Petit Verdot, and Malbec grapes, and white wines are produced from Sauvignon Blanc, Semillon, and Muscadelle. The exact proportions of these mixtures vary according to location and soil composition. Around 131 million gallons (or 4,950,000 hectoliters) of wine are produced every year in Bordeaux, and the size of this region's vineyards is equivalent to that of the much larger areas of Germany or South Africa.

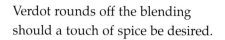

Verdot rounds off the blending should a touch of spice be desired.

UNITED STATES

In California—the temple of grape growing and winemaking in the United States—Cabernet Sauvignon has become the classic grape. It thrives in the Redwood Valley, a Region III type according to the Winkler scale that is home to the Fetzer winery, one of the largest wine producers in the country. In Napa Valley, Sonoma County, Alexander Valley, and Knights Valley, perfect conditions have created a mecca for Cabernet Sauvignon grapes. The top wineries are Kistler in Sebastopol, Laurel Glen in Glen Ellen, and Peter Michael in Calistoga.

In some other parts of California, yields are phenomenal. The vineyards yield up to 29 tons per acre (or 400 hectoliters per hectare). These figures are possible only through the use of the trunk system to train the vines. (Training systems were discussed in Chapter 2.) However, although these yields may well result in pleasant and easy drinking wines, these grapes will never produce truly great wines.

Sauvignon brings color and tannins that ensure aging potential, as well as a solid structure (body). Merlot adds fruit and plumpness, while Cabernet Franc brings a touch of perfume. Petit

*C*alifornia Cabernet Sauvignon

Cabernet Sauvignon may be best known as a crucial part of most wines that come out of Bordeaux, but it has also played an increasingly important role in the success of the wine industry of California in recent years. The list below includes the vineyards that produce some of California's best Cabernet Sauvignons.

DIAMOND MOUNTAIN DISTRICT
- Al Brounstein's Diamond Creek
- Andrew Geoffrey Vineyards
- Constant Diamond Mountain Vineyard
- Lakoya
- Randy Dunn's Howell Mountain
- Von Strasser Post Vineyard

NAPA VALLEY
- Caymus Special Selection
- Diamond Creek Volcanic Hill
- Etude
- Portfolio Winery

OAKVILLE
- Dalla Valle
- Joseph Phelps' Backus Vineyard

SANTA CRUZ MOUNTAINS
- Bill & Brenda Murphy's Clos la Chance
- Elias Fernandez's Shafer Hillside in Stag's Leap District
- Marston in Spring District Mountain

California is also characterized by the clear separation between grape growers and winemakers. Winemakers who have gained their credentials at large wineries, such as Mondavi, Fetzer, and E. & J. Gallo, often go on to establish their own wineries, and buy grapes from growers. In addition, because of less restrictive legislation, Californian winemakers are great innovators in the art of winemaking when compared with their European counterparts. Not only do they rely on research from their leading institutions such as University of California at Davis, but they also constantly experiment with grape-planting density, hybrids, and organic grape growing.

Some of California's Cabernet Sauvignons rival those of Bordeaux. Robert Mondavi was instrumental in bringing the best out of the grape in wines such as Opus One, a joint venture with the owners of Château Mouton Rothschild (though Mondavi has since sold his share). The inset on page 92 lists some of the best Cabernet Sauvignon from California.

CHINA

In China, Cabernet Sauvignon has become the backbone of the red wine industry. It is planted in vineyards in Shandong, Jixian, Ningxia, Gansu, Xinjiang, Shanxi, Hebei, Henan, Anhui, Jiangsu, and Shacheng. Its sturdiness and resistance to vine diseases make it the ideal grape variety for China, where temperature differences between winter and summer can range by as much as 122°F (or 50°C).

China is second only to France in terms of total Cabernet Sauvignon plantings. There are 110,000 acres (or 45,100 hectares) of these plantings throughout the country. The industry's major players are large wine companies such as Changyu, Great Wall, Dynasty, and Dragon Seal. On the boutique side, there are quality-driven wineries such as Huadong Winery and Grace Vineyard.

MOLDOVA

The wine industry in Moldova dates back to 4000 BC. Although in a state of dereliction at the time of the country's independence from the Soviet Union in 1991, the wine industry has gradually been benefiting from outside investment. It is now being actively modernized with the help of overseas concerns such as Penfolds from Australia and

French oenologist Jacques Lurton. Moldova's wine industry relies on European grapes such as Chardonnay, Sauvignon Blanc, and Cabernet Sauvignon. Excellent Cabernet Sauvignon made from old vines is produced in the country's southern region of Tarakliya.

BULGARIA

Bulgaria was also part of the Soviet Union until it dissolved. Around that time, this country saw a drive towards quality over quantity. It also searched for grapes more suitable for export. As a result of this search, Cabernet Sauvignon is now Bulgaria's dominant red wine grape variety.

Today, it annually produces around 58 million gallons of wine (220 million liters) from eighty industrial wineries harvesting grapes planted on 314,825 acres (128,500 hectares) of land. The largest producer, Vinprom Rousse (also known as Boyar Estates), relies on new plantings, together with the advice of Australian winemakers and the introduction of quality standards, to further the success of its business and industry.

Astringency is the puckering, roughing, and drying sensation encountered in the mouth during ingestion of certain foods or beverages, such as persimmon fruit, strong tea, and, of course, red wine.

The trunk system enables weight-load to be shared among a number of trunks. This system enables higher yields, but also exhausts the vine resources much faster. This leads to replanting every fifteen to twenty years, rather than the standard forty years.

Figure 6.3.
Cabernet Sauvignon plantings in Dynasty Vineyards in Ningxia province, China.

ROMANIA

One of the largest wine-exporting countries worldwide, Romania benefits from a continental climate suitable for the growing of grapes of international standard and recognition. Cabernet Sauvignon is one of the successfully grown grapes of Romania. This grape represents around 5 percent of the country's total grape plantings.

There are eight recognized wine regions in Romania: the knolls of Dobrudja (also called Dobrogea), Moldavia, Muntenia, Oltenia, Transylvania, Danube Terraces, Crişana, and Banat. Cabernet Sauvignon is mainly produced in Banat, Oltenia, Muntenia, and Moldavia. Most of the wineries are now privately owned. Dobrudja produces an interesting late-harvest Cabernet Sauvignon which is sweet. Otherwise, the

Cabernet Sauvignon wines produced in Romania are all dry, although of different quality levels depending on grape quality, winemaking techniques, and aging.

Quality standards applied to the wines in Romania rely mainly on an appellation system similar to that of Germany. It is based on must weight—the concentration of sugars in the unfermented grape juice.

AUSTRALIA

Although known as the Land of Shiraz, Australia also produces Cabernet Sauvignon in each of the four states where grapes for wine are grown: Victoria, South Australia, New South Wales, and Western Australia.

Victoria

In Victoria, almost every climatic condition can be found. The most dramatic variations are between the very hot and dry Sunraysia to the much cooler Macedon Ranges and Mornington Peninsula. The best Cabernet Sauvignon wines in Victoria can be found in the King Valley in the northeast of the state and in the Yarra Valley, a region located to the east of Melbourne. Reputable producers include Dalwhinnie in Moonambel, and Coldstream Hills and Mount Mary in the Yarra Valley. Excellent Cabernet Sauvignon is also produced in the region of Pyrenees.

South Australia

The Barossa Valley is one of the key birthplaces of the Australian wine industry. The other main regions, Padthaway and Adelaide Hills, have developed more recently and are currently producing many fine wines. The best Cabernet Sauvignon, however, comes from Coonawarra, Langhorne Creek, and McLaren Vale. These three regions were established at the end of the nineteenth century. South Australia is also home to Australian giants including Lindemans, Hardys, Seppelt, Mildara, Penfolds, Wolf Blass, and Wynns, whereas wineries such as Peter Lehmann, Jeffrey Grosset, and Charles Melton epitomize the possibilities for smaller producers. Grange from Penfolds, one of the greatest Shiraz-based Australian wines, is usually blended with a small amount of Cabernet Sauvignon to give it additional structure and body.

TABLE 6.2 RECENT CABERNET SAUVIGNON PLANTINGS

Country	Acres	Hectares	% of Worldwide Plantings
France	127,400	52,000	21.4
China	110,495	45,100	18.5
Chile	96,000	39,260	16.1
Moldavia	49,000	20,000	8.2
United States	46,550	19,000	7.8
Bulgaria	44,100	18,000	7.4
Romania	29,400	12,000	5
Australia	28,200	11,500	4.8
Yugoslavia	24,500	10,000	4.1
South Africa	12,250	5,000	2.1
Italy	6,125	2,500	1
Argentina	5,750	2,350	1
Spain	4,900	2,000	0.8
Hungary	4,900	2,000	0.8
Mexico	3,920	1,600	0.7
Others: Austria, Brazil, Cyprus, Germany, Greece, Honduras, Israel, Japan, Lebanon, Morocco, New Zealand, Peru, Russia, Turkey, and Uruguay.	1,960	800	0.3

New South Wales

In New South Wales, the Hunter Valley stands as the foremost area for grape production, mainly for Shiraz and Semillon. Cabernet Sauvignon wines, on the other hand, are mainly produced in the subregions of Mudgee, Orange, and Cowra, all situated on the other side of The Great Dividing Range—Australia's large mountain range—from Sydney.

Western Australia

Western Australia has traditionally been the home of smaller wineries, almost all of which are located along the southwestern tip of the state. Along the Margaret River, producers concentrate on both Bordeaux blends and Cabernet Sauvignon wines. Recently, most small wineries have been taken over by larger companies, notably Southcorp and B.R.L. Hardy. Rich and surprisingly European in style, Cabernet Sauvignon wines are also made by the likes of Cape Mentelle's David and Mark Hohnen—who are also involved with the French Champagne house of Veuve Clicquot—and Leeuwin Estate. Both wineries are located in the Margaret River region.

MERLOT

A vigorous and fast-growing vine with thick, dark green leaves, Merlot grows bunches that are large, cylindrical shaped, sometimes winged, and loosely hung. They consist of early-ripening or unevenly ripening dark berries. Suitable for both blending and as a varietal wine, Merlot is currently enjoying a rediscovery by wine drinkers, particularly those on the western coast of the United States.

There is a simple reason for this: Merlot wines are less tannic than Cabernet Sauvignon while exhibiting appealing aromatic characters, thus generating pleasant wines that are ready to be drank even at an early age. They also bring a fruity character to harsher grapes, as well as velvety sensations on the palate.

The grape is ranked seventh in terms of worldwide plantings with around 500,000 acres (or 200,000 hectares). Merlot is present in most countries where climatic conditions allow it to ripen properly. It is the basis of Château Petrus, a Pomerol wine from the Bordeaux region that is one of the most expensive wines in the world. The grape is also extremely popular in the Italian regions of Friuli, Veneto, and Trentino-Alto Adige, as well as Bulgaria, Yugoslavia, Russia, and Romania.

In the Eden Valley region of South Australia, winemaker and consultant James Irvine has been trying since 1985 to produce the best Merlot-based wines in the world. He may be inspired by Tenuta dell'Ornellaia of Tuscany, Italy and its 100-percent Merlot named Masseto. This fabulous wine reaches just a few people, thanks to a very limited production—and a very hefty price tag.

In California and Chile, Merlot is typically made with ripe fruit and is easy to drink when young. Fruit flavors of plum and currant predominate, while tannins are soft. On the other hand,

Figure 6.4.
Merlot.

Casa Lapostolle, a joint venture between Chilean and French interests, produces remarkable Merlot-based wines such as the Rapel Valley Cuvée Alexandre that should be cellared for five to ten years before being consumed.

The Merlot grape is slightly easier to bring to ripeness than Cabernet Sauvignon, rendering Merlot a more feasible option when climatic conditions are borderline. It is a variety that buds early, making it fragile in the face of spring frosts and coulure (a vine disease capable of dramatically reducing a crop's yield). It is also a grape that thrives better in heavier soils, such as the clay found in St-Emilion and Pomerol, than in the well-drained soils of the Médoc and Graves regions—where Cabernet Sauvignon reigns supreme.

Other names employed for this grape include Merlot Noir, Merlau, Plant Médoc en Bazadais, Sémillon Rouge, and Begney. Merlot clones numbered 181, 182, 342, and 343 are recommended for the Bordeaux area.

History

Merlot probably originated in the Bordeaux region in the southwest of France, and was first officially documented in the eighteenth century. Named Craburet Noir by Dupré de Saint-Maur in his 1746 *Essai sur les Monnoies ou Réflexion sure le rapport entre l'argent et les denrées*, the Merlot grape was described for the first time in an encyclopedia of the grapes of the Bordeaux region by Victor Rendu in 1857.

Ampelography

With cuneiform (wedge-shaped) leaves of average size and a very dark green color, bunches of Merlot come in cylindrical shape consisting of small to average-sized berries with skin of average thickness. Yields of Merlot vary considerable from 1.4 to 6 tons per acre (from 20 to 80 hectoliters per hectare). In Bordeaux, the permitted yield is from 3 to 4.5 tons per acre (from 40 to 60 hectoliters per hectare).

Ideal Soil

Merlot grows best in soils such as clay where humidity is partially retained by the earth, especially during the warm (and hot) summer months. In well-drained soils, its berries remain small and unable to reach their potential in terms of aroma and taste. As a result, it loses its fruity character.

Climatic Conditions

The best climatic conditions for Merlot are similar to those for Cabernet Sauvignon. They are therefore often planted alongside each other. Unfortunately, Merlot is more sensitive than Cabernet Sauvignon to spring frosts, mildew, and grey rot because it both ripens two weeks earlier and has very thin skin.

Olfactory Characteristics

In good years, and given the most appropriate soil and climatic conditions, Merlot shows jammy fruits like cherries, raspberries, mulberries, and plums. (When a wine is described as "jammy," it has intense and concentrated fruit flavors reminiscent of jam.) Depending on the level and length of oak-barrel maturation, flavors such as Asian spices, vanilla, caramel, and chocolate notes can readily surface. Black fruit is the dominant aroma in older vintages, which may also give off flavors of herbaceous tea, smoke, truffle, and olive.

Geographic Spread

Merlot is planted on 515,995 acres (or 210,600 hectares) of vineyard throughout the world. It is often planted in regions that also grow Cabernet Sauvignon, because the two enjoy similar climates. In Bordeaux, for example, an area known primarily for its yield of Cabernet Sauvignon, Merlot is actually the most planted grape with a staggering 170,275 acres (or 69,500 hectares) of vineyards. Grape growers in China, another temple of Cabernet Sauvignon, have discovered that Merlot planted in certain soils on the confines of the Gobi desert generate wines of utmost quality.

FRANCE

Merlot is the fourth most widely planted grape in France. It can generate exceptional wines, particularly in the Pomerol and St-Emilion regions of Bordeaux. According to Robert Parker, Jr, the richest wines of Pomerol are Châteaux Clinet, La Conseillante, l'Eglise-Clinet, l'Evangile, La Fleur de Gay, Lafleur, Petrus, Le Pin, and Trotanoy. The proportion of Merlot in these wines reaches up to 95 percent. In St-Emilion, the wines are based on 50- to 75-percent Merlot, with the remaining percentage filled with Cabernet Franc and/or Cabernet Sauvignon. The top wines of this region are Châteaux Angélus, Ausone, Canon-La-Gaffelière, and Cheval Blanc.

In other regions of France where Merlot is important, it appears either as a single varietal or a blend approved by the local Appellation d'Origine Contrôlée (AOC). Some such blends include Roussillon, Languedoc, Minervois, Fitou, Corbières, and Côtes de Provence.

ITALY

After local grapes Sangiovese, Catarratto Commune, Trebbiano Toscano, and Barbera,

TABLE 6.3 RECENT MERLOT PLANTINGS			
Country	Acres	Hectares	% of Worldwide Plantings
France	245,000	100,000	47.5
Italy	78,400	32,000	15.2
United States	41,650	17,000	8.1
Bulgaria	38,000	15,500	7.4
Chile	31,850	13,000	6.2
Russia	24,500	10,000	4.7
Yugoslavia	19,600	8,000	3.7
Romania	16,660	6,800	3.2
Australia	6,125	2,500	1.2
South Africa	5,635	2,300	1.1
Argentina	2,940	1,200	0.6
Hungary	2,450	1,000	0.5
Switzerland	2,205	900	0.4
Others: Brazil, Canada, China, Cyprus, Israel, Mexico, New Zealand, Portugal, and Uruguay.	980	400	0.2

*I*talian Vineyards and Grapes

There are vineyards through the whole of the peninsula of Italy, enabling grape growers and winemakers to work with a wide variety of climates and grapes. Covering roughly 3.5 million acres (or 1.4 million hectares), the land under vine falls into a number of diverse regions: Piedmont, Lombardy, Emilia-Romagna, Valle d'Aosta, Liguria, Trentino, Alto Adige, Friuli, and Veneto in the north; Tuscany, Umbria, Marches, Latium (Lazio), Campania, Abruzzi, and Molise in the center; and Campania, Basilicata, Apulia, Calabria, and the islands of Sicily and Sardinia in the south.

Although the quantity is always high, the quality of Italian grapes ranges from bad to exceptional. The output from Italian vineyards can be mind-boggling because of its diversity, but also because of how difficult it can be to identify the grapes from which individual wines are made. The Italian wine market also has its own system of regulations, which is described on page 156.

The number of different grapes cultivated in Italy is tremendous. White wines are produced from Chardonnay, Malvasia (in Lazio), Pinot Bianco (in Lombardy, Veneto, Friuli, Trentino, and Alto Adige), Vernaccia (in Tuscany's San Gimignano and Sardegua's Val di Tirso), Verdicchio (in Marches), Trebbiano (in Veneto's Bianco Di Custora and Lazio's Frascati), Prosecco (in Veneto), Moscato (in Asti), Inzolia (in Sicily's Marsala), Traminer (in Alto Adige and Friuli), and Tocai (in Veneto and Friuli). Riesling, Vermentino, and Sauvignon Blanc are also used in various regions. Red wine grapes produced in Italy are Pinot Grigio (used for the production of white wines in Collio, Friuli, Alto Adige, and Tuscany, but classified as a red wine grape due to the color of its berries), Barbera (in Piedmont and Lombardy), Dolcetto (in Piedmont), Sangiovese (the basis for Chianti and Brunello, among others), Corvina (in Veneto and Lombardy), Montepulciano (in Abruzzi), Pinot Nero, Nebbiolo (the basis for Barolo and Barbaresco), Negroamaro (in Apulia), and Schiava (in Trentino and Alto Adige). Cabernet Sauvignon and Merlot are also produced throughout Italy.

The most innovative wines of Italy are Tignanello and Sassicaia, the so-called Super Tuscans. Like the traditional Chianti, these wines include Sangiovese. However, the Super Tuscans do not comform to the rigid rules in place for Chianti. As a result, these wines are designated table wines despite their wide appeal.

Merlot is the fifth most important grape in terms of plantings in Italy, and is suited to most provinces. In the regions of Trentino, Friuli, and Veneto, it must be incorporated in all wines bearing a *Denominazione di Origine Controllata* (DOC) label. There are oceans of mediocre Merlot-based wines being produced in Italy, but there are also some serious attempts by Tuscan winemakers and viticulturists, such as Antinori, to come up with wines that could one day rival those of Pomerol.

UNITED STATES

Washington State, California, and Long Island are home to the most important Merlot plantings in the United States. Since the early 1990s, this grape has seen much revival, due to the ability of Merlot to display a softer and more fruity finish than Cabernet Sauvignon. In California, the most reputable vineyards are located in the Russian River, Stag Leap, and Santa Ynez Valley districts. Meritage, a quality label and trademark, must be made according to the "Bordeaux Blend" described on page 91.

SWITZERLAND

Although the quantity of Merlot produced in the Ticino region of Switzerland is relatively low when compared to its production in Italy or France, those wines are arguably the best reds in a country better known for its whites.

SYRAH

The Syrah grape is known as the King of Grapes in Australia. Its origins are quite obscure, and its name varies from country to country. It is called Syrah in France, while it is known as Shiraz in California and Australia. In the *Oxford Companion to Wine*, Jancis Robinson, MW names the old city of Syracuse, in Sicily, as the inspiration for the name "Syrah." The alternate name "Shiraz" was probably given because it may have been brought back by a crusader from Mesopotamia and Persia, likely from or around the old Iranian city of Shiraz. Other names for this grape include Sirah, Syra, Schiras, Sirac, Syrac, Serine, Balsamina, Biaune, Plant de Biaune, Entournerin, and Hermitage.

Syrah grows quite vigorously. Its vines produce long, cylindrical bunches, with small-to-medium berries of oval shape which have relatively thin skins and are quite sweet and juicy. Yields have to be kept below 6 tons per acre (or 80 hectoliters per hectare) to preserve the characteristic aromas of the grape. In France, sixteen clones are approved for the growing of Syrah. Clones 383 and 470 yield quality over quantity, while 99 and 100 yield quantity over quality. Syrah wines are produced in many countries, but Australian winemakers are particularly keen on the grape and vinify excellent Syrah wines. They utilize the grape both alone and blended.

History

Some historians date the appearance of the Syrah grape to the third century AD. For the prior 200 years, the planting of wine grapes had been prohibited in the Roman Empire to favor other crops. This prohibition was finally lifted in 276 AD by Emperor Probus. Although stories imply that Syrah's origins can be traced back to this time, little is known of this particular grape's true history.

Ampelography

Characterized by an average-sized bunch containing small berries, the Syrah grape displays a very deep black and blue color covered by an abundant white pellicle (thin protective membrane). Its flesh is very juicy and melts in the mouth with an enjoyable taste. Syrah is a late budding grape but its yield is generally low when compared with other red wine grape varieties. Galet posits that any yield above 6 tons per acre (80 hectoliters per hectare) results in a considerable loss of aromatic component in the final wine. The genetic ancestors of Syrah are two varieties called Dureza and Mondeuze from France in the Ardèche and Savoie regions respectively.

Ideal Soil

The soils best suited for Syrah contain rocks and stones, which absorb heat from the sun during the day and keep the vineyard relatively warm during the night. In Australia, the best Shiraz vines tend to be cultivated in terra rossa, a kind of clay or loam topsoil which covers well-drained limestone subsoil. This soil type is typically found in the Coonawarra region of South Australia.

Climatic Conditions

The best climatic conditions for Syrah are found in Regions I and II on the Winkler scale. This grape needs mild winters and warm summers. Syrah is a late budder and not-so-late ripener, and can be picked at least two weeks before Carignan, another black grape growing in both the Rhône Valley and the South of France.

Olfactory Characteristics

The Syrah grape is generous in terms of its aromas. Grapes grown in soils on the steep slopes of the Rhône River Valley usually have primary aromas of violets, cherries, and raspberries combined with a bouquet of spice, licorice, anise, truffle, blackcurrant, tobacco, chocolate, tar, coffee, and eucalyptus. A longer maceration of French Syrah emphasizes a spicy, peppery character, while a shorter vinification preserves fruit. This peppery character is less pronounced in Australian Shiraz. Instead, Australian

Figure 6.5. Syrah.

wines tend to have characteristics reminiscent of tar. *Tar* is an aromatic component naturally present in some grape varieties, including Syrah, Nebbiolo, and Pinot Noir. The smell of tar develops further as a wine ages. The blending of Shiraz grapes from various regions produces a wine with fewer tar characteristics and more fruit aromas.

Geographic Spread

The Australian version of this wine has become increasingly popular in recent years. However, there remains more Syrah plantings in France than in Australia. The total worldwide plantings of this grape are 342,733 acres (or 139,890 hectares).

AUSTRALIA

James Busby first introduced Syrah rootstocks to Sydney, Australia in 1832. The most famous Australian wines made out of the Syrah are Grange, a long-lasting wine made by Penfold's winery in South Australia, and Hermitage, Cornas, and Côte Rôtie from the Northern Rhône Valley.

There are also top Shiraz in both Western and South Australia. In Western Australia, these include Plantagenet in Mount Barker, and Great Southern and Vasse Felix in Wilyabrup in the Margaret River region. Henschke, located in South Australia at Keyneton in the Eden Valley, produces Hill of Grace, which many consider a rival for Grange. In Victoria, Yarra Yering at Coldstream in the Yarra Valley produces Dry Red No. 1, a highly sophisticated Shiraz. Wines produced from this grape at Mount Langhi Ghiran Vineyards in the Grampians are also of extremely high quality. In New South Wales, large wineries such as Lindemans, Tyrrell's, Rosemount Estate, and Rothbury produce both decent Shiraz and Shiraz-based wines blended with Cabernet Sauvignon.

FRANCE

Reputable French Syrah producers include the large wineries of Jaboulet, Guigal, and Chapoutier. Notable small producers in the Northern Rhône are André Perret at Chavannay, Domaine Jean-Luc Colombo (which produces controversial wines that are subjected to shorter

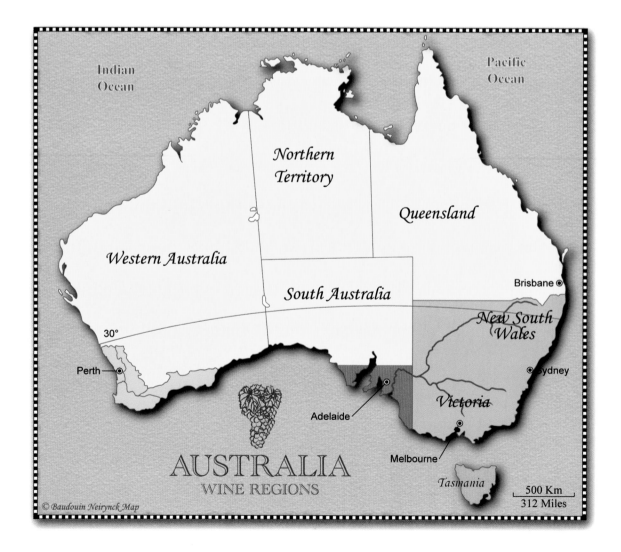

South Australian Wine Regions

Running from the Gulf of St. Vincent up to the Murray River, the state of South Australia is divided into two distinct wine-producing areas. One of these areas, located along the Murray River, uses water from the river to keep the land irrigated. It produces ordinary wines for everyday consumption. This area yields the highest production of the whole country, accounting for more than 40 percent of total wine output.

The other wine-producing area generates quality dry wines. Its planted vines are subject to various weather elements that depend on microclimates created by various topographies. This area includes Clare Valley, Barossa Valley, Adelaide Hills, McLaren Vale, Fleurieu, Wrattonbully, Mount Benson, Padthaway, Coonawarra (these last four regions are collectively known as the Limestone Coast), and Eden Valley.

The Clare Valley, located northwest of the Eden Valley, is renowned for the quality of its crisp yet delicate Riesling wines, as well as those made from Shiraz, Semillon, and Grenache. Vines have grown in this region, which enjoys a warm climate and low average rainfall, since 1842. Some of the most reputable producers are Leasingham, Pikes, Knappstein, Grosset, and Mitchell.

Barossa Valley was first populated by German-Lutheran immigrants, and is a large area with a wide range of soils and microclimates. Wines made with Shiraz, Grenache, and Riesling have all earned the area an excellent wine-producing reputation. This region's Shiraz wines are particularly successful, with Grange from Penfolds, Hill of Grace from Henschke, and Black Pepper from E&E jockeying for the title of the world's best Shiraz. Red grapes Merlot, Grenache, and Cabernet Sauvignon are also widely planted, as are white grapes Riesling, Chardonnay, and Semillon.

Adelaide Hills, located between the Barossa Valley and McLaren Vale, is part of the Mount Lofty Ranges, with an altitude of between 1,312 and 1,968 feet (or 400 and 600 meters) above sea level. This region is influenced by cool and windy oceanic air streams. In the north, soil and climatic conditions are particularly suitable for the production of Shiraz and Cabernet wines, whereas conditions in the south are favorable for Chardonnay and Pinot Noir (to be vinified for sparkling wines). The Lenswood subregion, on the other hand, yields Pinot Noir, Sauvignon Blanc, Riesling, and Merlot. High-quality wines of the region include Starvedog Lane and Ravenswood Lane.

McLaren Vale lies 25 miles (or 40 kilometers) south of Adelaide. Ironstone soils combined with a Mediterranean climate provide ideal conditions for the two stars of the region: Shiraz and Chardonnay. Rhône blends based on Grenache, Mourvèdre, and Shiraz have also been recognized for their excellent quality, as have Semillon, Sauvignon Blanc, and Verdelho.

Coonawarra is famous for its terra rossa—limestone soil—which generates excellent Bordeaux blends made principally of Cabernet Sauvignon. Shiraz wines from this region have also achieved a respectable reputation.

macerations and less new oak, resulting in wines that are drinkable earlier) at Cornas, and Domaine François Villard at Saint-Michel-sur-Rhône. Other producers with enviable reputations include Barge, Champet, Gaillard, J. M. Gérin, Jasmin, Rostaing, and Vidal-Fleury. In the southern Rhône subregion, Clos du Joncuas from the Chastan family and La Réméjeanne in Sabran have both earned peer recognition. Château La Nerthe and Domaine du Pegau are particularly impressive among Chateauneuf-du-Pape producers. Other top producers include Domaine du Vieux Telegraphe, run by the Brunier family on soils covered by the famous round galet stones, and Château de Beaucastel, run by the Perrin family and which produces wines from vines at least fifty years old and yields always below 2.2 tons per acre (or 30 hectoliters per hectare).

TABLE 6.4 RECENT SYRAH PLANTINGS			
Country	Acres	Hectares	% of Worldwide Plantings
France	168,070	68,600	49
Australia	90,650	37,000	26.5
Argentina	29,400	12,000	8.6
South Africa	24,010	9,800	7
United States	20,580	8,400	6
Chile	6,125	2,500	1.8
Italy	2,548	1,040	0.7
Others: Brazil, Cyprus, Greece, and New Zealand.	1,350	550	0.4

SANGIOVESE

Sangiovese is a famous Italian black grape that generates low-yield wines with a high acid and tannin content. It is also the most widely planted grape variety in Italy. Particularly important to the wine industry of Tuscany, it is the base for wines such as Chianti, Brunello di Montalcino, and Vino Nobile di Montepulciano. In Tuscany alone, Sangiovese is required in twenty-five appellations. Today, it is also planted in France, the United States, and several other countries.

According to famous ampelographer Pierre Galet, the grape is also called Sangiovese dal Cannello Lungo, Sangiovese Romagnolo, San Gioveto Grosso, Prugnolo Gentile di Montepulciano, Prugnolo di Montepulciano, Niellucio, Brunello di Montepulciano, and Lambrusco. Sangiovese is a notoriously unpredictable grape, generating huge variations from one clone to another. There are fourteen different clones of Sangiovese. The best well known of these is the Brunello clone. The Grosso clone, another well-known Sangiovese clone, is used to make Montalcino wines.

Recent Sangiovese trends have seen winemakers moving towards soft, rather than harsh, tannins. This is accomplished by using new oak barrels for maturation, and ensuring that malolactic fermentation is carried out.

Figure 6.6. Sangiovese.

History

A Tuscan legend credits a local friar for giving the name Sanguis di Jovis to this grape in the sixteenth century. The moniker is based on the name of a mountain called Monte Giove, located near the city of Sant'Angelo di Romagna. "Sanguis di Jovis" later became "Sangiovese." In recent years, this grape has become increasingly popular as viticulturists and winemakers in Italy and California have produced it following strict viticultural practices and stringent winemaking standards to much success.

Ampelography

Upon maturity, Sangiovese displays average to large bunches with average-sized berries of a deep blue to dark black color. Its juice is already colored pink during pressing, unlike some other red wine grapes such as Pinot Noir.

Ideal Soil

The best Italian Sangiovese-based wines are produced in the limestone soils of Montalcino, which are composed of clay, chalk, and schist. Wines of a lesser quality can be found in the Colli Aretini, where the soil is predominantly clay and loam. The soils of the coastal plains display a higher sand content, thereby rendering the wines relatively light. The grape also requires constant sunlight but cannot tolerate heat. There is constant debate in Tuscany as to whether plantings of Sangiovese should be restricted to only the best suitable sites, rather than being allowed in the whole of central Italy.

Climatic Conditions

Most of the best Sangiovese is grown in Tuscany, a region known for its long warm summers and cold winters, but more accurately characterized by its myriad of microclimates. The coastal plains are affected by the Mediterranean climate, while pockets of continental climate influence inland vineyards. The Chianti and Montalcino growing areas, on the other hand, fall under the influence of a mix of Mediterranean and continental climates.

Olfactory Characteristics

Montalcino wines must be made of 100-percent Sangiovese grapes. Therefore, this wine is a great reference as to the grape's olfactory characteristics. An earthy first impression is usually followed by aromas of black cherries, plums, cranberries, herbs, and leather. Capable of aging for many years, older Sangiovese wines develop an excellent, harmonious bouquet.

Geographic Spread

Worldwide, there are 232,750 acres (or 95,000 hectares) of Sangiovese grapes planted. The vast majority of these plantings are in Italy, but the grape has recently been planted in other countries, as well.

ITALY

Over 90 percent of the world's Sangiovese grapes are grown in Italy. Although the Sangiovese grapes of the best quality are from Tuscany, they are grown throughout the entire country. Winemakers in Tuscany have found that this grape is at its best when blended with Cabernet Sauvignon, rather than with Malvasia and Trebbiano, the other two traditional grapes authorized in the Chianti appellation in Tuscany.

Chianti and Chianti Classico are both DOCG red wines based on Sangiovese grapes. For many producers, the percentages of the final blend and aging process of these wines are both regulated by a *consorzio* (association) of producers. Today, 80 to 100 percent of the wine consists of Sangiovese, and the blend is then topped off with a red grape variety such as Cabernet Sauvignon. At the same time, many top producers no longer choose to be part of the *consorzio*, so its influence on winemaking practices has diminished considerably.

Top Chianti Classico producers are Antinori, Cacchiano, Cafaggio, Carobbio, Casa Emma, Collelungo, Coltibuono, Le Corti, Fonterutoli, Isole E Olena, Ispoli, La Massa, Le Macie, Monsanto, Nittardi, Palazzino, Paneretta, Panzanello, Poggerino, Poggio al Sole, Querciabella, Rampolla, Roca di Montegrossi, Ruffino, San Felics, Selvole, Terre di Montefili, and Volpana. A few excellent producers share the Montalcino market and its two million bottles per year: Argiano, Castello Banfi, Biondi-Santi, Campogiovanni, Capanna, Tenuta Carpazo, Casanova di Neri, Castelgiocondo (owned by Marchesi de Frescobaldi), Cerbaiona, Col d'Orcia, Costanti, Tenuta Friggiali, Greppone Mazzi Tenimenti Ruffino, Lisini, Il Marroneto, Mastrojanni, Nardi, Siro Pacenti, Il Poggione, and Val di Suga dei Tenimenti Angelini.

UNITED STATES

In the United States, winemakers have learned to manage the grape to produce high-quality wines. Craig Parker, winemaker at Flat Creek Vineyard in Texas, received a double gold award in San Francisco in 2005 for his 2003 Super Texan based on Sangiovese blended with 10-percent Cabernet Sauvignon.

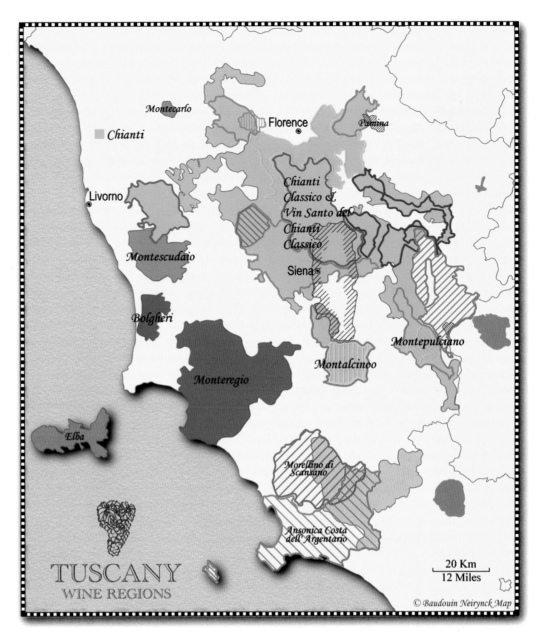

TABLE 6.5 RECENT SANGIOVESE PLANTINGS			
Country	**Acres**	**Hectares**	**% of Worldwide Plantings**
Italy	211,200	86,200	90.2
Argentina	7,350	3,000	3.1
France	4,410	1,800	1.9
Romania	4,165	1,700	1.8
Australia	1,765	720	0.8
Others: Algeria, Brazil, and United States.	5,120	2,090	2.2

GRENACHE

Grenache is the most widely planted black grape worldwide. Both France and Spain are home to around 245,000 acres (or 100,000 hectares) of Grenache plantings. Although rarely seen as a varietal on wine labels except in the New World (particularly in Australia), Grenache is a versatile grape. When grown in poor soils and pruned extensively, it can be used to produce wines with good aging potential. Grenache is the basis for renowned vins doux naturels (naturally sweet wines) such as Banyuls, Rivesaltes, and Maury, but can also be vinified as a rosé, and as such has established a good reputation under the Tavel label. On the other hand, it can also act as a supporting grape, bringing lovely fruit to the final blend. It matches well with Syrah, Mourvèdre, and Cinsaut in the Côtes du Rhône of France, and with Tempranillo in the Rioja region of Spain.

Grenache's robust trunk and canes render it particularly resistant to the strong winds originating from the Mediterranean Sea. Yet it is relatively fragile. It is sensitive to mildew, grey rot, and dead arm. Dead arm is a fungal vine disease that is also known as excoriose and caused by *Phomopsis viticola*, a fungus that causes the grape to rot.

With thick skin and abundant juice, Grenache buds relatively early and grape growers have much success with either bush-training systems or the short goblet training method. Bush-training requires no support such as steel wires, since the vine is kept close to the ground to avoid it being adversely affected by wind, and can yield around 1.5 tons per acre (or 20 hectoliters per hectare). The short goblet training method is utilized in less-exposed areas and permits higher yields of around 4.4 to 5.9 tons per acre (or 60 to 80 hectoliters per hectare).

Figure 6.7. Grenache.

The majority of synonyms for Grenache are of Spanish origin. These include Granacha, Granaxa, Garnacho, Granaxo, Garnacha Negra, Garnacha del Pais, Garnacha Tinta, and Aragonés. Cannono, Cannonau, Cannonao, and Cannonadu are Sardinian alternatives. In France, this grape is known as Grenache Noir, Alicante, Alicante de Pays, and Roussillon.

History

The earliest traces of Grenache in Spain and France can be found in the first millennium. By the year 1200, Grenache was already planted and cultivated in the Priorat region in Spain, and it thrived during the 400 years of Spain's Kingdom of Aragon. It also appeared around this time in Sardinia. Although it is unknown whether the Sardinians' Cannonau (as this grape is known there) became known as Grenache when it was exported to Spain or vice versa, it is the most important grape of modern-day Sardinia, with close to 29,400 acres (or 12,000 hectares) planted.

Ampelography

With a cuneiform leaf of a shiny light green color, Grenache's bunches are above average in size with wings and relatively compact. The Grenache berries display an ovoid shape and large size with abundant juice.

Ideal Soil

Grenache planted in the arid, rocky soils of the Côtes du Rhône and the South of France usually generates wines with high alcohol content (14 percent or even higher). This is accomplished by reducing the yield. In more fertile soils, yields increase substantially, while alcohol content and strength of the wines decrease. The Grenache grape is adaptable to various soil types but is not suited to those that are sandy.

Climatic Conditions

Grenache grows best in areas with warm climates, such as those in Regions II and III on the Winkler scale. Cold weather prolongs the flowering period, and may lead to coulure (which results in underdeveloped grapes and reduced yield).

Olfactory Characteristics

Grenache has flavors of berries and spice. More specifically, it can be reminiscent of blackcurrant, blackberry, and black cherries, as well as roasted nuts, leather, honey, and coffee. Younger Grenache tends to be more vigorous than older bottles and can taste of strawberries and raspberries.

Geographic Spread

The Grenache grape is planted on approximately 621,255 acres (or 249,900 hectares) worldwide. A majority of these vineyards are located around the Mediterranean Sea. As Grenache is a grape

TABLE 6.6 RECENT GRENACHE PLANTINGS			
Country	Acres	Hectares	% of Worldwide Plantings
Spain	257,250	105,000	42
France	231,100	94,300	37.7
Italy	29,400	12,000	4.8
Algeria	24,500	10,000	4
Tunisia	22,000	9,000	3.6
Mexico	18,850	7,700	3.1
United States	13,000	5,300	2.1
Australia	4,900	2,000	0.8
Others: Argentina, Cyprus, Greece, Israel, Morocco, Portugal, South Africa, and Uruguay.	11,270	4,600	1.9

Vineyards of the Rhône Valley

France's Rhône Valley consists of a 140-mile stretch of vineyards located along the Rhône River. It is divided into two main regions: the northern Rhône and the southern Rhône. This area, which has been cultivated since Roman times, covers more than 196,000 acres (or 80,000 hectares) and supports 8,000 estates.

Granite soil is the mainstay of the region, characterized by south- and southeast-facing slopes so steep that only manual harvesting is possible. The climate is very warm throughout the ripening season, producing grapes which make strong, heady, and well-structured wines that benefit from bottle aging.

The best red wines, called *crus* in French, from the northern Rhône are produced in the appellations Côte-Rôtie, Cornas, Crozes-Hermitage, Hermitage, Saint-Joseph, and Saint-Peray. The best white wines from this region are from Condrieu and the tiny but very famous Château-Grillet. Southern Rhône appellations that produce excellent wines are Châteauneuf-du-Pape (red and white), Gigondas, and Lirac (mainly reds), Tavel (rosé), and Vacqueyras (mainly reds).

While some wines are single varietal (such as Tavel, which is produced from Grenache), others are blends. Red Châteauneuf-du-Pape, for example, accommodates up to thirteen different grapes, and is representative of the varieties found in the region. Alexis Lichine, famous wine writer and critic from Bordeaux, pointed out that to the wines of this region, Grenache gives mellowness and alcohol; Mourvèdre, Syrah, Muscardin, and Vaccarese add body, color, and firmness; Counoise, Picpoule, and Cinsault give vinosity, bouquet, and freshness; and Clairette and Bourboulenc bring finesse and warmth. Terret Noir, Picardan, Grenache Blanc and Roussanne are also permitted in the blend.

While red wines predominate in the Rhône Valley, some exceptional white wines have emerged. Château-Grillet and Condrieu are both made from the Viognier grape and exhibit dry but rich characteristics reminiscent of spices, apricots, peaches, and pears. Marsanne and Roussanne also yield exceptional white wines under the name of Hermitage. Chapoutier, Jean-Louis Chave, Clape, and Guigal are the top producers of quality wines.

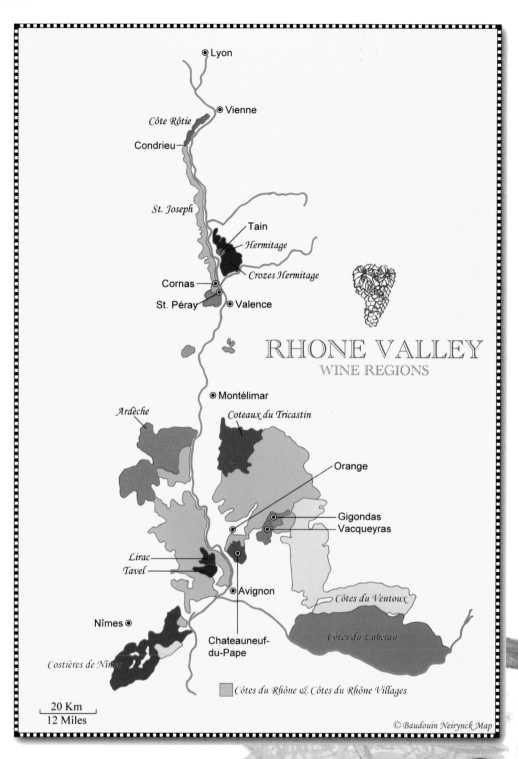

that needs plenty of sunshine, it is at home in most of the New World countries as well. However, its best terroir is indisputably Priorat, Spain. The Priorat village of Gratalops produces particularly fantastic Grenanche, which represents 40 percent of the village's plantations.

TEMPRANILLO

Considered by connoisseurs as the perfect mid-point between the austerity of Cabernet Sauvignon and the elegance of Pinot Noir, Tempranillo is a classic grape variety. It enjoys a cult following, and is responsible for some of the best Spanish wines.

Tempranillo is often thought of as the perfect variety to counterbalance the overpowering influence of noble grapes such as Cabernet Sauvignon and Pinot Noir. Displaying low acidity, soft tannins, strong fruit aromas, and an attractive color, Tempranillo generates wines capable of aging as well as being consumed while fairly young. It has been grown in Argentina for the past three hundred years, and can be found in the Iberic Peninsula's best wine, Vega Sicilia.

Tempranillo is called Cencibel in certain Spanish regions such as La Mancha and Valdepeñas. It was given the name Ull de Llebre in Catalonia, Tinta de Pais and Tinto Fino in the Ribera del Duero, Tinta de Madrid in Madrid, and Tinta de Toro in Toro. In Portugal, it takes on the name of Tinta Roriz along the Douro River.

History

The origins of this grape are difficult to trace. Pierre Galet refers to a Spanish "upbringing" and it is often reported to be native to Spain. Other historians believe the Spanish plantings came as a result of the Crusaders passing through the country while carrying cuttings bound for the Middle East. In any event, the name "Tempranillo" is derived from the Spanish word *temprano*, which means early and is a reflection of the variety's early ripening characteristic.

Ampelography

With a wide leaf showing five very distinct sections and a bunch of average to large size, Tempranillo berries are perfectly round and display a dark blue and black color. Their skin is rather thick, ensuring the presence of plenty of anthocyans (flavonoids that cause pigmentation) to color resulting wines. Tempranillo leaves become entirely red in autumn. In terms of yields, the Rioja region maintains maximum levels of 3.3 tons per acre (or 45 hectoliters per hectare). In some other regions, scarce water resources cause planting density and yield to drop.

Ideal Soil

Tempranillo vines can be planted in a wide variety of soils, from sandy or granite to gravelly. Planting in each of the various soils produces a slightly different style of wine.

Climatic Conditions

This grape is fairly adaptable, developing a thicker skin in hot and dry climates such as those of southern Spain, but becoming more delicate—and sensitive to vine diseases—when exposed to cooler climates. Weather conditions such as drought and humidity can also cause harm to Tempranillo vines.

Olfactory Characteristics

Tempranillo grapes sometimes lack acidity, but can generate deeply colored wines with great aging potential. Raspberry and blackberry accents round off a very perfumed spectrum of aromas and jammy notes in good vintages or particularly hot climates.

Figure 6.8. Tempranillo vines irrigated by a drip system in Granmonte Vineyard, Khao Yai, Thailand.

TABLE 6.7 RECENT TEMPRANILLO PLANTINGS			
Country	**Acres**	**Hectares**	**% of Worldwide Plantings**
Spain	111,500	45,500	49.4
Algeria	24,500	10,000	10.9
Tunisia	22,000	9,000	9.7
Mexico	18,850	7,700	8.3
Argentina	14,455	5,900	6.4
Portugal	13,000	5,300	5.8
United States	11,270	4,600	5
Australia	4,900	2,000	2.2
France	3,626	1,480	1.6
Others: Argentina, Cyprus, Greece, Israel, Morocco, Portugal, South Africa, and Uruguay.	1,470	600	0.7

Geographic Spread

The total worldwide plantings of Tempranillo grapes cover 225,571 acres (or 92,070 hectares). They are cultivated throughout Spain, but can also be found in many other countries. For example, Tempranillo vines are very popular in Mexico. In addition, the grape's presence in Australia continues to rise as well, with plantings doubling every three years.

In Spain, the following regions are authorized to plant Tempranillo: La Rioja, Navarra, Aragon, Castilla-León, Madrid, Castilla-La Mancha, Catalunia, Valencia, Murcia, Estremadura, Andalucia, and the Baleares. In Portugal, Tempranillo plantings under the name of Tinta Roriz are concentrated around the Douro region where Port wines are produced. In the same country, in Alentejo, the grape takes on the name of Aragonez.

Tempranillo has traditionally had a strong presence in North Africa. In countries such as Algeria, Morocco, and Tunisia, the natural acidity of grapes grown helps balance wines sometimes too rich in alcohol. In France, Tempranillo is recommended in all regions around the Mediterranean Sea.

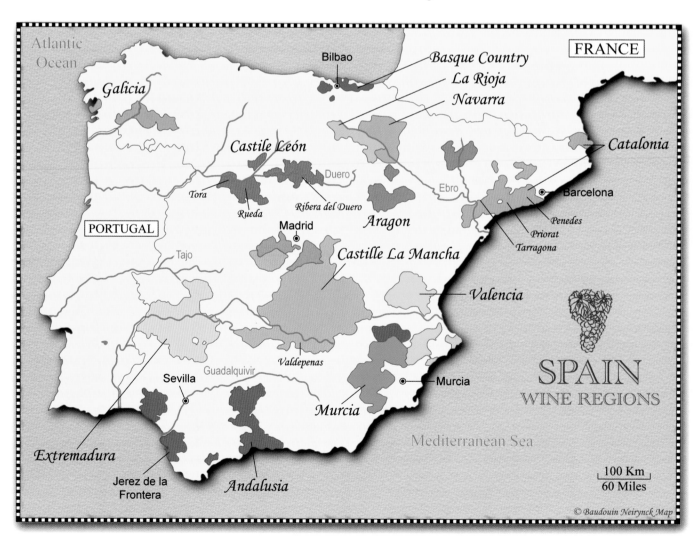

MALBEC

Malbec is a delicate grape similar to Merlot. It is prone to coulure and downy mildew (a plant disease which is also known as *pernospera* and is caused by the *Plasmopara viticola*). Also known under the names of Auxerrois, Cot, and Malbeck, the importance of its plantings has decreased in the last thirty years, particularly in France. Yet it is still used in some significant French wines.

Argentina, on the other hand, has soil and climatic conditions which suit this grape perfectly, and the resulting wines have shown great quality potential. The wines of Malbec are of a deep, ruby-red color and provide a depth of fruit aromas that can sustain aging in oak barrels.

Malbec, which is susceptible to coulure, powdery mildew, and grey rot, is also known by many different names. These include Beraou, Bérau, Bourguignon Noir, Calarin, Calavu, Quillot, and Plant Houdée.

History

According to Galet, Malbec originated in Cahors, France as early as the fourteenth century. Thereafter, this variety was exported to most of the other wine regions in France. In the nineteenth century, Malbec made its first appearance in Argentina, where it is currently considered king of the grapes, particularly in the region of Mendoza.

Ampelography

Characterized by an almost completely round leaf which becomes red in autumn, the two-winged bunch carries small round berries that are very dark, almost black, and generate little juice. Very sensitive to winter frosts, Malbec produces wines that are normally extremely tannic, mainly due to the poor juice to skin ratio. On the other hand, excellent extraction is usually achieved and results in opaque and deeply colored wines.

Ideal Soil

Malbec adapts to various environments relatively easily and can be found in a wide variety of soils. Provided the soil contains a minimum of clay and displays good drainage as well as poor fertility, the resulting wines are usually very impressive as long as the yields are low. Cahors in France and Mendoza in Argentina are the regions where the best Malbec is produced. They display relatively infertile soils and generally dry weather. In both these areas, Malbec constitutes more than 70 percent of the final blend.

Climatic Conditions

Malbec is highly sensitive to frost, and the warm regions of the New World are considered the most appropriate environment for growing this grape. At the same time, Malbec is also planted along the Loire River, where winter frosts can bring temperatures below zero. This is possible because these vineyards are planted on the river, which brings warmer air currents.

Olfactory Characteristics

According to Oz Clarke in *Grapes & Wines*, "At its best, carefully grown and skillfully vinified in Argentina, Malbec has a dark purple color, a thrilling damson and violet aroma, lush fat rich

Figure 6.9. Old Malbec Vines at Maison Jean Jouffreau in Cahors, France.

fruit flavours and a positively soothing ripe tannic structure. It can take new oak aging, but it's a pity to smother its natural delicious ripeness with wood. In Cahors, the flavor is more likely to be raisins, damson skins and tobacco. In both Chile and Argentina, you usually get the soft ripe lush texture."

For those who can afford to cellar Cahors wines, the rewards come after ten or twenty years, when the wines have developed tertiary aromas such as truffle and show an extremely long *finish*— the aftertaste and final impression of a wine.

Geographic Spread

Throughout the world, Malbec grapes are planted on 72,275 acres (29,500 hectares). Although originally grown in Hungary, Malbec was brought to France, where it was extremely popular for many years. Today, however, its plantings in France are diminished, while the grape has seen significant growth in Argentina.

FRANCE

The region of Lot boasts the best Malbec wines in France. A few producers, namely Jouffreau and Château du Cayrou, share the lion's part of this reputation. Château Lagrezette is another large producer of excellent Malbec wines. Its owner, Alain-Dominique Perrin, spares no effort in promotiong these wines around the world.

Malbec is one of the few grapes authorized in the making of Cahors wines. In fact, these wines are required to be composed of a minimum of 70-percent Malbec. This grape is also part of the blend for several of the South of France's "country" wines, such as Cabardès and Marcillac. Some Bordeaux viticulturists from Pomerol and St-Emilion utilize a very small percentage of Malbec (together with Merlot, Cabernet Franc, and Cabernet Sauvignon). In the Loire Valley, Malbec is used to produce fruity, aromatic rosé wines.

ARGENTINA

Most vineyards of Argentina are located along the Andes mountain range, in the north and west of the country. Here, the vines benefit from warm days and cool nights. Mendoza, a large city located on the west side of Argentina, is a particularly healthy location for vineyards because streams trickling down from the mountains provide beneficial irrigation. The Andean northwest (bordering Bolivia, Chile, and Paraguay) is another good vineyard location. Despite the heat due to their close proximity to the Tropic of Capricorn, these vineyards are located at an altitude of 6,232 feet (or 1,900 meters), making them the highest vineyards in the world. As a result, good dry wines are produced there. The Cuyo region stretches from San Juan province to the Colorado River, and produces the most reputable Malbec wines in the country.

Two excellent Argentine producers of Malbec wines are Bianchi and Terrazas. In Lujan de Cuyo, top producers include Fabre Montmayou, Bodega Norton, Bodega Enrique Foster (which was awarded the gold medal at the Argentina Wine Awards in February 2007), and Bodegas y Cavas de Weinert. In the Tupungato region of Mendoza, Salentein (under Dutch management) has established, in just a few years, an excellent reputation with its deeply colored wines and their extraordinary bouquets. The winery belonging to the Catena-Zapata family, also located in the Mendoza region, has been producing first-class Malbecs for more than a hundred years.

CHILE

The most reputable Malbec producers in Chile are Montes, located in Curicó, and Santa Carolina, located in Santiago. Because of the good results from producing this grape in South America, most producers of mass market Chilean wines have chosen to sell Malbec wines. MontGras, Valdivieso, Viña Casablanca, and Morandé are the most important group of wine labels for this particular grape variety.

TABLE 6.8 RECENT MALBEC PLANTINGS			
Country	Acres	Hectares	% of Worldwide Plantings
Argentina	53,900	22,000	73.7
France	16,000	6,500	22.8
Chile	2,450	1,000	3.5

CARIGNAN

Carignan is a red grape known for its long growing season and high yields. Of Spanish origin, it is commonly known as Carignane, Cariñena, Carignano, and Carinyena throughout various parts of the world. Generating wines with high acidity, tannin, and color, Carignan is usually produced as part of a blend or vinified on its own as an inexpensive table wine. However, plantings can also be manipulated for lower yields and better wine.

A grape that is not reputed for generating particularly pleasant wine, it has benefited from the introduction of carbonic maceration, which smooths its tannins while enhancing fruit flavors and aromas. It is part of some famous appellations such as Châteauneuf-du-Pape and Rioja, and produces at its best when harvested from old vines. Carignan is almost the most widely planted in France, and its name orginates from the eponymous city of Cariñena in the province of Aragon.

In flat lands, Carignan generates enormous yields of up to 15 tons per acre (200 hectoliters per hectare). It is very sensitive to oïdium and powdery mildew. There are more than twenty-five different clones of Carignan. It is frequently crossed with Cabernet Sauvignon. The resulting grape, Ruby Cabernet, provides a cherry flavor to many inexpensive table wines.

Figure 6.10. Carignan.

History

Carignan is a Spanish grape that was originally from the city of Cariñena in the region of Aragon. Pierre Galet suggests that it was introduced to France in the twelfth century, and subsequently became the most widely planted black grape there. It was most prolific in Languedoc and the southeast regions. In the last thirty-five years, its importance in terms of French plantings has been halved, as the AOC has restricted maximum plantings of Carignan in the South of France to 30 percent of total plantings.

Ampelography

The leaves of Carignan are probably the largest among all grape varieties and surround large cylindrical bunches. The berries are spherical and a very dark blue color with thick and astringent skin.

Ideal Soil

Carignan yields its best results in poor and rocky soils, but can be used as rootstocks in sandy soils.

Climatic Conditions

This is a grape that thrives in warm to very warm climatic conditions, due mainly to its late budding characteristics. Warm weather encourages the grapes to fully ripen.

Olfactory Characteristics

Carignan naturally produces very high yields, but can also be encouraged to produce grapes of lower yields and higher quality. From old vines and with low yields, Carignan is a variety capable of showing surprisingly good aromas such as violets, rose petals, and black fruits. Depending on the vinification, other aromas such as licorice, anise, and toast may appear. Contrary to most other red-wine-grape varieties, oak-barrel treatment is not indicated for Carignan, as it seems to enhance the roughness of its tannins.

Geographic Spread

Worldwide, Carignan vines are planted on 341,655 acres or (or 139,500 hectares). Its largest presence is in France and its former colonies Algeria, Tunisia, and Morocco, although the Carignan plantings in these areas are one-third to one-fourth of what they were in the middle of the twentieth century. Known in Spain as Mazuelo, it is not extensively planted in that country due to its tendency to be affected by powdery mildew. The Italian island of Sardinia, on the other hand, provides the ideal setting for Carignan plantings because of its warm and dry weather conditions. California has good plantings of this grape, which is known as Carignane in that region. In Australia, Carignan vineyards are primarily located in the Barossa Valley.

TABLE 6.9 RECENT CARIGNAN PLANTINGS			
Country	Acres	Hectares	% of Worldwide Plantings
France	210,700	86,000	61.7
Mexico	33,075	13,500	9.7
Tunisia	29,400	12,000	8.6
Spain	22,420	9,150	6.6
Morocco	11,025	4,500	3.2
United States	7,595	3,100	2.2
Italy	6,125	2,500	1.8
Australia	4,165	1,700	1.2
Algeria	3,675	1,500	1
Others: Algeria, Argentina, Australia, Chile, China, Cyprus, India, Lybia, South Africa, and Uruguay.	13,475	5,500	4

PRIMITIVO (ZINFANDEL)

Primitivo is the fifth most widely planted grape in Italy. It is also known on a global basis as the ubiquitous Californian Zinfandel, or Zin. This is a somewhat unusual grape in that it requires two harvests. The first one occurs by early September, while the second takes place in the first half of October. Despite being a hardy grape, Primitivo is very sensitive to coulure (poor fruit set that results in underdeveloped grapes), as well as grey rot and drought.

Primitivo grapes are versatile and can be vinified as white, red, or rosé wine. The resulting wines are usually extremely rich in color and consist of relatively good aromatic compounds. They often contain high volumes of alcohol. Taft Street in Sonoma County managed to produce its 2000 Zinfandel with 15.5-percent alcohol. Some of the best Zinfandel wines originate from the Lodi region, an area nestled between San Francisco Bay and the Sierra Foothills.

In Croatia, Primitivo is known as Plavac Mali; in California, it is called Zinfandel or Zin; in Italy, it goes by the names Primitivo di Goia, Primitivo Nero, Primaticcio, Gioia del Colle, Mrellone, Uva di Corato, Zaragese, and Uva della Pergola.

Figure 6.11. Primitivo.

History

Primitivo originated in Croatia, where it is today known and cultivated under the name of Plavac Mali. After crossing the Adriatic Sea and arriving in the Italian region of Apulia in the eighteenth century, it was given the name Primitivo throughout Italy.

Then, in the 1820s, the grape was imported to the United States via Vienna. It was first planted in California and became known as Zinfandel. Although it slowly spread to a total of fifteen states, it was the plantings in California that generated an amazing spectrum of wines from the pink beveraged White Zinfandel to luscious and full-bodied reds from the likes of Ridge Vineyards and Turley Cellars. It has become an all-time favorite of the American people.

Ampelography

Primitivo grape bunches are large and tight. The grapes themselves have thin skins and ripen easily.

DNA fingerprinting carried out in 2001 by scientist Carol Meredith outlined a relationship between Primitivo and Crljenak Kaštelanski, an obscure grape grown in Croatia along the Adriatic Sea. She found them to be two clones of the same grape variety.

Ideal Soil

Primitivo grows quite well in soil of limestone or granite and rock. Soils of this type retain heat at night, and the Primitivo grape develops a richness in this environment.

Climatic Conditions

Primitivo was born under the skies of the Adriatic Sea, and is best produced under sunny conditions. This grape has two harvests: one in early September and the other one with a lower yield by the end of October. For this reason, Galet proposed that warm and sunny weather but a long maturing period are necessary for growing this grape. In more humid climates, Primitivo suffers from coulure and is regularly affected by powdery mildew.

TABLE 6.10 PRIMITIVO PLANTINGS IN 2006			
Country	Acres	Hectares	% of Worldwide Plantings
United States	49,000	20,000	47.4
Italy	42,875	17,500	41.5
Mexico	9,800	4,000	9.5
Others: Australia, Brazil, Chile, Croatia, Portugal, and South Africa.	1,590	650	1.6

Olfactory Characteristics

Primitivo wines are generally relatively good aromatic compounds on the fruity and floral side. Scents are jammy and include raspberry, blackberry, and other fruit flavors. However, these aromas usually transform into spicy notes—such as cinnamon or black pepper—if the wines are aged.

Geographic Spread

Throughout the world, Primitivo is planted on approximately 105,350 acres (or 43,000 hectares). In its country of origin, Croatia, it is still cultivated, but represents only a small proportion of the vineyards. On the other hand, this grape has been planted extensively throughout Mexico and the United States. Zinfandel can be found in sixteen states: Arizona, California, Colorado, Illinois, Indiana, Iowa, Nevada, New Mexico, North Carolina, Ohio, Oregon, Tennessee, Texas, Virginia, Washington State, and West Virginia. In Italy, Primitivo is recommended in the provinces of Bari, Brindisi, Caserte, Foggia,

Lecce, and Tarente, and authorized for those of Benevent, Salerne, Matera, and Sardinia.

Zinfandel Wine Producers

The grape Primitivo is called Zinfandel in the United States, where it has become extremely popular. It is particularly present on the US wine scene as sweet rosé wine. There are many outstanding Zinfandel wine producers in California, including those on the following list.

- Behrens & Hitchcock
- Black-Sears
- De Loach OFS
- Dina's Vineyard
- Fanucchi-Wood Road
- Hartford Court Hartford Vineyard
- Hayne and Kuleto Estate Family Vineyard
- Lytton Springs
- Martinelli
- Mohr-Fry Ranches
- Pagani Ranch
- Pagani Vineyard
- Rafanelli
- Ravenswood
- Ridge Geyserville
- Robert Bialé
- Robert Mondavi
- St. Francis Winery
- Tofanelli
- Turley Cellars
- Valhalla Cellars
- Whitney Vineyards

The Growth of Wine Production and Consumption in the United States

According to a report prepared by wine educator Kevin Zraly in 2006, the United States will climb from its current position as the world's number three wine producer to number one in the year 2010. This report states that there were only 1,187 wineries in 1995—a number which has since increased to nearly 4,000. Almost every state, from the coolest (New York and North Dakota) to the warmest (Texas and Missouri), boasts wineries. There is quite a range between the number of wineries in each state. Ohio, for example, is home to 106 wineries while there are only 11 in South Dakota. Much of this growth is due to the love Americans have shown for American wine.

The increase in consumption and enthusiasm among Americans for American wine can be attributed to three main influences. The first is the French Paradox story aired on the TV show *60 Minutes* in 1992, which highlighted the health benefits of drinking red wine regularly (although in moderation). The second reason is a 1976 wine competition organized by respected British wine writer and critic Steven Spurrier, at which top French Bordeaux blends took on their Californian equivalents. The popularity of the latter skyrocketed after the New World wines finished ahead of the Old World Bordeaux. Lastly, a Supreme Court ruling in 2005 liberalized the shipping of wines across the country's state lines.

Originally, American wines were made from indigenous grapes such as Concord, a variety from the *Vitis labrusca* family discovered on the banks of the Concord River in Massachusetts. Then, Spanish conquerors imported grapes such as Merlot and Cabernet Sauvignon to the states of Texas and Mexico. Winemaking spread to California through the work of Spanish priests towards the end of the eighteenth century.

Today, California, Oregon, and Washington, and to a lesser extent New York, have become cult areas for winemaking. Although the styles of wines are very much inspired by Old World practices (Bordeaux blends, Rhône rangers, and Burgundian-style Pinot Noir), Americans have shown a great deal of imagination, creativity, and entrepreneurial spirit in their pursuit towards excellence in winemaking—and appreciation of these newer wines has followed accordingly.

CABERNET FRANC

Cabernet Franc is the parent grape of Cabernet Sauvignon. It is less well known than its descendant because it usually plays a supporting role in the elaboration of great Bordeaux rather than starring in its own varietal. However, some of the best wines worldwide contain 60-percent—or more—Cabernet Franc. This includes Château Cheval Blanc, a famous first-growth from St-Emilion in Bordeaux. Therefore, although Cabernet Franc is not a noble grape, it is an important part of any wine education.

Planted on all continents, this grape produces wines different in style than those based on Cabernet Sauvignon. Cabernet Franc wines have less tannins and *anthocyans*—flavonoids that produce color. (Having less anthocyans results in a paler-colored wine.) The lower tannin content causes Cabernet Franc wines to age faster than those based on Cabernet Sauvignon. Yielding between 2.2 to 3 tons per acre (or 30 and 40 hectoliters per hectare) under normal production conditions, this grape is susceptible to both black and grey rot and powdery mildew. The best growing locations for Cabernet Franc are the wine regions of Chinon and Bourgueil in the Loire Valley and on the right bank of the Gironde River in the vineyards of St-Emilion and Pomerol.

Cabernet Franc can be found under a variety of names. These include Bouchet in St-Emilion and Pomerol; Plant Breton, Cabernet, Bidure, Breton, Véron, Boubet, Bouchy, Gros Cabernet, and Capbreton Rouge in Bordeaux; Cabernet Franco in Chile; and Carbouet, Noir Dur, Trouchet Noir, Bordo, and Cabernet Frank in Italy. Cabernet Franc is often confused with Carmenère, a grape similar to Merlot that is grown extensively in Chile. The two, however, are unrelated, although they produce wines with similar aromas. Cabernet Franc wine tends to be fruitier than the more complex wine yielded from Carmenère.

History

Both Pierre Galet and Jancis Robinson, MW assert that Cabernet Franc can be traced back to ancient Roman times. The grape was introduced to France's Loire Valley in the seventeenth century by Cardinal de Richelieu, who cultivated it in his inherited wine estate in the abbey of Saint Nicolas-de-Bourgueil.

Ampelography

The leaf of Cabernet Franc reddens partially in autumn. Producing lower yields than its cousin Cabernet Sauvignon, its small cylindrical bunches display small spherical berries of dark blue color. Depending on the training method chosen and the climate, yields can reach 6 tons per acre (80 hectoliters per hectare), but are generally restricted to 2.2 tons per acre (30 hectoliters per hectare). Cabernet Franc's popularity is highlighted by the high number of scions produced currently in nurseries, particularly in France.

Figure 6.12. Cabernet Franc.

Ideal Soil

Cabernet Franc produces wines with spectacular raspberry aromas and finesse in the Loire Valley, where the ground is composed of chalky and tuffeau soils. The grape is much better suited to lighter soils such as these, as opposed to heavier soils such as the sandy and gravelly ones found in Bordeaux. However, a notable exception to this rule is Château Cheval Blanc. This St-Emilion vineyard consists mainly of gravel but produces fantastic wines.

Climatic Conditions

Cabernet Franc thrives in very different climates. Yet, although the climatic conditions of the vineyard is not as important to the quality of the Cabernet Franc grapes grown there as the soil content, the style of the resulting grapes is directly related to the amount of sunshine received during growth. In Napa Valley, Cabernet Franc wines produce opulent, full-bodied, and powerful wines, whereas in the Loire Valley, the same grape displays elegance rather than power.

Anthocyans, also known as *anthocyanidins*, are flavonoids (polyphenols) which contain the red or blue coloring substance found in plants and grapes. In the grape berry, anthocyans are found in the skin, and their antioxidant properties are well recognized.

Cabernet Franc is sometimes called Plant Breton, after the priest who was responsible for the transfer and planting of the grape in the Loire's sub-region of Bourgueil.

Olfactory Characteristics

When planted in the light tuffeau soils of the Loire Valley, Cabernet Franc produces wines with a certain degree of elegance. As exemplified by producers Chinon, St-Nicolas de Bourgueil, and Bourgueil, these wines display aromas of raspberries and blackcurrant leaves, yet show far less tannin than, for example, wines made from Cabernet Sauvignon.

Further south, on the other hand, Cabernet Franc is planted in the clay and sometimes gravelly and sandy soils of St-Emilion. Here, the grape is capable of producing rich and full-bodied wines which are matured in oak casks to reveal scents of minerals, exotic spices, menthol, tobacco, and rich black fruits. Château Cheval Blanc uses the highest proportion (66 percent) of Cabernet Franc in Bordeaux, and produces wine that is drinkable young but can also age beautifully. At its best, this grape is referred to as "exotic" for its capabilities of transporting the taster to remote countries on the Spice Route.

Tuffeau, known also as tufa in English, is a calcium-carbonate deposit omnipresent in the region of Saumur and the rest of France's Loire Valley. This type of porous rock constitutes the building material of many Loire Valley castles and estates. Tuffeau is also easy to dig and shape, and most of the region's wine cellars are dug in this material.

Geographic Spread

Found in many countries throughout the world, Cabernet Franc is grown on 110,250 acres (or 45,000 hectares) for a variety of different wine-related purposes. These uses include being blended with other grapes, used as a varietal, and even made into ice wine—a very sweet dessert wine—in countries such as Canada.

TABLE 6.11 RECENT CABERNET FRANC PLANTINGS

Country	Acres	Hectares	% of Worldwide Plantings
France	90,650	37,000	74
Italy	14,700	6,000	12
United States	2,570	1,050	2.1
Brazil	1,600	650	1.2
Yugoslavia	1,225	500	1
Hungary	1,225	500	1
Australia	1,000	400	0.8
Others: Argentina, Canada, China, India, Japan, Mexico, Morocco, New Zealand, Peru, South Africa, Spain, Tanzania, Tunisia, and Uruguay.	9,680	3,950	7.9

FRANCE

Cabernet Franc is authorized for all appellations in the southwest France region straddling Bordeaux, the Pyrénées, and Landes, but it is most heavily represented in the Loire Valley. In this region, Cabernet Franc is planted on almost 36,750 acres (or 15,000 hectares) and used to produce red and rosé wines, which best reflect the grape's character. Respected Cabernet Franc wines of this region include Chinon, Bourgueil, Saumur Champigny, and Anjou-Villages. Some of the best-known producers are Langlois-Château, Domaine Couly-Dutheil, Domaine Druet, Domaine Bernard Baudry, and Domaine Philippe Alliet.

In Bordeaux, Cabernet Franc is part of nearly all the great growths. It is blended in varying proportions, from as low as 0 to 30 percent in the Médoc to as high as 66 percent in St-Emilion. Some of the great-growth names associated with the use of Cabernet Franc in their wines are Ausone, Beauregard, Belair, La Conseillante, l'Evangile, Soutard, Trottevieille, and Vieux-Château-Certan.

ITALY

In Italy, Cabernet Franc vineyards are found mainly in the northeast of the country. They are particularly popular in the Friuli region, where the grape competes with local varieties such as Schioppettino and Pignola. Reputable producers are Ca'del Bosco, Quintarelli, Mario Schiopetto, Alessandro Princic, and Venica & Venica.

UNITED STATES

Even given their relatively short history—approximately forty years—of growing Cabernet Franc plantings, Californian winemakers have developed both a liking for varietal wines based on this grape and an appreciation of its value in Bordeaux blends. Bourriquot is one California wine, produced by Havens Wines, that contains 66.5-percent Cabernet Franc and 33.5-percent Merlot and has achieved a great reputation. Pride Mountain Vineyards also produces a wine—containing 75-percent Cabernet Franc and 25-percent Merlot—that highlights the potential of this grape when it is treated seriously both in the vineyard and the winery.

Cabernet Franc is also grown and produced in New York State with much success. On the North Fork of Long Island, Hargrave Vineyards produces a Loire-style Cabernet Franc of great appeal and with lovely flavors.

A RED WINE GRAPE LESS TRAVELED

The grapes discussed throughout this chapter are found in great abundance in the world wine market and in a variety of popular wines. There are, however, other important red wine grapes. Although some may not appear in wines with the same frequency or produce wines of the same quality as the grapes previously mentioned, they are an integral part of any wine education.

Petit Verdot

Petit Verdot is a complementary red wine grape that is used in a great number of châteaux wines. In the Médoc region, it usually comprises between 3 and 8 percent of the blend. Yet this figure has been decreasing over time due to the grape's tendency to ripen so much later than the other grapes used in the Bordeaux blends. When not allowed to ripen fully, the grape provides undesirable sharp and acidic flavors. In the United States, however, it is often used as a varietal wine. At its best, this grape provides high alcohol content, color, flavor, and tannins.

When fully ripe, Petit Verdot generates wines with an intense reddish-purple color; a fragrant nose characterized by banana, pencil shavings, violets, earth, leather, and cigar box; and richly textured flavors complemented by tannins that are generally soft. Total plantings in the Bordeaux region amount to less than 988.4 acres (or 400 hectares), and this measurement has decreased in recent years. Yet there are still close to one hundred Bordeaux wineries that are either using this grape in a blend or attempting to vinify Petit Verdot as a 100-percent varietal wine. In South Australia, on the other hand, enterprising grape growers have begun to plant Petit Verdot in Barossa Valley and McLaren Vale. Among these are Anderson Winery, d'Arenberg, De Bortoli, Giant Steps, Lilliput Wines, Millbrook Winery, Pettavel, Pirramimma, and Sevenoaks Wines. Petit Verdot has also generated a cult following in the warm wine regions of the United States, (namely California, Texas, Virginia, and Pennsylvania,) as the climates found there allow the grape to reach full maturity.

Nebbiolo

A native grape of Italy, Nebbiolo represents only a very small proportion—about 3 percent—of the wines produced in Piedmont in the North of Italy. Yet it generates some of the greatest and most traditional wines of Italy such as Barolo, Barbaresco, Ghemme, and Gattinara. Its wines are also known for needing much time to age in the bottle. About twenty years ago, a good Barolo had to be aged fifteen or twenty years because of its astringency from harsh tannins and notable acidity. Today, however, Nebbiolo wines—with a few exceptions—have been rendered more palatable at an earlier age.

Nebbiolo's first traces date back to the fourteenth century. It was mentioned as a cultivar in Valtellina in Lombardy, which is the only other Nebbiolo region outside of Piedmont in Italy. Its etymology may have two origins. *Nebbia* is the Italian name for fog, which prevails in the later part of the ripening season. On the other hand, the name may come from the word *nobile,* literally translated as noble. This grape is also known as Chiavennasca, Spanna, Picutener, and Nebieul.

Nebbiolo presents itself with thin skins but is notoriously difficult to grow, very much similar to Pinot Noir in Burgundy. Nebbiolo thrives best in calcareous soils. Found only in Piedmont and Lombardy, total plantings of Nebbiolo in Italy total a mere 3,100 acres. In Piedmont, reputable producers include Poderi Luigi Einaudi, Bruno Giacosa, Gaja, Falletto, and Pio Cesare. Most attempts to plant it elsewhere in the world have generated less than satisfactory results, although Argentina does have some large Nebbiolo vineyards. In the United States, the following AVAs boast some production of Nebbiolo: Paso Robles, Santa Ynez Valley, Shenandoah Valley, Red Mountain, and Rutherford.

Pinotage

Pinotage is a red wine grape that is a cross between Cinsaut and Pinot Noir. It was first bred in 1924 by Professor Abraham Perold in South Africa, where it was known as Hermitage. ("Hermitage" is also the name occasionally given to both Cinsaut and Shiraz grapes.) Pinotage has since become the symbol of the South African national wine identity.

Pinotage continues to perform well in South Africa because it is quite capable of coping with the humid climatic conditions. It is a vigorous grape and an early ripener, which are advantages in regions prone to early winter frosts. In addition, the resulting wine seems to have inherited the aging potential of Pinot Noir.

Recent Pinotage grape plantings covered up to 16,660 acres (or 6,800 hectares) in South Africa alone. At the present time, this grape is also being used to produce some remarkable wines in New Zealand and Argentina.

Cinsaut

A red wine grape particularly resistant to heat, Cinsaut is well adapted to the climatic conditions of the South of France, where it is principally found. One of the oldest grape varieties in France, it probably originated between Provence and Languedoc.

There are many names for this grape. In France, it is called Bourdalès, Picardan Noir, Espagnen, Salernes, and Cinsault. In South Africa, the grape has taken the name of Hermitage, while in California it is called Black Malvoisie.

Cinsaut produces fragrant rosé wines with aromas of berries, peaches, strawberries, and raspberries. It can also produce red wines which, if aged for a few years, highlight aromas of red fruit, raspberry, mint, spice, and almond.

Total worldwide plantings of Cinsaut are estimated to be around 110,250 acres (or 45,000 hectares). France alone accounts for 73 percent of this total, to the tune of 80,360 acres (or 32,800 hectares). The other 23 percent of the plantings are found in Morocco, South Africa, Australia, Bulgaria, Cyprus, Lebanon, Portugal, Romania, and Russia.

Gamay

Gamay is grown with great success throughout the eastern French region of Beaujolais. At one time, it was planted all over Burgundy, but was banned from this region by Philip the Bold at the end of the fourteenth century. Today, Gamay is an authorized grape in Burgundy but only for two appellations: Bourgogne Passe-Tout-Grain and Bourgogne Grand Ordinaire.

This grape thrives on poor soils, such as those composed of granite and sand. The most famous appellations of Beaujolais, namely Brouilly, Chénas, Chiroubles, Côtes de Brouilly, Fleurie, Juliénas, Moulin-à-Vent, Régnie, and Saint-Amour, are home to these types of ideal soils.

Young Gamay wines exhibit smells of bubble gum and fruit, such as strawberry and banana, particularly when they have undergone carbonic maceration. Only a handful of Gamay wines show dramatic improvement after fermentation or maturation in oak barrels. Those fermented in oak give off aromas similar to those found in Pinot Noir. The Gamay-based wines with aging potential come from vineyards planted on the best soils and with the best sun exposure. The Burgundian house of Louis Jadot makes a series of exceptional Gamay wines under the labels Château de Jacques and Bellevue.

Mourvèdre

Mourvèdre is a very important grape variety in France as well as regions around the Mediterranean Sea. In New World wine regions, Mourvèdre is associated with Grenache and Syrah. The three grapes are blended to make a wine known as GSM (which stands for Grenache Syrah Mourvèdre).

Mourvèdre-based wines have long been appreciated for their robustness and aging potential. French literary references to this grape can be found as early as the fourteenth century. Mourvèdre was abandoned during the phylloxera epidemic of the nineteenth century, before enjoying a revival during the second half of the twentieth century.

With close to 34,700 acres (or 85,000 hectares) planted worldwide, its presence is particularly strong in the arid limestone Spanish plains of Jumilla and Yecla, where it generates wines high in alcohol. In Spain, Mourvèdre is called Monastrell or Morastell. According to Pierre Galet, this grape is called Mataro in the United States and Australia after a Spanish town of the same name.

Renowned for the high quality of the wines it produces, the Mourvèdre grape is part of the Rhône Valley stable, and is regarded as a welcome addition in an area that grows mostly grapes of lesser quality. Characterized by thick skins covering small berries, Mourvèdre grapes produce a rich, dark wine when long skin contact is allowed during maceration or fermentation.

Carmenère

Carmenère is a red wine grape. Although it has long been thought to be the same as Chile's Merlot, genetic fingerprinting has proven the grape's separate identity. The two may, however, be distant relatives of each other. Carmenère used to be grown throughout Bordeaux, but has since been discarded by most of the region's viticulturists on accounts of its low productivity and late ripening when compared with the likes of Cabernet Sauvignon and Cabernet Franc.

The best Carmenère wines are made from grapes harvested in Chile's Rapel and Maule Valleys. The most respected producers and their esteemed Carmenère wines are Concha y Torro with its Terrunyo, Caliterra with its Arboleda, Ventisquero with its Grey, William Fevre with its Gran Cuvée Reserva, Santa Inès with its Carmenère Reserva, Errazuriz with its Don Maximiano Estate Carmenère, Montes with its Purple Angel, MontGras with its Reserva, and De Martino with its Single Vineyard.

Carmenère produces carmine-red wines with violet tints. When the grapes are picked fully ripened, the wine usually has a very deep concentration of red fruit. When the grapes are picked earlier, on the other hand, the wine often displays flavors of green peppers.

Tannat

The grape "par excellence" in Uruguay, Tannat generates exceptionally tannic wines with a deep color and hefty structure. Its name is derived from its high tannin content when grown in the United States, Argentina, Australia, and Italy. When grown in Uruguay, however, its tannin content tends to be lower.

The best French Tannat wines are made at Château Viella Village and Château de Sabazan. In Uruguay, the best wines are from producers Casa Luntro, Progreso, Toscanini, Viñedo de los

Vientos, Viticultores del Uruguay Arerunguá, and Vinson Richards.

Today, areas planted with this grape amount to slightly less than 7,400 acres (or 3,000 hectares) in France. Tannat plantings cover about 12,250 acres (or 5,000 hectares)—or a quarter of all vineyards—in Uruguay, where Tannat is known under the name Harriague. It was imported there by Spanish and French settlers from the Basque country in the early nineteenth century. Plantings of the grape have also spread across the border to the northern part of Argentina.

Touriga Nacional

In the seventeenth century, Touriga Nacional was already being cultivated in its native home, the Portuguese regions of Dao and Douro. It is planted on 7,350 acres (or 3,000 hectares) through this country. In the Douro region, Touriga Nacional is planted on steep terraces with subsoil consisting of rocks and schist. These two elements encourage low yields and superb color and aromas extraction during vinification.

Despite generating very low yields—about half that of comparable red grape varieties—and appearing in small bunches, Touriga Nacional is well respected. This is due to its tannins and concentrated fruit aromas, both of which form the backbone of many of the best port wines. Australia, South Africa, and California have all recently imported the variety in attempts to produce quality port.

Genetic fingerprinting has revealed an association between Touriga Nacional, the Madeiran grape Tinta Negra Mole, and the Mediterranean grape Moscatel Galego. It has also been discovered that Touriga Nacional is a mutation of Touriga Francesa, another grape variety grown extensively in the Douro. Numerous synonyms for Touriga Nacional—including Bical Tinto, Mortágua, Mortágua Preto, Preto Mortágua, Touriga, Touriga Fina, Tourigao, Tourigo Antigo, Tourigo do Dão, and Turiga—exist around the Mediterranean Sea.

Conclusion

Although there are numerous wine grapes with excellent aromas or aging potential that were not studied in this book, the most popular varieties were reviewed in great detail. To continue to further their wine education, wine connoisseurs and amateurs alike should be provided with ample opportunities for experimentation with new tastes and aromas.

Regardless of whether wine is bought as an investment or for immediate drinking, your job as wine owner does not conclude with its purchase. Part 3 offers suggestions and tips on the storage and service of wine.

PART 3

The Pleasures of Wine

7.
Wine Service

Wine service has evolved considerably during the last forty years, from a deeply ceremonial act to a much more informal yet still respectful process in contemporary society. Wine-ordering patterns of clients in restaurants and the common practice of serving wine at home reflect this evolution.

Young Wines Versus Old Wines

There is an important distinction between a mature, prestigious wine carrying a certain price tag, and those wines bought from supermarket shelves to be consumed within the same year (if not the same month or even the same day).

Some wines today are produced mainly by machine. There are still many hours and much labor necessary to bring these bottles to the market. However, the mechanization of both viticulture and vinification has resulted in enormous productivity gains in an industry which not so long ago relied heavily on manual labor.

At the same time, a white wine harvested by machine is usually vinified in a few months and found within the same year on a supermarket shelf. Those bottles may not need as much consideration as wines produced from grapes harvested by hand from carefully selected Chardonnay vines located in some of the most valued vineyards in the world, such as those of the Côte de Beaune in Burgundy, France. The time, money, dedication, and painstaking care

expended to make the latter wine not only justify the far higher price tag, but also call for care and consideration in the serving process.

A young red wine can be uncorked at the table, does not need decanting, and can be drunk slightly below the recommended temperature of 61 °F to 64 °F (or 16 °C to 18 °C). Similarly, a young white wine, served chilled, does not usually require any special treatment before being served.

On the other hand, a mature wine can be a more challenging proposition. The first step is to settle the sediment to the bottom of the bottle by standing the bottle upright for a few hours. The next step is to uncork it. Any cork older than twenty to twenty-five years will likely crumble into pieces when brought out of the bottle. Therefore, particular care and caution, as well as special tools, may well be required when uncorking. It may also be necessary to decant the wine before it is served. (Decanting is discussed on page 126.)

The Service Steps

One needs to take quite a few preparatory steps to ensure wine service without a hitch. Temperature of wine and glasses, cleanliness and appropriateness of glasses, service container, and quantity of wine to be poured are all details that transform not only the wine itself but the sensory and emotional perception during tasting and drinking wines.

TEMPERATURE

Every wine needs to be served at its optimum temperature. A young, fruity, and slightly tart white wine—as well as Champagne and other sparkling wines—should be served relatively chilled, at around 43 °F to 46 °F (or 6 °C to 8 °C). Oaked and aged Chardonnay can be served at the slightly higher temperature of 46 °F to 50 °F (or 8 °C to 10 °C) to enhance secondary and tertiary flavors and aromas.

For red wine, the spectrum of service temperatures is very wide. Beaujolais Nouveau, for example, must be chilled. On the other hand, aged reds such as Bordeaux and Rhône blends are at least seven years old and must be served at room temperature. These wines express their best only if served at a temperature where aromas such as leather, cedar box, vanilla, chocolate, coffee, and spices can fully develop and caress the olfactory senses. Yet there is a tendency to serve them at too high a temperature. No reds should be served at greater than 65 °F (or 18 °). In a room where the ambient air is set at 72 °F (or 22 °C), the temperature of a 4 ounce (or 120 milliliter) serving of wine poured in a crystal glass will rise about 3 °F (or 1 °C) for every minute spent in the glass. (The same is true for white wine.) Thus, to keep wine at an appropriate temperature in the serving glass, smaller quantities (and frequent refills) are preferable to larger quantities.

Some wines from the early 1900s, particularly from Bordeaux, may appear as light in color as that of a rosé wine because of the sediment. Bordeaux, and other older red wines, should often be decanted to rid the wine of these particles.

In recent years, a unfortunate trend of serving wine in completely disproportionately large glasses has emerged. These glasses look more like fish bowls than appropriate containers for serving a respectable glass of red wine!

SERVICE CONTAINER

Wine can be poured from one of two receptacles: a bottle or a decanter. *Decanting*—pouring the wine from the bottle into a different container—allows for the separation of the sediment from the rest of the wine. Sediment is the accumulation of phenols and polyphenols which have precipitated during the aging process. This build-up is not a wine fault, but can be relatively unpleasant on the tongue.

Most wines aged for less than five years do not need to be decanted, although the server may decant if he or she wishes to either soften aggressive tannins or oxygenate the wine to enhance flavors and aromas. On the other hand, most red wines older than five years may need to be decanted, while most white wines of all ages should not be decanted.

Decanting red wine has the potential to significantly modify the beverage structure through oxygenation. To decant, take a large carafe that is much wider at the base than at the neck, a candle, and the wine bottle itself. Light the candle and place it behind the bottle. The wine is then gently poured into the carafe until sediment begins to appear in the neck of the bottle, detectable due to the candle light.

To be able to serve old and expensive wines by the glass, wine bars use machines where each open bottle of wine is topped up with nitrogen. This is a neutral gas which allows the bottle to remain open for days (if not weeks) without altering the original olfactory or taste characteristics of the wine.

RECIPIENT GLASS

The glass into which the wine is poured is quite important. To keep Champagne and other sparkling wine bubbles flowing from the bottom of the glass, a *flute*—or long-stemmed narrow glass—is a prerequisite for serving. The Champagne coupe, while adding a romantic touch, actually decreases the refreshing effect of the bubbles and disseminates aromas. White wines are served in glasses a little shorter and narrower than those used for reds for a simple reason. Red wines exhibit a greater spectrum of aromas and flavors, especially in the case of aged, oaked wines made with noble grapes, and need a wider bowl to help express this character.

Each wine does have its own perfect glass, including smaller versions for fortified wines. The most popular glasses in general are open or closed tulip-shaped bowls, with either a long or a short stem, depending on whether the use is occasional or heavy.

Most up-market glassware manufacturers, such as Schott Zwiesel, Spiegelau, and Riedel, sell complete lines of glasses for each particular grape variety. Recent research, as well as anecdotal evidence, shows that glass shape and material have a dramatic impact on the way a wine smells and tastes.

REMOVAL OF FOIL

Before uncorking wines, foils have to be removed. Initially, foils were made of alloys that included

Figure 7.1. Before opening a Champagne bottle, part of the foil is removed and the wire is untied.

lead, a poisonous metal. The foil's objective was to keep dust and other undesirable elements from appearing on the portion of the cork outside wine bottles. Although it is now forbidden to use any lead in bottle foils, it is still advisable to remove the foil or at least cut it below the reinforcing ring that is part of the bottle neck. As foils are part of bottle design and marketing appeal, to remove it completely may not be entirely appropriate. In old times, sommeliers and wine waiters would chisel a ring, still attached to the bottle, out of the foil. That ring would hold the cork, which was printed with winery logo and vintage, to prove that the wine was the genuine item. The wine would then be served in a basket.

REMOVAL OF CORK

Removing the cork from the bottle is usually the trickiest part of serving either still or sparkling wine from a bottle. It requires muscular strength to remove some corks, which have been crammed in the bottle neck for several years. The length of the cork and the drying or decomposing process affect this particular step.

Thousands of corkscrew models exist. Some date back a few centuries, while others are very modern in shape and efficiency. The fist corkscrew was patented by British citizen Samuel

Henshall in 1795. Today, collectors around the world bid on corkscrews at auction.

In recent years, some new bottle openers, such as the lever-style corkscrew and pump-style wine opener, have appeared on the market. They facilitate the removal of the cork. However, caution should be used since the condition in which the cork will emerge from the bottle during removal is unknown. Champagne corks may require a specific opener resembling pliers.

QUANTITY OF WINE

The level at which wine is served in each glass is a direct reflection of the quality of service. A glass filled to the rim is nonsense. Generally speaking, a wine glass should not be filled more than halfway and not less than one third. The only possible exception would be situations in which wines are served by the glass in commercial operations such as a restaurant and bar. However, rather than completely filling the glass, it would be appropriate to increase the glass's size.

SERVICE

Wine is always served from the right of the guest, and the neck of the bottle never touches the glass. To pour wine, the bottle neck should be lifted upwards. When pouring is complete, the bottle should be gently rotated clockwise to prevent spillage on the tablecloth.

Figure 7.2. Champagne bottles are opened by twisting the bottle and holding cork.

As wine drinking has become increasingly popular, more and more people have developed a basic wine knowledge. Therefore, it has become increasingly important to deliver competent wine service, in both restaurants and homes. This begins with clean and appropriate glasses, avoiding spillage on the tablecloth, no broken corks, and appropriate serving temperatures. These factors together deliver a memorable and pleasurable experience, particularly if the wines in question deliver their promise of aroma, taste, and length. The next chapter, which addresses formal wine tastings, will only serve to enhance your wine experience.

Figure 7.3.
Wine is always served from the right of the guest. The neck of the bottle never touches the glass.

8.
Wine Tastings

Many people have never had the opportunity to taste wine in a serious or professional setting. Yet wine is a beverage that should be not only enjoyed, but also fully appreciated. After all, much hard work, care, and passion has gone into it. Wine deserves consideration, time, and concentration, as well as an appropriate environment in which to experience it. When setting up a professional wine tasting, certain conditions should be considered to make the event both worthwhile and enjoyable.

Preparing the Venue

Ideally, a wine tasting should be held in a quiet, non-smoking, and well-ventilated room. There should be sufficient lighting so that participants can appreciate the wines' colors. French professional trade associations such as the BIVB (Bourgogne Vintners Association) and the CIVC (Champagne Vintners Association) have set up their own high-tech tasting rooms where each taster is isolated, and thus not influenced by the reactions of fellow tasters. However, this is not necessary. Many people prefer the social aspect of most tastings.

Regardless, seating should be comfortable. Tables should be covered with white tablecloths, although an easily washable white surface is equally appropriate. A white background is the best way to observe the colors in the glass. Indirect but powerful lighting is needed for tasters to appreciate the nuances and variations

in the color of the wines. Natural daylight may not be appropriate if the sun shines directly into the tasting room.

All necessary equipment should be gathered before the day of the tasting. Glasses need to be ISO-approved, with a medium-length stem and a wide bowl with a tapered top. There should be spittoons, a water pitcher, bread or unflavored crackers (to bring taste buds back into a neutral stance between wines), and a tasting sheet on which to record impressions.

Figure 7.1.
The new tasting room at the CIVC. Each seat is isolated from the others and lighting is designed so as not to detract from the color of the wines. The center of the room features a tasting table for both tasting panels and comparative tastings. Epernay, Champagne, France.

Tasting the Wine

Three senses—sight, smell, and taste—are in action during a wine tasting. Eyes, nose, and palate are each utilized. The brain then combines these sensations to reach an overall assessment of the wine.

SIGHT

First, the eyes appreciate and judge a wine's *robe*—color. This process helps determine the wine's age and concentration of alcohol. A pale yellow wine typically indicates a young white wine that has not been exposed to oak. A pronounced golden color may suggest an older wine with a high concentration of residual sugars and probably a high alcohol level. At this stage, the clarity of the wine is also assessed. Special attention is paid to whether colloidal material is still in suspension.

A wine's length, shape, and size of its *legs*—also known as *tears,* the drops of wine that remain on the side of a glass after it is swirled—can help a taster determine *viscosity*—the liquid's thickness or thinness. A wine's viscosity affects the ease with which the drink can be poured. It also indicates levels of glycerol, residual sugar, and alcohol.

To compare the alcohol contents of two beverages, take two identical glasses. Pour one wine into the first. Pour the same volume of a different wine into the second. Swirl both liquids, and examine the drops sliding down the inside surface of the glass. The drink with the higher alcohol content will have bigger drops that take longer to reach the bottom of the glass.

SMELL

Although there are people subject to *anosmia*—the inability to clearly distinguish between different smells and aromas—most of us are aware of certain daily smells: coffee, toast, cigarette smoke, and so on. Our recollections of these smells are stored in our olfactory memory. Some people possess not only a better memory of smells than others, but have also been exposed to a greater number of smells. The extent of exposure to differing smells can determine the extent of vinous olfactory memory—the ability to identify different aromas and associate them with specific fruits, herbs, wood, and other components of the aroma spectrum. Thus, assessing the nose of a wine can be easy for some tasters, and more difficult for others.

Swirling the glass increases the surface ratio of wine in contact with oxygen, which serves to concentrate the smells and aromas inside the glass. Young Chardonnay wines usually exhibit grape characteristics such as apple, pear, and peach, while young Pinot Noir wines smell like black cherries. Aged wines outline far more complex and sophisticated aromas.

When tasting wines, tasters should look for balance. There should be no predominant smell, either fruit-like or from another group which might reflect the processing of the grape, either during fermentation or maturation.

Some grape varieties are easier to identify than others. Even inexperienced tasters can often recognize the flavors of lychee, rose, and pepper in a glass of Gewürztraminer, the most aromatic white grape. On the other hand, differentiating between a Merlot and a Cabernet Sauvignon is far more difficult. Olfactory memory also affects tasting.

Ann Noble, a now-retired professor of the University of California at Davis, devised a way to determine wine aromas. Her aroma wheel classifies the various aromas into categories such as chemical, pungent, oxidized, microbiological, floral, spicy, fruity, vegetative, nutty, caramelized, woody, and moldy. Although the wheel has its detractors, it is very helpful for beginners, and it also integrates the Emile Peynaud school of thought. (See the inset "Categorizing Wine Smells" on page 131 for more information on Peynaud.)

It is very helpful to keep track of tasting experiences by recording the information on tasting sheets. (Tasting sheets are described on page 126.) Every tasting session brings additional material and experience to the memory of the taster.

When you are smelling wine, you are also trying to identify any wine faults. The wine's odor may imply cork taint (which smells like wet cardboard and was described on page 40) or excessive sulfur dioxide or oxidation (which has a sherry-like smell).

Spittoons are especially important if more than five or six wines are to be tasted. They are usually made of stainless steel and may contain sawdust to absorb the liquid. These buckets can be shared, but make sure they are emptied before they become too heavy to pass around.

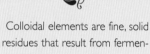

Colloidal elements are fine, solid residues that result from fermentation. Usually quite difficult to see because of their size, these elements are normally removed by membrane filters. However, some white and red wines only undergo racking and are marketed as unfiltered. It is in these wines that colloidal elements can be found.

Glycerol is a by-product of fermentation. It is falsely credited with having a positive contribution to *mouth feel*—the sum of sensations elicited inside the mouth when tasting or drinking wines.

Categorizing Wine Smells

Emile Peynaud was a wine teacher who revolutionized many common wine ideas. Through his efforts, grapes are no longer picked if they are unripe or rotten, and the quality of wine improved. He also made many advances in the vinification process.

On page 175 of his remarkable book *Le Goût du Vin (The Taste of Wine)*, Peynaud categorizes wine smells into the following nine groups. Each group name is followed by a short description of its smell.

- Animal odors: game, venison, and beef.
- Balsamic odors: pine trees, resin, and vanilla.
- Woody odors: new wood of oak barrels.
- Chemical odors: acetone, mercaptan, yeasts, hydrogen sulfide, acidity, and fermentation.
- Spicy odors: pepper, cloves, cinnamon, nutmeg, ginger, truffles, anise, and mint.

- Empyreumatic odors: crème brûlée, smoke, toast, leather, and coffee.
- Floral odors: violets, roses, lilacs, and jasmine.
- Fruity odors: blackcurrants, raspberries, cherries, plums, apricots, peaches, and figs.
- Vegetal odors: herbs, tea, mushrooms, and vegetables.

TASTE

For a long time, it was thought that the mouth was able to distinguish four basic tastes via the taste buds: sweetness, sourness, saltiness, and bitterness. However, recent studies have highlighted the role of the retro-nasal palate in identifying a range of aromas. Thus it can be said that the action of the mouth helps not only in tasting, but also in smelling. Some wine faults are only found in the mouth, such as excessive sweetness or tartness, vinegary characteristics, excessive astringency, and excess alcohol.

In addition, the so-called fifth taste or sensation—*umami*—is sometimes found in aged wines, as a result of several chemicals combining to trigger heightened olfactory and tasting sensations. Recent research in wine chemistry has focused on the role of amino acids in the umami tasting experience. Typically, a bottle of wine contains about 0.03 to 0.11 ounces (or 1 to 3 grams) of amino acids. As far as eating is concerned, the umami experience is due to a combination of glutamate, inosinate, and guanylate.

ASSESSMENT

Professional tasters use a specific vocabulary to describe their findings. For example, when tasting a 1990 Chateau Beauséjour (Duffau-Lagarosse), a St-Emilion first growth, Robert Parker Jr. described his May 1998 experience as follows: "I have had the 1990 Beauséjour-Duffau a half-dozen times since [bottling]. I believe this wine may, in fifteen to twenty years, be considered to be one of

the greatest wines made this century. It is in a league with such legends as the 1961 Latour à Pomerol. Beauséjour-Duffau's 1990 has always been the most concentrated wine of the 1990 vintage. The color remains an opaque murky purple. The nose offers up fabulously intense aromas of black fruits (plums, cherries, and currants), along with smoke, a roasted herb/nut component, and a compelling minerality. The wine is fabulously concentrated, with outstanding purity, and a nearly unprecedented combination of richness, complexity, and overall balance and harmony. What makes this effort so intriguing is that as good as Beauséjour-Duffau can be, I know of no vintage of this estate's wine that has come remotely close to this level of quality. In several blind tastings, I have mistaken this wine for either the 1989 or 1990 Pétrus! However, the 1990 Beauséjour-Duffau is even more concentrated than those two prodigious efforts. It should be at its best between 2000 and 2030."

Parker gave this wine the seldom-attributed 100 mark out of 100. All the information one may need is there, except perhaps for the grape varieties, which are included in an earlier paragraph in Parker's book. For those less familiar with "purple prose," the tasting sheet provides a more down-to-earth approach to wine notes. The inset on page 132 explains how to write or improve your tasting notes.

Researchers from the Australian Wine Centre at the University of Adelaide and the Cooperative Research Centre for Viticulture in South Australia devised a mouth-feel wheel. It was similar to that developed by Professor Ann Noble from the University of California at Davis for wine smells and aromas.

The retro-nasal palate is the upper part of the human palate, where the inner roof of the mouth is linked to the nose. This area is responsible for around 25 percent of flavors experienced during the ingestion of foods and beverages.

Writing a Tasting Sheet

Your enjoyment and appreciation of any tasting event will be enhanced if you take notes. These notes, called tasting sheets, will later allow you to clearly recall the impression you had of each wine. You may also find that these notes will help when you have wine discussions, as you will already be familiar with putting your reflections into words.

Before you start, you may find it useful to read some tasting notes of wine critics. Notice the consistency that critics have in their various notes. Similarly, your notes should eventually have their own style, too. The following information should be found in each tasting note. However, you should also include notes of any other observations you may make.

BACKGROUND INFORMATION
- Date of tasting
- Name of wine
- Vintage
- Origin (estate, region, country)
- Grape variety or varieties (if known)
- Proprietor, merchant, bottler, or shipper
- Date of supply
- Price (if known)

SIGHT OR VISUAL ASSESSMENT
- Depth
- Hue
- Clarity
- Viscosity

NOSE OR SMELL IMPRESSIONS
- General appeal or harmony of the various olfactory components
- General appeal or harmony of the aroma(s)
- General appeal or harmony of the bouquet (if any)

MOUTH OR TASTING SENSATIONS
- Tartness or acidity levels
- Sweetness or the amount of residual sugars
- Tannin levels or astringency
- Body
- Balance
- Length in the mouth

OVERALL ASSESSMENT ON THE QUALITY OF THE WINES

This section of your tasting note is highly personal, but most people either sum up their opinions in one or two sentences or assign the wine a numbered rating, a practice that has become increasingly popular over the years.

ADDITIONAL INFORMATION

You can include any pertinent information not mentioned in the above categories. This can include expected maturity or potential foods with which to match the wine.

Since the 1980s, there has been a tendency to score or apply a rating to wines, as exemplified by the success of Parker's wine books. This rating system has the merit of providing the public at large with an easy basis for comparison. However, the system is highly controversial. Scoring is a valid exercise, but only if it is always undertaken by the same person, and if it follows a strict set of criteria. For beginners, it is very useful to file this tasting information so as to provide a readily available reference on which to build olfactory memory.

The Tools of Tasting

Le Nez du Vin (*The Nose of Wine*) is a kit consisting of fifty-four small bottles. Each is filled with a different wine aroma, and comes with a description of the aroma. This kit helps novice tasters to identify the various smells found in a variety of wines. (Lenoir has also issued a twelve-bottle kit containing the scents of various wine faults, which are discussed on page 133.)

Alternatively, it is similarly educational to take a basic dry white wine, pour it into a number of glasses, and then macerate various fruits, herbs, and other ingredients in each of those glasses. These are then covered with plastic film, which is removed after half an hour. At that point, the concentration of specific smells and aromas is quite marked and easily observed.

Further, the research and development department of France Telecom has devised a computer peripheral consisting of six aromatic, gel-equipped micro fans, each connecting via USB ports. It diffuses smells according to instructions from specific software (Exhalia). In other words, it sends smells and aromas in the same way that a printer delivers printed sheets of paper. Once connected to specific websites such as that of the BIVB, students are able to experiment with all the smells associated with viticulture, vinification, and wine tasting, while at the same time building their olfactory memory.

FAULTS IN WINE

The most common faults found in wine are relatively obvious to an experienced nose. These faults variously emanate from the base material itself; the processing during pressing, fermentation, racking, and filtration; and storage inside the cask or bottle.

Grape Faults

During harvest, it may happen that vine leaves and stems remain with the grapes, either inside the white-wine press or in the red-wine fermentation vessel. This results in the presence of a molecule that brings a vegetal smell and taste perceptible in concentrations of 0.05 percent (or 0.5 grams per liter).

Corked Wine or Cork Taint

Said to be occurring in 5 to 7 percent of all wines, TCA (2,4,6-trichloroanisole) emanates from a fungus that infects cork manufactured from the bark of oak trees (*Quercus suber*). Its presence in cork results in *cork taint*, and the wines in which it occurs are called *corked wines*. Characterized by the smell of wet cardboard, mould, or dirty socks, corked wine lacks a fruit component in the aromas spectrum, and may taste bitter. Corked wines can be returned to the merchant for an exchange. It is more perceptible in white and sparkling wines than in reds.

Cooked Wine

Cooked wine is a direct result of inappropriate storage, either during transportation or in retail outlets. Major temperature fluctuations affect the physical shape of the wine inside the bottle, triggering expansion and contraction. This pressure on the bottle's closure can cause oxidation if oxygen is allowed to seep through the cork, which may result in a lack of structure and dull aromas on the wine, and leading to the taste of cooked fruits or jam.

Sulfur Dioxide

Used to prevent the development of undesirable microorganisms, sulfur dioxide (SO_2) enables a better control of fermentation, but most importantly prevents a second fermentation from occurring inside the bottle. However, a strong smell like a struck match is a good indication that too much SO_2 has been added. This usually occurs during bottling. Too much SO_2 can also be the fault of *Saccharomyces* yeast, which is present during fermentation. This occurs mainly in light white wines and rarely in reds.

Oxidation

Oxidation happens when wine is exposed to sufficient amounts of oxygen to trigger the formation of acetaldehyde, a compound that overpowers all others. Wines opened for a few days or suffering undue exposure to oxygen during racking and bottling exhibit a rather unpleasant smell of walnut and brown apple.

Techniques to prevent oxidation, such as bottling under neutral gas and adequately filling and topping up all bottles, are gradually being implemented in wineries around the world, thus reducing occurrence of oxidation. It happens more frequently in young wines and in those with low alcohol. Drinking an oxidized wine can trigger a serious hangover.

Barnyard

The presence and concentration of *brettanomyces* determines whether the wine outlines a wonderful leathery character (at a concentration of 0.0002 percent or 2 milligrams per liter) or a strong and unpleasant horse manure or band-aid type of smell (at a concentration of 0.0004 percent or 4 milligrams per liter). Very much desired in some Burgundy or Californian red wines, it seldom appears in white wines.

Barnyard smell can also be the result of unsanitary conditions in the winery, which can

Saccharomyces are a family of yeasts including the *saccharomyces cerevisiae* and *saccharomyces bayanus*, which are both used in the process of winemaking, as well as in beer brewing and bread-making.

Acetaldehyde is the chemical responsible for the "hangover" feeling. It results from the conversion of ethanol in the liver by the enzyme alcohol dehydrogenase.

Brettanomyces belong to the same yeast family as the *saccharomyces*. Minute quantities in wine are highly desirable as it adds complexity of aroma and flavor. However, it becomes a fault when the concentration exceeds these levels. Also known as "brett," the resulting faulty wine is generally coined "mousy" or "bretty."

encourage the presence of the bacteria responsible for the degradation of certain phenolic compounds in wine. Maturation of the wine in used barrels may also generate the presence of *brettanomyces*. This fault can be eliminated by the sterile filtration of the wine before bottling.

Volatile Acid

A wine affected by *acescence* has been infected by acetic bacteria and gives off a vinegary smell. Naturally present in all the wines at the rate of 0.02-percent concentration or 200 to 300 milligrams of acetic acid per liter, it becomes very unpleasant when the wine contains 0.07- to 0.08-percent concentration or 700 to 800 milligrams per liter. Caused by damaged fruit, insufficient SO_2, or poor hygiene in the winery, acescence is never pleasant, and gives a hot and hard sensation in the mouth. It smells like nail polish remover or solvent.

Sulfides

Sulfides represent several chemical compounds in which sulphur oxidizes at its lowest level. The presence of sulfides in wine can take three forms: hydrogen sulfide, which is characterized by an unpleasant smell reminiscent of boiled egg; mercaptans, which give off aromas of onion, garlic, and burnt rubber; and dimethylsulfide, which smells of canned or cooked vegetables (most notably asparagus). These unpleasant odors are caused by a lack of amino acids (particularly nitrogen) during fermentation, and can be avoided by the addition of *diammonium phosphate* (DAP)—a water-soluble chemical compound commonly used as an agricultural fertilizer.

While grape-growing requires a good deal of attention in relation to soil, grape variety, climate, and pests and insects, vinification is equally demanding. After all, a minimum level of chemistry knowledge is necessary to avoid many faults. The incidence of faulty wines has dramatically decreased over the last two decades, but a number of unacceptable practices are still observed. Unsanitary conditions in the winery and a lack of basic precautions can still be witnessed, even in large winery operations. In the next chapter, you will read of the importance of having guaranteed quality and aging ability, particularly if wines are to be purchased as an investment.

Acescence is characterized by the presence of acetic acid and ethyl acetate in the wine, which slowly transform into vinegar as a result. The sensory experience highlights a sharp and sour attack of the tongue, similar to a salad dressing made with too much vinegar.

DAP can also be used in minute quantities as energy material to feed yeasts during fermentation. Such use helps to avoid a build-up of nitrogen, so that fermentation can be brought to safe completion.

Figure 8.2. Refrigerating your wines at the proper temperature will help maintain their flavor until your next wine tasting.

9.
Wine Storage and Investment

In June 2006, Bordeaux estates and merchants released the prices of the 2005 vintage to the stupor of the wine world. Some cases—such as those from Château Quinault L'Enclos in Saint Emilion—had increased in price from the previous vintage by 85 percent! Price hikes of this nature render many wines out of reach for most wine drinkers, but serve to trigger much interest in the wine-investment community.

Yet care for such this high-price commodity does not end with the writing of a check. Wine—particularly when expensive—must be stored appropriately. This chapter addresses both wine investment and wine storage in detail.

Wine Storage

Wine usually needs to be stored before it is consumed. Some wines (such as Beaujolais Nouveau) require only two to three weeks storage before they can be appreciated. On the other hand, others (such as Grange from Penfolds winery in Australia) need fifteen to twenty years in the bottle before they reach full maturity.

To determine the length of time that a wine should be stored, the type of wine should be considered. Only a few white wines—such as Burgundian Chardonnay, Loire Valley Chenin Blanc, Bordeaux blends of Sauvignon Blanc and Semillon, and most botrytized wines—age gracefully. The majority of other white wines should usually be opened within the first five years of their lives.

Many red wines are suitable for immediate consumption. Yet others—such as those based on Cabernet Sauvignon, Cabernet Franc, Malbec, Sangiovese, and Syrah—may need to be stored for as long as five years. While it is possible to drink Merlot-based wines four to five years after the harvest, they can also age and mature for much longer periods.

Regardless of how long you plan on storing your wine, there will come a point when you must bring the bottle home. When a bottle of wine is transported by car or other means, it will be subject to *bottle sickness*. This is a flattening of fruity aromas and flavors that can be caused by any shaking motion. The only cure for such a condition is to rest the bottle for at least three weeks.

Whether your wine is being stored until it matures or merely until the liquid settles after having been jostled around, there are certain factors to consider when seeking ideal storage conditions. These include light, temperature, humidity, and vibrations.

LIGHT

The *anthocyanins,* or coloring agents contained in the wine, react with the amount of daylight to which they are exposed. Therefore, wine bottles should be exposed to as little light as possible. In a wine cellar that is 100 square feet (or 10 square meters), a single sixty-watt bulb is sufficient—but should not be permanently switched on.

Botrytized wines are produced from grapes affected by the aphid botrytis cinerea, also called noble rot. Those grapes are brownish, shriveled, and rotten, but reveal a very high sugar content. These grapes are transformed into luscious, long-lasting wines with superb aging potential.

Fluorescent or neon tubes flicker light at a high speed, and should be completely avoided. Although the human eye hardly detects this flicker, exposed wine quickly reacts to the light and undergoes a color change. The bar code scanner at the cashier counter where the wine was purchased can cause changes, too! Specialists recommend laying down such bottles for three weeks before consumption.

TEMPERATURE

The ideal temperature for wine storage is a constant 52˚F (or 12˚C). For both red and white wines, this allows for good conservation and maturation at a controlled pace. Yet a temperature of 42˚F to 44˚F (or 6˚C to 7˚C) kills the aromas and results in flat and unappealing wines, while also hardening corks, rendering them less watertight. A temperature of 68˚F (or 20˚C) accelerates the maturation and development of some wines, resulting in a reduced life span.

Steven Spurrier is a British wine writer and consultant. In 1976, he organized the famous wine tasting "Judgement of Paris," at which Californian Chardonnay and Cabernet Sauvignon wines were deemed better than their prestigious counterparts from Burgundy and Bordeaux—much to the surprise of the French wine world.

However, the constancy of temperature is more important than the temperature itself. Even in a basement wine cellar, bottles should be stored at the far-north corner, where they will be less subject to temperature change—not only fluctuations throughout the day, but with seasonal changes. At the same time, most wine experts, such as Steven Spurrier, agree that seasonal variations are not detrimental to the safe-keeping of wines, as long as the bottles are kept in the basement or in a place where the impact of such variations is attenuated.

HUMIDITY

While a certain level of humidity is beneficial to the cork, excessive moisture inevitably causes problems for a wine collection. It can damage both the cork and label, creating the conditions for the emergence and propagation of moulds and bacterial growth.

Anything above 75-percent humidity is considered excessive, and below 50-percent humidity is insufficient. With the arrival of screwcaps and plastic and silicone closures, the requirement for minimum humidity levels may change in the near future.

VIBRATIONS

Wine is a living product. High-end bottles undergo tremendous positive changes throughout their lives. However, these changes can only occur correctly if the wine is disturbed as little as possible. Every vibration creates a chaotic environment inside the bottle. As a result, even wine that does not need to mature should be allowed to settle down for two to three weeks after being purchased from a wine merchant. This will help eliminate any resulting bottle sickness.

Therefore, wine cellars should be located in buildings away from train, tram, and underground lines and roads with heavy vehicle traffic. They should even be kept apart from domestic appliances such as washing machines. Most wine storage cupboards and refrigerator brands such as Eurocave, Liebherr, Vintec, Ecovin, and Frigidaire are equipped with anti-vibration systems.

The conditions in which quality wine is stored is very important. Therefore, some people may find that the ideal storage conditions aren't plausible in their home. On the other hand, some wine collectors may find that they have collected too many bottles for the space they set aside. Luckily, professional storage facilities are always available for a small fee.

The Composition of Wines With Aging Potential

To properly mature, a wine needs the right combination and balance of acidity, tannin, and alcohol. It is typically at harvest time that such a combination is decreed. Fully ripened red grapes harvested at low yields generate high sugar content, and their skins contain maximum tannins. Subsequent skin-contact and temperature-controlled fermentation ensure optimal tannin extraction. The aging environment is equally important. The bottle itself has to be of high-quality, colored glass, while the cork has to provide an airtight seal to eliminate virtually all oxygen.

TANNINS

Tannins are to wine what the skeleton is to the human body: they provide the structure to both maintain it and keep it in good shape as it matures. With time, harsh tannins usually soften and add a subtle note of support to the primary and secondary aromas. In other words, they become part of the complex bouquet associated with older wines. While tannins are most often found in substantial quantities in red wines, the exposure of white wines to new oak during maturation can also result in a reasonably high degree of tannin. New oak can add as much as .007 ounces per 1.06 quarts (or 200 milligrams of tannin per liter) of wine in one year.

ACIDITY

If the acidity level in a grape bunch is too high at harvest time, the finished wine will have a tart sensation. Too little acidity, on the other hand, gives rise to unduly high levels of alcohol, an undesirable by-product of over-ripened grapes. The right balance has to be found, not only by the viticulturist during the harvesting period, but also by the winemaker before and during fermentation. For white wines, acidity is directly related to aging potential, as these acids soften with time and uncover special aromas and flavors. Yet the sweetest of wines also have extraordinary aging potential. These wines may continue to mature for fifty—or even one hundred—years, because high residual sugar acts as a preserving agent.

ALCOHOL

High alcohol content helps prevent oxidation. It is the high alcohol level in fortified wines, and in some still wines, that allows them to age for many years, possibly decades. The alcohol helps to preserve a wine's qualities, and also contributes to its structure.

Wine Investment

Anyone considering wine as an investment should bear in mind some of the constraints associated with buying, storing, and re-selling wine over a period of time. The investment horizon in wines is certainly a minimum of five to six years—and a lot more for some wines.

In the investment world, the goal is always to buy low and sell high. It is only worth investing in a wine that has a value that will continue to rise over time. In general, wines produced in small quantities following stringent vinification methods are worthwhile investments.

The classified growths of Bordeaux are tried and true examples of good investment wines. Other good investment wines are single-vineyard Rhône Valley wines made from Syrah, Super Tuscan blends made from Sangiovese and Cabernet Sauvignon, top Burgundy reds and whites, Champagne, and some wines of Portugal. To find out which wines make it to the top grade, it is best to consult the records and catalogues of auction houses. Christie's and Sotheby's are the two major auction houses.

BUYING LOW

For top-grade wines, the first indicator of potential future appreciation in value is quality at harvest time. Together, sugar concentration, level of maturity of the grape berries, thickness of the skins, length of the growing period, yield, and the prevailing climate during the growth period give important indications as to the future quality of the wine.

However, it is only after the first fermentation and some time in the barrel that the first tasting by wine experts takes place. This is usually around seven months after harvest. After the tasting, wine experts—such as the notable Jancis Robinson, MW, Robert Parker, Jr, Steven Spurrier, and James Suckling—publish their findings on websites and in columns. A positive consensus opinion by five or six experts is usually a good indication that the wine possesses all the necessary aging potential attributes, will mature in an elegant fashion, and—most importantly—see its value increase with time.

The key to buying low is to buy before bottling. This can be done by buying either in futures—purchasing the wine before the vintage—or *en primeur*—purchasing the wine one year after its harvest. Futures involve considerable risk since nothing is known of the coming vintage, but experts generally predict that out of ten years, three will generate a good to excellent vintage. If a buyer chooses to take this risk and buy futures, he takes an option on a certain quantity of bottles produced from the forthcoming vintage. It can be extremely helpful

The ability of a wine to age is based on many factors, including the amount of sugar it contains. In wine, sugar acts as a preserving agent—just as it preserves fruit in jams.

Master of Wine (MW) is the highest academic qualification delivered by the Institute of Masters of Wine. Worldwide, only around 260 people have achieved it. Masters of Wine are true experts who are able to not only taste, appreciate, and judge wines, but also consult and write on almost any related topic such as wine marketing, viticulture, and vinification.

to look at statistical information as to which chateau or winemaker manages to produce consistently good wines across bad and good vintages alike.

To buy wine en primeur, one needs to rely on the opinion of wine experts. The 2003 vintage is a good example. This was a very dry year across Europe, compounded by exceptionally hot weather, producing yields way below the usual quantity, as well as uneven results across varying wine regions. Some winemakers (such as Le Pin in Pomerol) actually chose not to make any wine. As a result, this vintage's investment grade wines were much more limited in number compared with previous vintages. Prices were, therefore, very high and the wines sold out very quickly. These 2003 wines, delivered in 2006, have subsequently seen their price increase by more than 50 percent.

One year later, on the other hand, the 2004 vintage yielded far larger quantities, and saw en primeur prices down by 20 to 30 percent—even 50 percent in some cases. Premier prices for 2005 Bordeaux in the same league shot to stratospheric levels in April 2006, after most of the influential tasters rated the vintage as good as that of the remarkable 1945. They highlighted fabulous tannin levels, sustained acidity, and reasonably high levels of alcohol—the three main characteristics that give a wine best aging potential.

There is a simple explanation as to why wine prices constantly fluctuate. Only a limited number of bottles are produced in any given vintage

> The first wine sale at auction took place in December 1766 in London at Christie's. This was also the very first auction held at this now-famous auction house. In 1769, Christie's held its first auction dedicated completely to the sale of wine.

for most of the top-grade wines, and every time someone anywhere in the world opens one of these investment-grade bottles, the remaining ones from the same estate and vintage instantly become rarer, and thus more valuable.

However, one more dimension is added to the equation in the case of wine, as opposed to other collectibles: it is a living product that evolves with age. In the life cycle of a wine bottle, there is an ascending curve followed by a peak period before a stage of decline. The key is to sell at the most appropriate time. Tasting the wine at regular intervals and reading tasting notes in wine magazines will help provide an indication as to a time frame during which to sell the wine.

SELLING HIGH

The only aspect of wine investment more important than buying at a low price is selling at a higher one. As a collector, one should only acquire wine bottles when their *provenance*—history of ownership—and previous storage conditions can be established. There are specific storage locations that guarantee optimum conditions in terms of temperature, humidity, and lighting, and serious investors always ensure they can produce records from the storage companies at selling time.

The price of a bottle of wine is also determined by its *ullage*—the level of wine in the bottle. In their catalogues, auction houses always mention the ullage of Bordeaux wines (and wines bottled in Bordeaux bottles) by indicating where in the upper part of the bottle, from its bottom shoulder to upper neck, the liquid reaches. For wines bottled

Maintaining Provenance

Movement of older wine, particularly that bought as an investment, should be kept to a minimum. Temperature changes, as well as vibrations and shocks, greatly affect the delicate balance achieved by the winemaker. While young wines are usually able to quickly recover from this trauma, older wines can be destroyed by transportation. That is why bottles that have been shipped and re-shipped to several continents usually fetch lower prices at auction, particularly with ten or twenty years of bottle age.

To keep this information accurate, all French wines imported to the United States bear an additional label that identifies the bottle as having taken the trip. This label was created specifically to meet the requirements of the Bureau of Alcohol, Tobacco and Firearms. If the bottle is then proposed for sale at an auction in London, its price will be negatively affected. However, the same bottle will probably see its price unaffected if auctioned in New York or San Francisco.

in other shapes, such as from Burgundy and Germany, and wines bottled in other sloped-necked bottles, the ullage is measured from the base of the cork to the wine level in inches or centimeters, depending on the auction location.

Some top-grade wine houses provide Wine Clinics whereby the bottles are opened every fifteen to twenty years. The wine is tasted, and then topped up with the same wine from the same vintage. Wine Clinics are held in important cities where large collections can be found. In May 2005, the collection of 500 bottles of Chateau Palmer 1961 belonging to Dr. Stanley Ho in Macau, PR of China, underwent such a treatment. Seventeen of the bottles were used to compensate for the evaporated wine in the other bottles. The remaining bottles were then re-corked. They were also given an additional label which mentioned the date of the opening, tasting, and topping up, as well as the name of the person who did it. Usually, this process is carried out by the winemaker.

Another factor that can determine potential selling price is the state of the bottle's label. A perfectly readable label in good condition suggests good storage conditions. Some estates deliver their bottles wrapped in soft, transparent paper which allows the label to be read, while at the same time protecting it against excessive humidity.

WINE AT AUCTION

The most well-know auction houses around the world are the multinational Sotheby's and Christie's; the United Kingdom's Bonham's; and the United States' Acker Merrall & Condit, Zachys, Hart Davis Hart, and Bonhams & Butterfield.

Prices can reach phenomenal levels for much sought-after wines. On November 18, 2006, a single lot of fifty cases (600 bottles) of Château Mouton-Rothschild 1982 sold for $1,051,600 (£781,208)—$1,753 (£1,302) per bottle. In this case, the provenance and pedigree of the wine from the Park B. Smith collection was clearly established, and helped push auction prices to a new record.

Using wine as an investment opportunity usually brings handsome returns, as well as portfolio diversification. Specialized British houses, such as Berry Bros. & Rudd or John Armit Wines, offer the wine investor a one-stop shop. They purchase the wine, store it, and then suggest its best possible selling time. This is particularly relevant for investment-grade wine held in large quantities.

Another possibility for wine investment is a wine fund. These companies allow you to invest in wine of which they are in possession. On average, three key London-based wine funds outperform the Dow Jones Industrial Average, the FTSE 100 Index, and a British government bonds index (Kumar, 2006). Similarly, the Vintage Wine Fund, an offshore investment company managed by OWC Asset Management Limited, showed an appreciation of 69 percent for the period from February 2003 to February 2007. Another company, The Fine Wine Fund, has shown a portfolio appreciation of nearly 22 percent from August 2006 to April 2007.

While wine funds represent an interesting diversification opportunity, they do not allow collectors to actually own their wine. In case of a substantial market value decrease, wine collectors can always console themselves by consuming their bottles—something not possible with a wine fund. On the other hand, this type of investment often makes its investors substantial profit.

Starting a wine collection demands dedication, capital, and a great deal of patience. Unlike many other collectibles, however, the investment is "liquid"— and can thus usually provide much satisfaction even if its price drops to a very low level. On the other hand, the temptation to open a good bottle that has reached optimum maturity can sometimes be hard to resist! Try to be careful if the urge comes to drink your investment. At the very least, make sure to enjoy it.

On the other hand, if purchased wines are intended for home consumption, wine storage no longer calls for the perfect underground cellar. The wine refrigerators available today provide highly appropriate storage conditions, even for apartments located in high-rise buildings in tropical cities.

If you do plan on drinking the wine you have purchased, you already learned how to serve it in Chapter 7. The next chapter will explain pairing wine with food.

The largest single-owner cellar sold at auction was that of Russell H. Frye, which was sold for $7,832,755 (£5,816,694) in 2006. This outperformed the high-profile auction of Sir Andrew Lloyd Webber's cellar which, in 1997, brought in $6,100,000 (£4,531,274).

10.
Matching Food and Wine

Although some wine experts, sommeliers, and chefs may indeed say otherwise, there are no absolute rules in the world of food-and-wine matching. This is because, quite simply, we all taste differently. Yet this chapter will provide you with basic rules to help you make particularly enjoyable decisions.

There are many different types of foods that are eaten in various cultures. People living in tropical areas tend to eat very spicy food, while many Arab people eat very sweet food, and Japanese people have a particular liking for raw food. There are also, of course, many likes and dislikes among people of a culture.

It may seem daunting to consider reconciling such varying preferences with wine—but it can be done. The spectrum of wines on offer is certainly as extensive as the range of cuisines around the world. Wines, after all, range from bone dry to sweet, from light to heavy, from young to aged, from mild to spicy, and from white to crimson red.

The large variety of flavors, aromas, and textures, present not only in food but also wine, means that there are endless potential combinations. This chapter will examine certain aspects of both wine and food to aid your discovery of delicious pairings. It will also provide some tried-and-trusted pairings on which almost everyone can agree.

Main Considerations

Conventional wisdom matched white wines with fish and white meat, and red wines with red meat. Unfortunately, a successful marriage requires a little more direction than this.

The first criterion for the match is to decide whether the wine or the food is more important. Perhaps there is in the cellar a special wine which has been aging for twenty years, and is now at the peak of its maturity. This wine will take precedence over the food—though it will dictate discretion and neutrality in the choice and preparation of this eagerly anticipated dinner.

On the other hand, there may have been in the market some super-fresh seafood which would be great for lunch. Here, then, the food is the dominant element in the equation. Yet a wine

Figure 10.1. Champagne served with cheese.

Wine and Cheese

A popular food to pair with wine is cheese. Yet in a 2005 study undertaken at the University of California at Davis and published in both *New Scientist* and *American Journal of Enology and Viticulture*, Dr. Hildegard Heymann and fellow researchers found that wine tasters were unable to characterize the aromas, smells, and flavors of berry, oak, sourness, and astringency when wine was paired with cheeses.

Why are certain wine flavors indiscernible when tasted with cheese? One possibility is that the fat content of cheese coats the palate and impairs the function of taste buds, as well as that of the retro-nasal palate. Another is that cheese proteins bind with wine compounds, making the flavors more difficult to detect.

Regardless of the reason, these findings challenge decades-long beliefs that the pairing of wine with cheese was a perfect match. Although it is certainly possible to enjoy the two together, cheese should clearly not be served at a wine tasting or with particularly high-quality wine. When wishing to truly relish the wine's flavors and aromas, you may want to find a better food for the accompanying meal than cheese.

can be chosen that will not only match the food, but also enhance it.

You then need to decide whether you are going to match food with a similar, contrasting, or opposite wine. A similar pairing would be a sweet port wine or Banyuls with chocolate dessert. Contrasting wine and food would be a crisp, light unoaked Chardonnay with juicy rich oysters. Opposites can be a full-bodied botrytized Sauvignon or Semillon, which are sweet, served with a British Stilton or Berkshire Blue cheese from Massachusetts, which are salty. This is further explored in the next section.

Figure 10.2.
Champagne can be served with warm oyster, gooseliver, and lobster.

The Basic Rules

There are other considerations when pairing food and wine. Once you decide whether to match the food with a similar, contrasting, or opposite wine, you must also consider whether this should be based on aroma or taste. This section will provide some examples. More specific suggestions are shown in Table 10.1 on pages 144 to 146, including some of the most popular pairings of wine with food. The food in this table is representative of typical western and Asian cuisines. Using this table and the following advice, even the most inexperienced food-and-wine matchmakers will be pleased with their choices.

Realize, though, that the following categorizations should be seen as generalizations. After all, unoaked Chardonnay can have a very crisp, dry, and acidic finish with very fruity aromas. On the other hand, if it has undergone malolactic fermentation and wood-barrel maturation, it will appear richer, rounder, more luscious, and less tart. When you are choosing a wine, make the decision based on your determination of the specific qualities of that exact wine.

MATCHES BASED ON SIMILAR AROMAS

The strong aroma of some bottles of wine can match with similarly smelling food. A grilled steak, for example, requires an oaked wine such as Cabernet Sauvignon. A dish served with pepper sauce demands a wine with a spicy character such as a Syrah or even a Gewürztraminer.

MATCHES BASED ON SIMILAR TASTES

Wine and food can be matched based on similar tastes. Pick out a dominant flavor in your meal, and match it to a wine that has a similar flavor. For example, dishes from Provence based on olives and herbs such as thyme, bay leaf, and rosemary may find their match in red Northern Rhône wines. This meal and wine show a very similar olfactory spectrum.

MATCHES BASED ON ACIDITY

The acidity found in some foods prepared with lemon juice or vinegar, such as salads with Italian dressing, needs to be counter-balanced with rich and "fat" wines such as those found in Spain, California, Provence, or the Rhône Valley. Acidic foods tend to reinforce the perception of tannins in red wines, as well as the tartness of white wines.

MATCHES BASED ON SWEETNESS

Sweet food items tend to cause tannic red wines to taste even drier, as well as underline any bitterness in both red and white wines. Therefore, they should be balanced with sweet wines, such as botrytized, fortified, or ice wines. The intensity of the dish must also be taken into account: chocolate desserts demand wines with more body and intensity—such as Banyuls—than cream-based desserts.

MATCHES BASED ON INTENSITY

The wine's intensity (often referred to as its spectrum) must always be considered. This ranges from light to heavy, for both white and red wines. The intensity of the wine should match—or at least be similar to—the intensity of the food.

Figure 10.3.
A glass of sweet Champagne with strawberry tart

*P*airing Food and Wine

The following considerations should be used as guidelines on getting the most out of both wine and food. When paired with the information given in the section "The Basic Rules," this advice is invaluable toward creating a special meal.

■ White wines are usually more acidic than red wines.

■ Most red wines have a much higher tannin content than white wines.

■ Wines based on Cabernet Sauvignon, Cabernet Franc, and Syrah (or Shiraz) are more tannic than those based on Pinot Noir or Merlot.

■ Sweet foods with a high sugar content tend to emphasize the acidic character of dry wines, so it is advisable to avoid serving dry white wines with sweet food.

■ Tannic wines appear softer when served with heavy foods.

■ Some foods are decidedly difficult to match with any wine. Artichoke and asparagus, for example, are difficult to match because of their herbaceous smell and taste.

■ The way in which a dish is prepared and the sauce with which it is served are as important as the main ingredients. For example, grilling caramelizes the surface of meat, producing a strong flavor. Such meats should be matched with a wine equally strong in flavor. A grilled black-pepper steak needs a strong, full-bodied red wine with a pepper-spice character such as Syrah (or Shiraz).

■ Wine should complement food, rather than being dominant.

■ During a meal, white wines should usually be served first, with red wines to follow. The rare exceptions are some white dessert wines, such as Sauternes, which can be served last.

■ During meals, younger wines should be drank before older wines.

TABLE 10.1 POPULAR WINE-AND-FOOD COMBINATIONS

Food	Wine
Cold Appetizers	
Antipasto	Light Sauvignon Blanc, Semillon from Bordeaux or Western Australia, or any dry and unoaked Italian white wine such as Soave
Caviar or salmon roe	Vodka or extra-brut Champagne
Fish, raw (oysters, sashimi, and fish carpaccio)	Unoaked New World Chardonnay, Chablis, Muscadet, Chenin Blanc, Sauvignon Blanc, or Sylvaner
Meat, raw (beef carpaccio)	Italian Merlot or Sangiovese
Salad, spicy meat	New World Chardonnay, Semillon, Pinot Grigio, Pinot Bianco, Primitivo, Nero D'Avola, or Negroamaro
Salad, vegetables	New World Chardonnay, Semillon, Pinot Grigio, Pinot Bianco, Primitivo, Nero D'Avola, or Negroamaro
Shellfish (lobster, clam, shrimp, and scallops)	Chardonnay, Riesling, Chablis, Semillon, Chenin Blanc, or Sauvignon Blanc
Smoked fish (salmon, marlin, and trout)	Bone-dry Gewürztraminer, Pinot Gris, Viognier, or Pinot Blanc
Warm Appetizers	
Beef stew (red-wine based)	Malbec, Pinot Noir, Carignan, Merlot, Cabernet, or Syrah. You can drink the same wine as used to cook the dish.
Cocktail frankfurters	Light dry white
Fish, deep-fried	White dry Graves or Sauvignon Blanc
Fish, grilled and served in a hollandaise or buttery sauce	Oaked Chardonnay, Semillon, Riesling, white Bordeaux, white Rhône, or Albariño
Fish, pan-fried	New World Sauvignon Blanc
Fish, poached	White Burgundy, including Chablis
Fish, steamed (also mussels and clams)	Pinot Grigio, Soave, Verdicchio, Chenin Blanc, or Sauvignon Blanc (Loire)
Mushrooms, stuffed	Pinot Grigio, Pinot Gris, Marsanne, or Roussanne (Rhône Valley)
Sauerkraut	Alsatian Tokay
Sausages with onion gravy	Malbec (Argentina or Cahors)
Cheese	
Blue cheese	Botrytized Semillon, late-harvest Gewürztraminer, or tawny port
Goat cheese, fresh	Sauvignon Blanc or Fumé Blanc
Hard cheese (Parmesan)	Cabernet Sauvignon or Chianti
Mozzarella	Sauvignon Blanc or Fumé Blanc
Soft cheese (Camembert and Brie)	Chardonnay or Chenin Blanc

Soups

Bouillabaisse	Chardonnay, Sauvignon Blanc, or Chenin Blanc
Clam chowder	Chardonnay, Sauvignon Blanc, or Chenin Blanc
Fish	Chardonnay, Sauvignon Blanc, or Chenin Blanc
French onion	Cahors or Madiran
Minestrone, ribollita (Tuscan vegetable and bread soup)	Riesling, Cortese, Valpolicella, or Pinot Grigio
Oxtail	Gamay or Sauvignon Blanc
Rouille broth or consommé broth, with mushrooms	White Marsanne or Roussanne
Tomato	Dry sherry
Vegetable soup (leek, watercress, and Vichyssoise)	Alsace Riesling, Viognier, or dry sherry

Meats

Goose liver	Gewürztraminer or Sauternes
Pork products (ham, smoked sausages, and pâté)	Riesling, Gamay, Pinot Noir, young red and rosé Rhône wines, Valpolicella, or Montepulciano
Roast beef	If cooked rare: tannic Cabernet Sauvignon, or young Northern Rhône (Syrah). If well-cooked: low tannin, mature red Bordeaux, particularly St. Emilion, Pinot Noir, or Barbera
Roasted turkey, chicken, guineafowl	Ripe Chardonnay, Pinot Noir, light Cabernet Franc

Pasta

With cream sauce	Barrel-fermented Chardonnay
With olive oil and Parmesan	Sauvignon Blanc, Semillon, or Trebbiano
With tomato sauce	Gamay, Pinot Noir, Sangiovese, or Barbera

Main Courses

Beef, grilled	Cabernet Sauvignon
Confit of duck or goose	Merlot-based wines, Malbec, Cabernet Sauvignon, Syrah, or Tokay-Pinot Gris
Duck with orange sauce	Tawny port
Fowl, roasted	Merlot from Pomerol or St. Emilion
Lamb, roasted or pan-fried	Pauillac or Cabernet Sauvignon
Pork	Pinot Noir or Beaujolais
Pork with apple sauce	Chardonnay
Poultry, roasted or grilled	Pinot Noir, Light Cabernet Franc, or ripe Chardonnay
Roast beef	Shiraz, Pinotage, or Cabernet blends
Steak	Cabernet Sauvignon
Steak with pepper sauce	Syrah/Shiraz (either Rhône or Australian)

Asian Dishes	
Barbecued meats	Riesling or Gewürztraminer
Chili crab	Gewürztraminer
Curry, green	Gewürztraminer or Riesling
Fish with lemongrass sauce and cilantro	Coastal Plain Californian Chardonnay
Fried rice, Cantonese-style	Chablis-like Chardonnay or Riesling
Fried rice, noodles, and beef	Chardonnay, Sauvignon Blanc, or Riesling
Nasi Goreng	White Zinfandel
Oyster sauce-based dishes	Oaked Chardonnay
Peking duck	Pinot Noir, Gewürztraminer, or Cabernet-Merlot blends
Sashimi	Sake, Sauvignon Blanc, or Champagne
Seafood in curry sauce	Zinfandel or Shiraz
Steamed fish with coriander, ginger, and soy sauce	Riesling, Chardonnay, White Bordeaux, or Pinot Blanc
Sushi	Sake, Sauvignon Blanc, or Champagne
Thai seafood soup	Gewürztraminer
Wokked beef dishes	Oaked Chardonnay
Desserts	
Chocolate	Banyuls
Custard	Reciotto di Soave, Sauternes, Barsac, or Monbazillac
Ice cream	Demi-sec white wines, sparkling or otherwise
Fruit	Asti Spumante or medium-sweet Muscat
Pastry	Asti Spumante or ice wine
Puddings	Monbazillac

Although tastes for both food and wine change over time, the process of combining the two does not. The basic principles governing these matches remain the same. In a restaurant, a wine steward is usually available to recommend the best choice. However, you are now prepared to make the decision on your own, be it in a restaurant or the comfort of your home. To further educate you in your ability to choose a proper wine bottle, the following chapter explores the world of labels and the myriad of information they carry.

II.
Wine Labels From Around the World

The very first wine label laws were promulgated by the Babylonian King Hammurabi around 1700 BC. These laws highlighted compulsory indications such as price and expiry date. This date usually declared that the wine had to be sold within a few days of the fermentation's completion.

From 1500 BC to 1000 BC, Egyptian law stated that not only the origin of the wine, but also the name of the winemaker and the name of the Pharaoh reigning during the harvest, be declared. These details were written directly on the *amphorae*—elongated, baked clay containers with two handles that were used to store and transport wine during the time of this ancient civilization. The shape of the amphora was often an indication of the wine's origin, so fraud consisted of imitating this shape to obtain higher prices for wines of an inferior quality.

In various forms, labels have been around through many ages. Wine consumers have always been eager for more information regarding the quality and origin of their favorite beverage. Yet it is only during the last fifty years that additional and strict regulations have given consumers the information they desire. While these labels have become more informative, however, inexperienced wine collectors may find them more difficult to read.

This chapter includes explanations of all the information found on a wine label, both compulsory and otherwise. It will remove the mystery from reading wine labels so that you can be an informed consumer.

Information Found on a Wine Label

To properly read a wine label, you should be aware of the information that is found there. This can include the name of the winery, vintage, region of origin, bottle contents, and alcohol content. You will also learn how to decipher a wine's *appellation*—the name given to the wine because of its origin, grape variety, or type of vinification. The label may also include information pertinent to quality.

NAME OF THE WINERY, WINEMAKER, OR ESTATE

The wine label contains information regarding the name of the winery, winemaker, or estate. However, the exact information given can take several forms because the rules vary from country to country.

French wine labels vary according to region. In Bordeaux, most wines are called "Château" (which literally translates as "castle" but means vineyard), followed by the name of the estate, the name of the estate owner, or a historical reference. For example, Château Margaux is named such because it is from Margaux. Château Mouton-Rothschild was named after both its owner— Rothschild—and a historical reference—wine from that château was originally called Château Brane Mouton. In Burgundy, on the other hand, the only wine name appearing on the label is that of the area of production, followed by the exact name of the vineyard. One wine label may read, for example, "Chambertin-Latricières." Alsace is one of the few regions in France where the wine is named by grape variety. The grape variety may stand on its own or be followed by the vineyard name, as in the wine Riesling-Schoenenburg.

In Italy, most wine names are taken from the appellation of origin. Brunello di Montalcino, for example, is Brunello wine that was produced in Montalcino, while Barbera d'Asti is made of Barbera grapes grown around the town of Asti. Brand names, such as Tignanello, Sassicaia, and Villa Antinori, are more recent developments. Californian wine names include all types of names, including Portfolio (which refers to an artistic production) and Stag's Leap (which refers to an animal movement). Neither language nor format are regulated, as exemplified by Le Cigare Volant (literally, "The Flying Cigar")—a Californian wine made at Bonny Doon Vineyard.

In Australia, everything is permitted in terms of wine name, from yellow tail [sic] to Bin 28. These names are usually coupled with the grape name. Behind every wine name, there is usually a story.

VINTAGE

The year on the label indicates the year in which the grapes were harvested. It allows consumers to reflect on the particular climatic conditions prevailing in that year. However, the vintage should not be confused with bottling time, which can take place months or even years after the vintage year itself. The wine indicated by the Portfolio label below is of the 2001 vintage. Its grapes were harvested during the second half of 2001.

Figure 11.1.
Wine labels, back and front: Portfolio.

REGION OF ORIGIN

Many countries, particularly those of the Old World, classify wine, and often its quality, according to grape origin. Burgundy's Meursault Genèvrières, for example, is so named because it comes from a village called Meursault, and a particular parcel within that village called Les Genèvrières. This is a tiny piece of land that delivers particular—and particularly good—olfactory characteristics in wines produced from its grapes. In Bordeaux, the quality (and price) of wine usually increases with the narrowing of the origin. A St-Julien is a wine whose origin is anywhere within the boundaries of the commune (geographic district of 2,222 acres or 907 hectares), while a Château Léoville-Barton covers only 115.25 acres (or 47 hectares) within this commune, and corresponds to a very defined vineyard with its own soil and climatic conditions. This second wine, as a result, is considered of a higher quality.

Similarly, labels from most European countries, including Spain, Italy, Germany, and Portugal, prominently display the wine's origin. This is a guarantee that the grapes have been both grown and harvested in that region, usually indicating a certain level of quality.

In the New World, on the other hand, the origin of the grapes is deemed far less important than the location of vinification. However, Californian winemakers have started to recognize the importance of grape origin, as well as the influence of the soil and climatic conditions on the resulting wines. The New World Portfolio label to the left, for example, prominently displays that its origin is Napa Valley, while the region, California, does not garner as much attention. The country (United States) is not shown at all on the front label.

In New Zealand, the Marlborough region has reached cult status as "the" area capable of achieving utmost quality in the production of Sauvignon Blanc wines. Thus, the name Marlborough is as much a marketing tool as a name used to define origin. However, all other indications—such as vintage, bottle contents, alcohol content, grape variety, and name—remain mandatory.

The information found on the wine label regarding region of origin differs from place to place. Most regions display the information that best suits the wine produced there.

ALCOHOL CONTENT

In most countries where wine is produced and sold, this indication is compulsory. It is expressed in either percentage of alcohol to total volume, or degrees of alcohol. Usually, a beverage cannot be called wine if its alcohol level falls below 7 percent. On the bottle of Portfolio from which the label on page 148 came, the alcohol content is indicated on the back label and is 14.5 percent.

GRAPE VARIETY

This indication reflects the varietal which makes up the majority of the wine. In some countries, a wine can be declared Cabernet Sauvignon even if only 75 percent of the grapes used are Cabernet Sauvignon. Usually, if the wine is made from noble grape varieties, the grape names are mentioned on the label. This occurs particularly on New World wine labels. On the Portfolio label, however, grape varieties are not mentioned, as it is a blended wine. This indication is not compulsory by law.

QUALITY AND/OR APPELLATION

References to quality ratings vary according to country of production. Many of these denominations are explored in the following section.

Wine Labels by Region

Although the rules are occasionally amended, each country has determined the best ways in which to showcase its wines. This section will explore the information that appears on each country's wine labels, as well as the ways in which the country's wines are classified.

AUSTRALIA

The Australian Wine and Brandy Corporation regulates many aspects of the Australian wine trade. The following information, extracted from its Wine Law, explains which information is mandatory and which is optional for Australian wine labels.

■ Winery name/trademark/business or brand name: optional.

■ Name of wine, grape varietal name, or generic style name (such as dry red/white): name is

mandatory; variety is optional. It is interesting to note that in this particular part of the legislation, wine is considered to be "food"—the same labeling laws apply to both commodities.

■ Geographical indication: optional.

■ Vintage: optional.

■ Volume: mandatory and must appear on the front label in letters of a height of at least 3.3 millimeters.

■ Alcohol content: mandatory but exact wording is optional.

■ Allergens declaration: mandatory if the wine contains at least 10 milligrams of added sulphites per kilograms; nuts; or fining agents (which clarify the liquid) such as casein, potassium caseinate, egg white, milk, evaporated milk, or isinglass.

■ Name and address: mandatory. This information must include the name and street address of responsible entity rather than just the postal address.

■ Country of origin: mandatory.

■ Cask labeling: cask wine, as well as wine in any other non-glass container, may require a "Best Before" date which is to be stated in one of the two following formats: "Best Before Dec. 05" or "Best Before 12 05."

> The degree of alcohol in white wines ranges from 8 to 15 percent. In red wines it ranges from 10 to 16 percent. In fortified wines, such as port, it ranges from 16 to 22 percent. .

Figure 11.2.
Australian Label: Penfolds' Grange.

Winery name: Penfolds

Wine name: Grange

Region of Production: South Australia
Grape Variety: Shiraz
Vintage: 1998 (Bottled in 1999)

Bottle Contents: 750ml
Other Information: Bottled by Penfolds Wines Pty Ltd
Country of Origin: Wine made in Australia
Alcohol Content: 14.5%

Three Levels of Qualitätswein Austrian Wine

High-quality Austrian wines are labeled Qualitätswein. Yet even within this prestigious category, wines are divided further into three levels of quality. These subcategories are as follows.

PRÄDIKATSWEIN

Wines in the *Prädikatswein* category are of the highest quality. They have a very high sugar concentration level and are made using grapes that were specially ripened and harvested. Wines within this subcategory are divided into levels used in the German wine classification system. These terms include *Spätlese, Auslese, Beerenauslese, Kabinett, Trockenbeerenauslese,* and *Eiswein,* and are described in the inset on page 151.

KABINETT

Kabinett wines are *Qualitätswein* wines. They are of lesser quality than *Prädikatswein* wines but higher than *Qualitätswein mit Staatlicher Prüfnummer* wines. They have a higher sugar concentration level, a reflection of better maturity of the grapes at harvest. Wines of this category are indicated as *Kabinett* or *Kabinettwein.*

QUALITÄTSWEIN MIT STAATLICHER PRÜFNUMMER

This subcategory of *Qualitätswein* indicates that the bottle contains quality wine, but of lesser quality than a *Kabinett* wine. It can be labeled *Qualitätswein mit Staatlicher Prüfnummer, Qualitätswein bestimmter Anbaugebiete,* or *Qualitätswein b. A.*

Figure 11.3. Austrian Label: Kracher.

Nouvelle Vague: Non compulsory, indicates a botrytized wine

Vintage: 2002

Winery Name: Weinlaubenhof, Kracher, Burgenland

Brand: Number 7. Indicates level of sweetness

Bottle Contents: 375 ml

Federal Inspection Number: LE726904

Grape Varieties/Type: Not indicated here, instead White Table Wine. (But it is known to be made from Chardonnay and Welschriesling.) Trockenbeerenauslese (TBA—a sweet wine made from botrytized grapes)

Alcohol Content: 9%

NOUVELLE VAGUE
2002
WEINLAUBENHOF
KRACHER
BURGENLAND
GRANDE CUVÉE
TROCKENBEEREN
AUSLESE
NUMBER 7
White Table Wine
ALC. 9,0% BY VOL.
NET CONT 375 ML
LE726904
Österreichischer Qualitätswein
PRODUCED & BOTTLED BY
KRACHER
A-7142 ILLMITZ
PRODUCT OF AUSTRIA

AUSTRIA

Austria has several wine classification systems. The one used most often divides wines on the basis of their grapes' sugar content at harvest. The term used for wine of quality is *Qualitätswein.* Within this classification, there are three subcategories. These categories are described in the inset above.

The Austrian Wine Law dictates what information must be found on each Austrian wine label. The following must be included unless otherwise stated.

■ *Abfüller* (bottler) or *abgefüllt durch* (bottled by). In the case of *abgefüllt für* (contract bottling), name or company name, community or area of the village/town, state of the head office, and, if applicable, the actual place of bottling.

■ Coding is permitted (company number and postal code as well as information about a marketing participant/distributor).

■ Federal inspection number.

■ *Erzeugerabfüllung* (bottled by producer), *gutsabfüllung* (estate bottled), or *hauerabfüllung* (bottled by grape grower).

■ *Trocken* (dry or *sec*), halbtrocken (medium dry or *demi-sec*), lieblich (semi-sweet or *demi-doux*), süß (sweet or *doux*).

GERMANY

German wines are classified according to their own system. The information on their labels includes much of the same information as found on labels from other countries, but can also list other helpful facts such as quality and taste indication. The terms used to describe the level of quality are as follows.

■ *Deutscher Tafelwein* indicates that the wine is entry level and comes from grapes harvested in Germany.

■ *Deutscher Landwein* indicates that the wine is entry level but made with higher quality grapes than those used in wine labeled *Deutscher Tafelwein*. The grapes were harvested at one of the *Landwein*—officially recognized regions of production.

■ *Qualitätswein Bestimmter Anbaugebiete* (QbA) indicates a light, refreshing, and fruity wine that was produced in one of thirteen specified wine-growing regions.

■ *Qualitätswein mit Prädikat* (QmP) indicates that the wine is of the highest quality. Wines in this group are classified in six different subcategories. See the inset below for a listing of these categories.

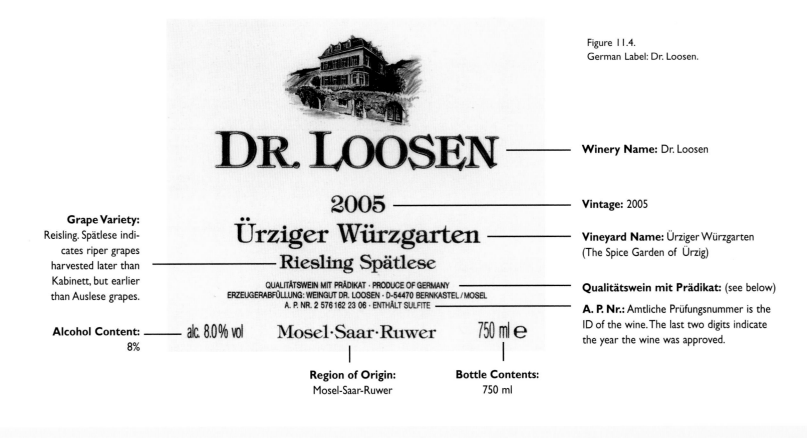

Figure 11.4.
German Label: Dr. Loosen.

Winery Name: Dr. Loosen

Vintage: 2005

Vineyard Name: Ürziger Würzgarten (The Spice Garden of Ürzig)

Qualitätswein mit Prädikat: (see below)

A. P. Nr.: Amtliche Prüfungsnummer is the ID of the wine. The last two digits indicate the year the wine was approved.

Grape Variety: Reisling. Spätlese indicates riper grapes harvested later than Kabinett, but earlier than Auslese grapes.

Alcohol Content: 8%

Region of Origin: Mosel-Saar-Ruwer

Bottle Contents: 750 ml

Subcategories of High-Quality German Wines

German wines of the highest quality are labeled *Qualitätswein mit Prädikat* (QmP). They are then divided into the following, more specific subcategories. These categories are also used to classify high-quality Austrian wines, or *Prädikatswein*.

■ *Auslese*: sweet wines from very ripe grapes, producing intense aromas and taste.

■ *Beerenauslese*: rich, sweet dessert wines from individually selected and over-ripe grapes.

■ *Eiswein*: made from grapes harvested and pressed at 9°F (-13°C).

■ *Kabinett*: light wines made from fully ripened grapes.

■ *Spätlese*: wines of superior quality made from a late-harvest crop. Sometimes but not necessarily sweet.

■ *Trockenbeerenauslese*: rich, sweet, and luscious wine produced from a harvest of individually selected and over-ripe berries.

FRANCE

There are wine-labeling laws that apply to most French-produced wines. As you will read, however, there is a separate set of rules and abbreviations that is used for labeling Champagne wine bottles.

Most French Wines

As dictated by French law, there is information that must be found on all French wine labels. Other information, on the other hand, is optional.

■ Country of origin: mandatory on all exported wines with the phrase *"Produit de France,"* which means "Product of France."

■ Grape variety: optional. The likelihood of this appearing depends on the region. Wine labels from most French regions do not usually mention grape variety. In Alsace, however, most wines are varietals so the name of the grape is often equivalent to the name of the wine. In Languedoc and Roussillon, too, the varietals are often named, so as to better compete with New World wines.

■ Bottle contents: mandatory in either milliliters (ml) or centiliters (cl).

■ Location of bottling: optional. *"Mis en bouteille au Château"* means "estate bottled"; *"mis en bouteille à la propriété"* means "property-bottled"; *"mis en bouteilles dans la région de production"* means "bottled in the region of production"; and *"mis en bouteilles dans nos caves"* means "bottled in our cellars."

■ Vintage: indicates the year of the harvest for the grapes used to make the wine.

There are numerous quality-based French wine classification systems, but the nationwide *Appellation d'Origine Contrôlée* (AOC) is used most frequently. It is a four-tier classification system that guarantees the standards of certain French products, including most types of wine. It is regulated and monitored by the appellation syndicates as well as the *Institut National des Appellations d'Origine* (INAO), the institute which looks after all the appellations of origin. The INAO applies its categories based on the following guidelines.

■ AOC wines are labeled with the name of the area where their grapes were grown. They are subject to strict regulations as to grape varieties used, alcohol content, yield, ripeness of the grapes, and viticulture and vinification methods.

Figure 11.5. French Label: Château La Conseillante.

Winery Name: Château La Conseillante

Region: Pomerol

Quality: Appellation Pomerol Controlée

Vintage: 1989

Alcohol Content: 13%

Country of Origin: Produce of France

Owners: Héritiers (Inheritors) of L. Nicolas

Bottle Contents: 750 ml

Estate Bottled: Mise en bouteilles au chateau

■ *Vin Délimité de Qualité Supérieure* (VDQS) is the level below AOC. Grape varieties used are controlled and production methods are rather strict. Although the official classification positions them below AOC wines, VDQS wines are actually considered of superior quality.

■ *Vin de Pays* (VdP) translates literally into "country wines," and represents the third level of the AOC hierarchy. The origin of such wines can be from any size vineyard. These wines are usually named Vin de Pays, followed by the region name. For example, wine from the Cévennes region is called Vin de Pays des Cévennes.

■ *Vins de Table,* or table wines, are labeled *"Vin de Table Francais"* if of exclusively French origin. If the wines are a blend from various countries of the European community, they must bear the label *"Mélange de vins de différents pays de la Communauté européenne"*—which means, literally, a "blend of wines from different European countries."

Champagne and Sparkling Wines

The wines of Champagne are some of the most regulated in France. Classified vineyards, grape varieties, and clones are restricted; the quantity of juice pressed out of grapes is controlled; and the release date after vinification is also prescribed. On the wine label, there is also a unique set of abbreviations that indicate the business nature under which the bottle's producer operates.

■ RC (*Récoltant Coopérateur*): a grape grower who sells wine from his own grapes but made by a cooperative winery. An example is Michel Baudvin. There are 4,015 RC in Champagne.

■ RM (*Récoltant Manipulant*): a grape grower who produces his own Champagne from his own grapes. An example is Champagne Janisson-Baradon & Fils. There are 3,649 RM.

■ NM (*Négociant Manipulant*): a producer who vinifies grapes bought from grape growers. Examples are Champagne De Castellane and Moët et Chandon. There are 1,320 NM.

■ CM (*Coopérative Manipulant*): a cooperative winery (group of growers) which also produces

and sells Champagne under its own name. An example is Nicolas Feuillatte. There are 233 CM.

■ SR (*Société de Récoltants*): a company set up by growers who produce and sell their Champagne under one or more brand name. Examples are Guy Charlemagne and André Clouet. There are 31 SR.

■ ND (*Négociant-distributeur*): a company marketing and selling Champagne it does not make. There are 148 ND.

■ MA (*Marque d'Acheteur*): a brand name owned by the purchaser, who may represent a hotel, restaurant, retail house, or wine merchant. An example is The Peninsula Hotel in Hong Kong. There are 2,994 MA.

Most Champagne bottles bear no indication as to their grape variety. However, a few producers do emphasize the composition of their wines. The following phrases are found on these bottles.

■ *Blanc de Blancs* indicates that the wine has been obtained from the pressing of solely Chardonnay white grapes.

■ *Blanc de Noirs* indicates that the wine has been obtained after the pressing of only black grapes Pinot Noir and/or Pinot Meunier.

■ *Rosé* indicates that the wine was made by adding a small amount of still red wine to a white base to reach the desired color.

Figure 11.6.
Champagne Label: René Geoffroy.

Most Champagne wine labels include the abbreviation NV, which means that the wine is non-vintage. If a vintage is mentioned on the label, it indicates all the grapes used in the production of the wine have been harvested only during that particular year.

UNITED STATES

The following rules and regulations apply to all US wine labels. They have been extracted from the Federal Regulations published by the Bureau of Alcohol, Tobacco and Firearms.

■ Appellation of origin: legally required on label.

■ American Viticultural Area (AVA): a "defined area for grape growing" and not an indication of quality. For the AVA to be used on the label, at least 85 percent of the grapes used to make the wine must come from the same AVA. If a wine grower wishes to display the state or county of origin, on the other hand, 75 percent of the grapes used to produce the wine must be grown in that state or country.

■ Grape varieties: the names of one or more grape varieties may be used as the type designation of a grape wine only if the wine is also labeled with an appellation of origin. In most states, wines with a single grape variety label must contain at least 75 percent of that grape, and the entirety of the 75 percent must be grown in the appellation of origin area. Wines produced from *Vitis labrusca* grapes are an exception to this rule—the minimum content of the labeled grape is 51 percent. However, there are also several states with different labeling regulations for all grapes. In California, the minimum quantity of any single grape variety increas-

es to 85 percent, while it increases to 95 percent in Washington State. In New York, on the other hand, only a minimum of 51 percent of the single grape is necessary.

■ Estate bottled: a term that may be used by a bottling winery on a wine label only if the wine is labeled with a viticultural area appellation of origin and the name of the bottling winery.

■ Vintage wine: wine labeled with the year of its grapes' harvest. At least 95 percent of the wine must be derived from grapes harvested in the labeled calendar year, and the wine must be labeled with an appellation of origin rather than a country of origin.

■ Declaration of sulfites: must be stated for any wine bottled after July 9, 1987 that contains any sulfate or sulfiting agent that causes a content level of ten or more parts per million (ppm), measured as total sulphur dioxide. This can appear on the front, back, strip, or neck label, and must appear as "contains sulfites," "contains (a) sulfiting agent(s)," or a statement identifying the specific sulfiting agent.

■ Brand name: cannot be misleading in terms of age, origin, and identity. For example, a wine made in Oregon cannot bear a brand name such as Washington's Delight.

■ Class and type: descriptor of the wine in terms of sugar, carbon dioxide content, and so forth, using common wine terms such as "table," "dessert," "sparkling," "crackling," or "Champagne" wine.

■ Name and address: must include name of bottler or packer, as well as the place where the bottling or packing took place. This must be immediately preceded by the words "bottled by" or "packed by," except if the bottler or packer made less than 75 percent of the wine, in which case the words may be changed to "blended and bottled (packed) by," or "rectified and bottled (packed) by."

■ Alcoholic content: stated in terms of percentage of alcohol by volume. It must be stated in the case of wines containing more than 14-percent alcohol by volume. Wines containing 14-percent or less alcohol by volume must either be designated as "table" wine ("light" wine) or include a statement of alcoholic content. A 1.5-percent variation is allowed.

■ Net contents: must be provided in the metric system of measure, followed by the equivalent US volume.

Figure 11.7. American Label: Robert Mondavi.

Estate: Robert Mondavi Winery ⎯⎯⎯⎯⎯

Vintage: 2003 ⎯⎯⎯⎯⎯⎯

Region of Production: Napa Valley ⎯⎯⎯⎯⎯

Grape Variety: Cabernet Sauvignon ⎯⎯⎯

Other Information: Reserve ⎯⎯⎯⎯⎯

Alcohol Content: 14.5% ⎯⎯⎯⎯⎯

ROBERT MONDAVI WINERY

2003

NAPA VALLEY

CABERNET SAUVIGNON

RESERVE

ALC. 14.5% BY VOL.

Government health warning: any alcoholic beverage sold or imported into the United States after November 18, 1989 has to bear the following statement: "Government warning: (1) according to the Surgeon General, women should not drink alcoholic beverages during pregnancy because of the risk of birth defects; (2) consumption of alcoholic beverages impairs your ability to drive a car or operate machinery, and may cause health problems."

Other requirements: the size of wine labels, language, location of the label on the bottle, packaging, ethical nature of the wording, and copyright laws, as well as any additional properties of the wine, have to be clearly defined so as to avoid any misunderstanding.

SOUTH AFRICA

All wine labels produced in South Africa have to be approved by the South African Wine & Spirit Board. This organization regulates and standardizes the information found on the labels as explained below.

Quality: The highest quality is represented by the Wines of Origin moniker. It appears on the wine label next to the viticultural area designation.

Grape variety: at least 75 percent of the bottle's total contents must be of the grape variety mentioned on the label. For exports to the European Union, this percentage rises to 85 percent.

Appellation of origin: can include an estate, a ward, a district or a region. According to the Wine of Origin (WO) classification system, a wine must contain 100 percent of the grapes from a specific and designated area to be labeled WO.

The WO areas are clearly demarcated and published in the country's *Government Gazette*. The country is broken into three Geographic Units. Within these areas, the land is further divided into estates, which consist of one or several farms where grapes are grown, harvested, and vinified together on the premises; wards, which consist of either one farm or a combination of different farms with only one type of growing condition (or terroir); districts, which consist of several types of growing conditions; and regions, which regroup several districts together.

South African wine legislation is constantly evolving, as is the exhaustive list of WO areas. For a complete and up-to-date list, visit the website of the South African Wine Information and Systems, a research institute, at www.sawis.co.za.

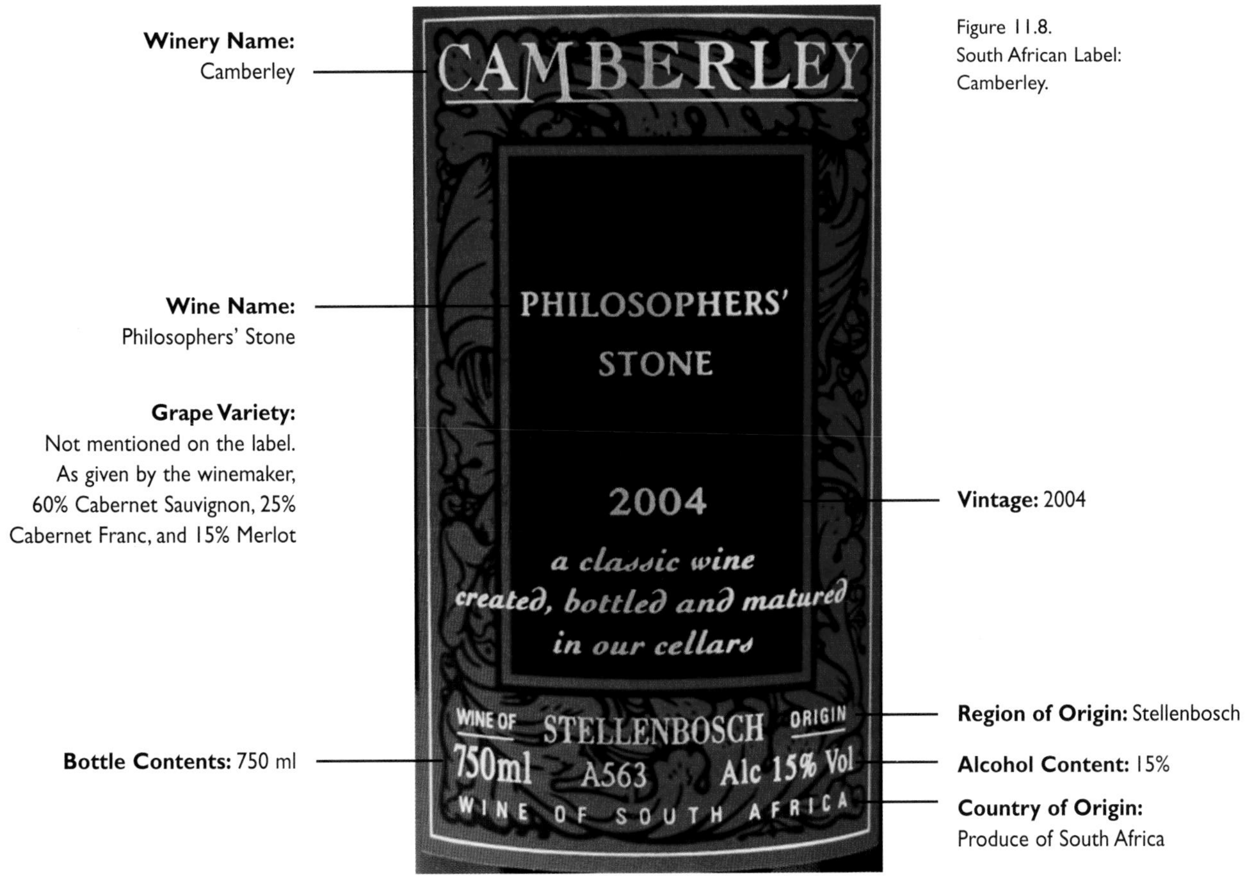

> The wine-producing areas of the country of South Africa are divided into three Geographical Units: Western Cape, Northern Cape, and KwaZulu-Natal.

Winery Name: Camberley

Wine Name: Philosophers' Stone

Grape Variety: Not mentioned on the label. As given by the winemaker, 60% Cabernet Sauvignon, 25% Cabernet Franc, and 15% Merlot

Bottle Contents: 750 ml

Figure 11.8.
South African Label: Camberley.

Vintage: 2004

Region of Origin: Stellenbosch

Alcohol Content: 15%

Country of Origin: Produce of South Africa

NEW ZEALAND

New Zealand wine has been around for years but recently entered the world market in a big way. With its entrance came more strict regulations than were previously applied. Some are listed below. The other labeling requirements are identical to those promulgated in Australia—except for geographic indications. These were the subject of a separate act enacted in 1995. There are currently ten major wine regions in New Zealand.

In all countries, alcoholic beverages are generally taxed according to their alcohol content. In accordance with this progressive rate, wine that contains a greater percentage of alcohol is taxed higher.

■ Grape variety, region of origin, and vintage: must be 85-percent accurate. This regulation applies to the 2007 and subsequent vintages, and brings the country in line with international wine-labeling practices. Prior to the 2007 vintage, only 75 percent of the grapes used had to be true to the variety, the region of origin, and vintage.

■ Alcohol content: wines that contain below 15-percent alcohol can be sold as table wine in New Zealand. When the alcohol volume is above 15 percent, higher rates of excise tax are usually imposed. In most other countries, table wine must contain less than 14-percent alcohol.

ITALY

Wine laws in Italy have been in effect since the ancient Romans first defined wine-production areas. The current wine regions that produce top-quality wines are listed in the inset on page 157. Today, there are four different quality categories that describe most Italian wines.

■ DOCG (*Denominazione di Origine Controllata e Garantita*): top-quality Italian wine. (See the inset on page 157 for examples.) All wines labeled DOCG have to be controlled and guaranteed by the producer. They are also often analyzed by government inspectors and closed with a government seal. Moreover, the label must state the net contents, alcohol strength, name of grower and bottler, venue for bottling, and zone of origin.

■ DOC (*Denominazione di Origine Controllata*): second-tier Italian wine. There are 242 wines that fall into this category. DOC and DOCG wines include wines that range from white to red, from still to sparkling, from dry to sweet, and even fortified.

■ IGT (*Indicazione Geografica Tipica*): wines of very high quality, although often considered of a lower tier than DOCG and DOC wines. Created in 1992, it is the equivalent of French *Vin de Pays* (country wines), and requires the bottler or winemaker to

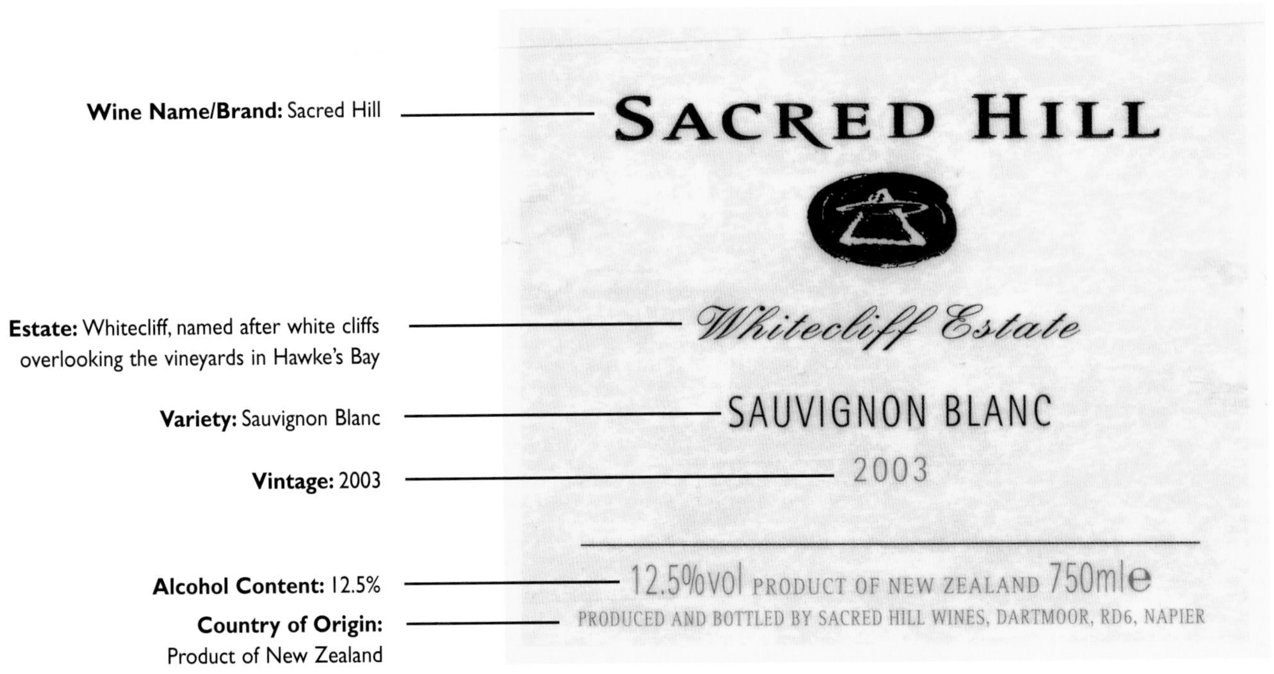

Figure 11.9. New Zealand Label: Sacred Hill.

Wine Name/Brand: Sacred Hill

Estate: Whitecliff, named after white cliffs overlooking the vineyards in Hawke's Bay

Variety: Sauvignon Blanc

Vintage: 2003

Alcohol Content: 12.5%

Country of Origin: Product of New Zealand

SACRED HILL

Whitecliff Estate

SAUVIGNON BLANC

2003

12.5%vol PRODUCT OF NEW ZEALAND 750ml℮

PRODUCED AND BOTTLED BY SACRED HILL WINES, DARTMOOR, RD6, NAPIER clearly state the geographic provenance of the grapes on the bottle's label. The label may also include vintage and grape variety. There are currently around 100 IGTs.

■ VDT (*Vino Da Tavola*): wines produced anywhere in Italy. They do not usually display grape variety or vintage and may be of inferior quality. However, some excellent wines are classified in this category because their grape variety blend does not conform to the restrictions in place for the specific region in which they were produced. The price tag can often be used to determine a wine's quality. Super Tuscans, for example, are in the VDT category—but can cost as much as five to six times more than some DOCGs.

"Super Tuscans" represent a new wave of red wines from Tuscany which began to appear at the beginning of the 1980s. Exemplified by the likes of Tignanello, Sassicaia, Nardo, Siepi, Ardingo, Solengo, Solaia, and Ornellaia, these wines were created to circumvent the traditional, rigid blending laws prevailing at the time

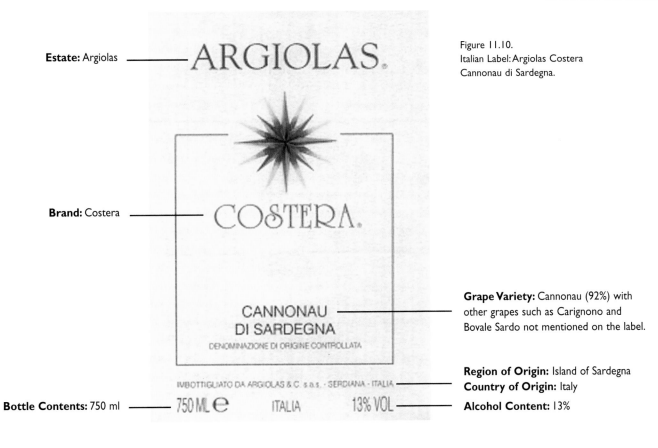

Estate: Argiolas

Brand: Costera

Figure 11.10.
Italian Label: Argiolas Costera Cannonau di Sardegna.

Grape Variety: Cannonau (92%) with other grapes such as Carignono and Bovale Sardo not mentioned on the label.

Region of Origin: Island of Sardegna
Country of Origin: Italy

Bottle Contents: 750 ml

Alcohol Content: 13%

*I*talian Wine Regions Categorized as DOCG

There are nine wine zones in Italy in which wines that can be labeled DOCG (Denominazione di Origine Controllata e Garantita) are produced. The following list of these nine regions also includes examples of their high-quality wine.

■ Campania: Taurasi
■ Emilia-Romagna: Albana di Romagna
■ Friuli: Ramandolo
■ Lombardy: Franciacorta and Valtellina Superiore
■ Piedmont: Barolo, Barbaresco, Gattinara, Moscato d'Asti, Asti, Brachetto d'Acqui, Gavi, and Ghemme
■ Sardinia: Vermentino di Gallura

■ Tuscany: Brunello di Montalcino, Chianti, Chianti Classico, Vino Nobile di Montepulciano, Carmignano Rosso, and Vernaccia di San Gimignano
■ Umbria: Torgiano Rosso Riserva, and Sagrantino di Montefalco
■ Veneto: Recioto di Soave, Bardolino Superiore, Classico Superiore, and Soave Superiore

SPAIN

Spanish wine laws differ from those in other European countries. The following are the most common terms found on Spanish wine labels and their explanations.

■ *Sin Crianza*: the wine has not been aged.

■ *Crianza*: the wine has been aged for at least six months in small oak barrels.

■ *Reserva*: the wine has been aged for at least one year in oak barrels.

■ *Grand Reserva*: the wine has been aged for at least two years in oak, and released only in the best vintages.

■ *Bodega*: the Spanish name for winery, generally followed by the name of the winery.

■ *Cosecha*: indicates the wine's vintage; followed by a year.

Spain also has its own classification system, used not only for wine but also for many food products. There are five levels to this hierarchy: DOCa, DO, VdlT, VC, and VdM.

■ DOCa (*Denominación de Origen Calificada*): the highest guaranteed quality from a particular region. These wines are reminiscent of the Italian DOCG (described on page 156). Only two wine regions qualify for this status: DOCa Rioja and DOCa Priorat.

Rioja was qualified as a DO (described below) until 1991 when it was granted DOCa status. This region comprises three subregions. Rioja Baja produces rustic wines based on the Garnacha grape variety. Rioja Alta produces excellent Tempranillo-based wines from a limestone soil riddled with clay. It also produces Garnacha-based wines. Rioja Alavesa consists of hills and limestone soils that yield very good Tempranillo wines.

Priorat is located in the province of Tarragona. Although the region is large, it produces extremely low yields, and is recognized as one of the star Spanish wine regions. The main red grape varieties used are Cariñena, Garnacha, Garnacha Peluda, Cabernet Sauvignon, Merlot, and Syrah. The most common white grape varieties found here are Chenin Blanc, Macabeo, Garnacha Blanca, Viognier, and Pedro Ximénez. There are approximately sixty-two *bodegas*—wine estates—registered in Priorat.

■ DO (*Denominación de Origen*): mainstream wines that accord to all the criteria of the region from which they are from. The inset on page 159 describes some of the regions that produce prominent wines enjoying this status.

Figure 11.11. Spanish Label: Muga.

Vintage: 2000

Brand Name/Winery: Muga

Alcohol Content: 12.5%

Bottle Contents: 75 cl

Name and address of winery:
Bodegas Muga S.A. Haro—España

Region of Origin: Roja

Quality: Denominacion de Origen Calificada + embotellado en la propriedad (estate bottled) + fermentado en barrica nueva de roble (new oak barrel fermented).

Producing Spanish Wines of the Denominación de Origen Classification

DO wines are mainstream, quality Spanish wines that completely conform to the wine rules of the region in which they were produced. Castile and León, Murcia, Catalunia, Navarra, Aragon, Galicia, Cantabria, Pais Vasco, La Mancha, Valencia, Extremadura, and Andalucia produce many of the most desirable wines of this categorization. Although notable wines emerge from each, this inset will explore those from the regions of Castile and León and Murcia.

CASTILE AND LEÓN

Castile and León is a large district that consists of nine provinces. The following five regions produce much of the area's popular wines.

Ribera del Duero

Ribera del Duero was named after the Duero River. This area generates excellent Tempranillo-based wines with good structure and excellent aging potential. Vega Sicilia is a popular wine that has the best reputation and highest price of any in the region.

Toro

Toro, characterized by a hot climate and arid soil, produces wines with alcoholic strength and low acidity. The main wine produced here is Tinto de Toro, another version of wine from the Tempranillo grape. The soil is sandy, which allows the region to largely avoid the problem of grapevine-eating insects.

Rueda

This region is particularly renowned for the production of white wines from the Verdejo grape. Limestone soils and a cooler climate contribute to the production of wines which are fresh, fruity, and medium-bodied, with good acidity and aroma.

Cigales

The region of Cigales mainly produces rosé wines. Red grape varieties grown are Tempranillo and Garnacha Tinta, while the most common white grape varieties are Verdejo and Albillo.

Bierzo

Referred to as the "gateway to Galicia," this region produces stunning red wines based on the Mencia grape, which is also called Negra because of its deep and opaque color. It also produces white wines made from the Godello grape. These wines have recently been making a small comeback after years in oblivion.

MURCIA

Murcia is a small area located on the river of Segura. It has extreme climate changes between summer and winter, and gets little rainfall throughout the year.

Jumilla

The specialty wines of Jumilla are the concentrated and rich red wines made from the Monastrell grape variety (known as Mourvèdre in France).

Bulas

The region of Bulas produces 15,000 hectoliters of wine at ten bodegas. The red grape varieties Tempranillo, Monastrell, Cabernet Sauvignon, Garnacha, Syrah, and Merlot are grown, as well as the white grape varieties Macabeo and Airén.

Yecla

Despite having only seven bodegas, Yecla manages to churn out 50,000 hectoliters of wine every year. Red grape varieties include Monastrell, Garnacha Tinta, Cabernet Sauvignon, Cencibel (Tempranillo), Merlot, Tintorera, and Syrah, while white wine grape varieties include Mersuguera, Airén, Macabea, Mavlasía, and Chardonnay.

■ VdlT (*Vino de la Tierra*): wine of a lesser quality than both DOCa and DO wine. Wine of this category is comparative to the VdP wines of France (see page 153).

■ VC (*Vino Comarcal*): wine of a lesser quality than both DOCa and DO wine. As far as quality is concerned, wine of this category is comparative to the VdM wines. However, these wines are produced with grapes from a variety of regions.

■ VdM (*Vino de Mesa*): table wine of lower quality.

PORTUGAL

Laws regarding Portugal wine-quality ratings are in a transition period, as legislation is slowly being passed to make the shift from the country's prior traditions to European standards. However, as it stands now, the rating system is similar to that of Spain, in that they both delimitate regions and outline the various categories under which the wine can be labeled. These categories are as follows.

■ VQPRD (*Vinho de Qualidade Produzido em Região Determinada*): means "Quality Wines Produced in a Specific Region." It can be shown as RD, *Região Demarcada*, or QWPSR. This indicates the wine is of a high quality, of limited production, and made from specific grapes produced from a delimited region. Specific taste, color, and aroma are required from the wine to qualify for this category. DOC and IPR wines both fall in this category.

■ DOC (*Denominação de Origem Controlada*) wines are made from grapes produced in a strictly delimited region. There are twenty-nine appellations registered as DOC. Some of these areas, along with their most popular wines, are listed in the inset on page 161.

■ IPR (*Indicações de Proveniência Regulamentada*) wines, on the other hand, adhere to many strict regulations, but are not produced in one of the DOC-registered areas.

■ *Vinho Regional*: table wines with labels that state the specific region in which the wine was produced.

■ *Vinho de Mesa*: table wines with labels that state

their producer and that they are from Portugal, rather than a specific region.

There are fifty-five officially recognized appellations in Portugal, across vineyards totaling around 980,000 acres (or 400,000 hectares). The production regions and the type of wines for which they are most popular are described below.

Minho

The region of Minho is located in northwest Portugal. Slightly fizzy and tart red and white wines are produced here. The most popular wine from this region is Vinho Verde. Although translated as "Green Wine," this name refers to its youthful qualities as opposed to its color, which can be either red, white, or rosé. Located nearby Minho in northern Portugal are the wine regions of Chaves, Valapacos, Planalto, Mirandes, Varosa, and Encosta da Nave.

Douro

The Douro region has long been most famous for its production of port wine, which is sweet and fortified. More recently, however, it has begun to attract attention for its dry, still red wines of high quality.

Dão

Dão, located in central-north Portugal, is best known for its elegant red table wines. The most famous of these red table wines are produced under the brand Grão Vasco. Both red and white wines produced in this region tend to have fruity flavors. Close to Dão are the two regions of Cova da Biera and Lafões.

Figure 11.12. Portuguese Label: Mouchão.

Winery Name/Brand: Herdade do Mouchão

Quality: Vinho Regional

Cuvee: Tonel No 3-4

Vintage: 1999

Country of Origin: Portugal

Region of Production: Alentejano

Alcohol Content: 13.5%

Bottle Contents: 750 ml

HERDADE — DO — MOUCHÃO
VINHO REGIONAL ALENTEJANO
TONEL N° 3-4
1999
PRODUCE OF PORTUGAL

Portuguese DOC Wines

Wines with the DOC label are of high quality and were produced in one of the DOC regions. The following list includes popular examples of these wines and the designated areas in which they were produced.

- Vinho Verde in Minho
- Trás-os-Montes in Transmontano
- Douro or Porto in Duriense
- Távora-Varosa, Lafões, Bairrada, Dão, and Beira Interior in Beiras
- Encostas de Aire, Óbidos, Alenquer, Arruda, Torres Vedras, Lourinhã, Bucelas, Carcavelos, and Colares in Estremadura

- Ribatejo in Ribatejo
- Setúbal and Palmela in Setúbal
- Alentejo in Alentejo
- Lagos, Portimão, Lagoa, and Tavira in Algarve
- Madeira/Madeirense on the island of Madeira
- Biscoitos, Pico, and Graciosa on the islands of Açores

Bairrada

Bairrada is in central-west Portugal, between the cities of Coimbra and Aviero. This region produces powerful, tannic red wines in soil that consists largely of clay. Nearly all of these wines are produced from the Baga grape.

Other Portuguese Wine Regions

A large number of small wine regions are juxtaposed in the region delimited by the cities of Lisbon, Santarem, and Leiria, located in central-west Portugal. These include Encostas D'aire, Alcobaco, Santarem, Obidos, Cartaxo, Alenquer, Arruda Bucelas, Colares, Carcavelos, Tores, Arrabida, Palmela, Coruche, Almeirim, Chamusca, and Tomar. Carcavelos is notable as one of the only wine regions in Europe to have remained phylloxera-free, owing to its sandy soils. Also located here and the most well known of the bunch is Setúbal. Setúbal is famous for its sweet, fortified wines, based on the Muscat grape.

There are also wine regions located on the eastern side of Portugal. Of these, Borba, Redondo, and Reguengos De Monsaraz have achieved IPR status. Portalegre and Vidigueira are also located there.

CHILE

According to wine laws of 1985 and a decree from the Ministry of Agriculture appended in 1994, Chilean wine labels must include all of the following declarations: winemaking zones, origins of denominations rules, indications of grape varieties, year of vintage, and any other aspects relating to the commercialization and labeling of Chilean wines. The country's viticultural zones and their subregions, as defined by the 1994 decree, are as follows.

- Atacama includes two subregions: Copiapó Valley and Huasco Valley.

- Coquimbo includes three subregions: Choapa Valley, Elqui Valley, and Limarí Valley.

- Aconcagua includes three subregions: Aconcagua Valley, Maipo Valley, and Casablanca Valley.

- Central Valley includes three subregions: Curicó Valley (which includes Teno Valley), Maule Valley (which includes Claro, Loncomilla, and Tutuven Valleys), and Rapel Valley (which includes Cachapoal and Colchagua Valleys).

- The South includes two subregions: Itata and Bío Bío Valley.

Figure 11.13.
Chilean Label: Almaviva.

Winery name: Viña Almaviva S.A. (Joint venture between Baron Phillipe de Rothschild and Viña Concha y Toro)

Vintage: 2003

Wine name: Almaviva

Origin: Wine of Chile, Puente Alto

ARGENTINA

The fifth largest wine producer in the world, Argentina produces large quantities of low-quality and a small number of outstanding wines. Although the country's wines have shown a substantial drop in domestic consumption—50 percent in less than thirty years—its export wine industry has flourished. Criolla and Cereza are the most planted grapes and cover about half of the vineyards.

> Most Argentine vineyards are at very high altitudes. In fact, this country is home to the highest vineyards in the world. They are at heights of up to 3,000 feet (or 915 meters) above sea level.

With the exception of the Rio Negro, the various wine regions of Argentina lie along the western part of the country. Argentina's rainfall is notoriously insufficient for grape-growing activity, but Salta, La Rioja, San Juan, and Mendoza benefit from natural irrigation from the Andean mountain range.

The country's highest quality wines are produced from grapes cultivated at high altitudes. There, the temperatures are cooler and there is less humidity. As a result, there are rarely problems with diseases or insects infesting vineyards.

Figure 11.14.
Argentina Label:
Catena Malbec.

Vintage: 2003

Grape variety: Malbec

Region of origin: Mendoza

Winery name:
Bodega Catena Zapata,
Mendoza, Argentina

The Northwest

The northern region of Salta produces high-quality Cabernet Sauvignon as well as Torrontés, a popular white wine. Calchaquí Valleys is located to the west of Salta, and includes many smaller valleys. Many excellent wines are produced in this area, which consists of a number of vineyards. The Catamarca Province is divided between the western and eastern areas, and is mostly known for the cultivation of table grapes and production of raisins.

Jujuy is located on the Argentine border, adjacent to both Chile and Bolivia. This region would normally not qualify for grape growing as it lies at a latitude of around 24° to 26°, and is at a very high altitude—up to 6,230 feet (1,900 meters) above sea level. Yet some cool climate grapes—most notably Torrontès, Malbec, and Cabernet Sauvignon—generate some excellent wines when grown here.

The grape variety Torrontès Riojano grows exceedingly well in La Rioja. Almost 50 percent of this grape's plantings are in this region, which consists of both plains and valleys. Wines for everyday drinking and wines of a higher quality are both produced here.

Cuyo

The province of San Juan, where the Pedernal Valley is situated, is home to some nonindigenous grape varieties such as Merlot, Cabernet Sauvignon, and Pinot Noir. Tulum Valley and Zonda, close to the capital city of San Juan, share the limelight with Ullum Valley, the site of bulk-wine production.

Mendoza, located on the western side of the country, accounts for about 75 percent of total plantings in Argentina. In this region, enormous quantities of everyday wines are produced from many different types of grapes. At the same time, Malbec, Tempranillo, Cabernet Sauvignon, and Chardonnay are also planted and generate high quality wines that find their way into export markets. Mendoza includes the subregions Maipu (Cruz de Piedra and Coquimbito), Luján de Cuyo (Drummond, Carrodilla, Agrelo, Pedriel, and Vistalba), and Uco Valley. San Rafael is another notable wine area.

Patagonia

Patagonia is the southern part of Argentina, and home to the Rio Negro and Neuquén wine regions. These areas are similar to Chile's Bio Bio because they are located at the same latitude. Both Rio Negro and Neuquén hold great promise for grapes which thrive in cooler climates.

CHINA

China's modern wine industry is relatively new. As a result, wine-labeling laws are rather loose. Information found on labels is much more a result

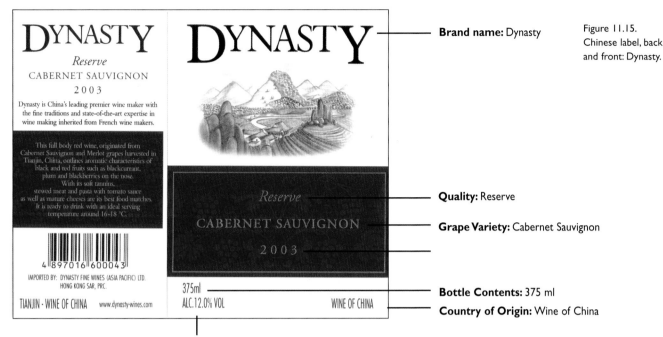

Brand name: Dynasty

Figure 11.15.
Chinese label, back
and front: Dynasty.

Quality: Reserve

Grape Variety: Cabernet Sauvignon

Bottle Contents: 375 ml

Country of Origin: Wine of China

Alcohol Content: 12%

of marketing decisions than legal requirements. Yet, in its quest to conquer new markets abroad, China will need to strengthen not only its labeling laws, but also the enforcement of these mandates.

As of December 2005, certain information must be found on the label of every alcoholic beverage as well as food product. There are also requirements regarding size and placement of some of this information. The following guidelines must be followed.

■ Product name: mandatory and must be a minimum of 0.07 inches (or 1.8 millimeters) in height. The words "grape wine" are sufficient, though it is advisable to qualify this with the wine's type, such as red, white, sparkling, semi-sparkling, or fortified. Position is not defined.

■ Volume statement: mandatory and must be a minimum of 0.16 inches (or 4 millimeters) in height and on the same label as the word "wine."

■ List of ingredients: mandatory and must be a minimum of 0.07 inches (or 1.8 millimeters) in height, but position is not defined. Because wine can be considered as made from a single raw material, it is exempt from the requirement of having an ingredient list. However, any added sweeteners, preservatives, acids, and color (which is only legal in fortified wines) must be declared. Substances such as sulphur dioxide, sorbic acid, and caramel need to be declared separately as well.

■ Alcohol content: mandatory and must be minimum of 0.07 inches (or 1.8 millimeters) in height, but position is not defined. This information must be expressed as the percentage of either alcohol per volume or alcohol per mass. The option may account for some of the reported disparity between results obtained from different Chinese testing authorities. The stated alcohol level is permitted to deviate from the actual alcohol content by plus or minus one percent.

■ Name and address: that of the Chinese-registered general distributor is mandatory. It must be written in Chinese characters and a minimum of 0.07 inches (or 1.8 millimeters) in height, but its position is not defined. However, the name and address of the producer is not mandatory and, if included, does not need to be translated into Chinese characters.

■ Volume statement: mandatory and must be on the same display panel as the word "wine." It is given as net content per millimeter or net content per liter. For packages up to and including 6.76 fluid ounces (or 200 milliliters), minimum print height is 0.12 inches (or 3 millimeters). For packages from 6.76 fluid ounces (or 200 milliliters) and up to and including one liter, minimum print height is 0.16 inches (or 4 millimeters). For packages greater than one liter, minimum print height is 0.24 inches (or 6 millimeters).

■ Country of origin: mandatory and must be minimum 0.07 inches (or 1.8 millimeters) in height. Position is not defined.

■ Bottling date: is required on Chinese labels and must be minimum 0.07 inches (or 1.8 millimeters) in height, but position is not defined. The bottling date can be expressed as, for example, "26 January 2007," "2007 01 26," "20070126," "2007-01-26," or "Jan, 26th 2007."

■ Minimum durability date: date when best drank by. It is mandatory for wines with an alcohol content of 10 percent or less. Wines with over 10-percent alcohol are exempt from this requirement.

■ Product type: mandatory and can be indicated by actual sugar content or by category. Still wines are labeled "dry" if they contain less than 0.4-percent sugar (or 4 grams per liter) or up to 0.9-percent sugar (or 9 grams per liter), provided the total tartaric acid (expressed as grams per liter) is within 0.2 percent (or 2 grams per liter) of the sugar. Wines are labeled "semi-dry" if they contain between 0.4- and 1.2-percent sugar (or 4 grams per liter and 12 grams per liter), or up to

1.8 percent (or 18 grams per liter) if the sugar content and acid content do not differ by more than 0.2 percent (or 2 grams per liter). A label that reads "semi-sweet" indicates that the wine contains between 1.2- and 4.5-percent sugar (or 12 grams per liter and 45 grams per liter). Wines are labeled "sweet" if they contain greater than 4.5-percent sugar (or 45 grams per liter).

Around the world, countries have different wine-labeling laws and different levels of enforcement. The European Union is undoubtedly at the forefront of wine label standardization, while many other countries still permit insufficient—or even false—information.

Yet many wines are exported to locations worldwide. It seems probable wine-producing countries will develop some level of product globalization in the near future, at least for mass-market wines. Global product standardization would improve the market for consumers because, as the laws stand now, the wine labels of many countries do not provide nearly enough information. More information would allow wine tasters the ability to determine whether their sensory evaluation corresponds with the wine's actual grape variety, vinification, and maturation. When this pertinent information is not provided on the label, this determination can often not be made.

12.
Wine and Health

In cooperation with Professor Georges M. Halpern, MD, PhD
Distinguished Professor of Pharmaceutical Sciences
Department of Applied Biology & Chemical Technology
Hong Kong Polytechnic University

In 450 BC, the great Greek physician Hippocrates recommended the use of wine variously to dress wounds, as a food supplement, as a diuretic, and to treat fever. Yet it is only recently that the medicinal benefits of wine, a beverage that for many subsequent years was largely regarded as a toxin, have again been researched and recognized.

Since these studies have begun, many articles and papers have been published on the merits of drinking wine on a moderate basis. None, however, caused a stir to the extent of a 1991 episode of *60 Minutes* featuring Professor Serge Renaud. He reported his findings of the so-called *French paradox,* the comparison of lifestyles—particularly eating and drinking habits—between French and Americans. Renaud highlighted a much lower incidence of cardiovascular disease among the French, despite a comparable consumption of fats between the two groups. The difference was attributed to the beneficial effects of moderate red-wine drinking.

Subsequent to Professor Renaud's study, there have been many further discoveries regarding the role of various wine components in preventing several major diseases. This chapter examines the components of wine from a chemical point of view together with their effects on the wine drinker's body. First, however, it is important to review the process by which wine is made, as well as those attributes that make wine unique.

Wine describes a diverse group of drinks composed of the yeast fermentation products of the *must,* or juice, pressed from grapes of the genus *Vitis.* Wine is a fruit product, but *fermentation*—the process by which sugar converts to alcohol—produces a variety of chemical changes in the must.

Fermentation alters the must in several ways. It changes the conjugation of organic acids and *phenolics*—chemical compounds found in plants. It both extracts and forms *copigments*—coloring agents. It allows the development of an anaerobic—able to occur without the presence of oxygen—and protective *redox potential*—which determines the extent to which wine can be oxidized. Wine, therefore, is not simply grape juice with the addition of ethanol.

Yet is wine different from other alcoholic beverages? Do different types of wine have different effects on the body? Throughout the years, animal studies have been performed to address these questions. From these studies, many of which are described later in this chapter, we can infer that wine is in fact different from other alcoholic drinks, and that various wines are different from other types of wine.

Although Professor Renaud popularized the theory of the French paradox, this discovery had been made prior to 1991. In the 1970s, the Framingham Heart Study in Massachusetts arrived at a similar conclusion.

Wine and other fermented products are safer and healthier than non-fermented ones, and can be kept for much longer periods of time. This is very important in warm or hot climates.

Wine Composition

Both clinical and experimental evidence suggests that wine, particularly red, offers greater health protection than other alcoholic beverages. Table 12.1 lists the main constituents of wine as well as the amount in which they are present. Some of the important and relevant components will be discussed in the following sections.

TABLE 12.1 COMPOSITION OF WINE, EXCLUDING PHENOLIC ACIDS AND POLYPHENOLS

Component	Concentration (grams per 3.38 fluid ounces/100 milliliters)
Water	80-90
Carbohydrates/sugars	0.20-0.45
Alcohol (mostly ethyl)	8.0-15.3
Glycerol	0.3-1.4
Aldehyde	0.01-0.05
Organic acid (tartaric, etc.)	0.3-1.1
Nitrogenous compounds	0.01-0.09
Mineral compounds (potassium, etc.)	0.15-0.40

POLYPHENOLS

Polyphenols (or polyphenolics) are chemical compounds commonly found in plants and fruits. They are classified into two groups: tannins and phenylpropanoids. Phenylpropanoids are then divided into further categories, one of which is flavonoids. The majority of grape polyphenols are present in skins and seeds. A summary of polyphenols in red and white wines can be found in Table 12.2 on page 167.

Although varietal and growing conditions do influence the spectrum of polyphenols in grapes, winemaking processes have a greater effect on total polyphenol content than grape variety. Skins and stems are left in contact with the must for prolonged periods to produce red wines. When white wines are being produced, on the other hand, the skins, stems, and must are rapidly separated after the crush. The resulting higher concentration of polyphenols in red wine is one of the reasons why it is considered more advantageous for health than white wine.

It is the high levels of polyphenols to which the beneficial effect of light-to-moderate drinking of red wine in decreasing the risk of coronary heart disease (CHD) is attributed. Red wine has also been found to increase high-density lipoprotein (HDL or "good" cholesterol), improve insulin function, and restrict hemorrhaging.

Copigmentation, or the production of copigments, is a phenomenon that occurs in a solution. Pigments, the coloring material, combine with other non-colored organic components to form molecular associations. Copigmentation significantly affects the color in young wines.

Aging wine—allowing the chemical properties to change over time—results in composition-altering processes. These changes are usually for the better, up to a certain point. Some take place in the winery, but most wines continue to age until they are consumed.

The production of dealcoholized wines begins with the production of regular wine. Once the process is complete, most of the alcohol is removed from the product. Note, however, that a small amount of alcohol remains in the drink. These beverages are available in most stores.

SULFITES

Sulfites are naturally occurring sulfur-based compounds commonly found in wine and certain food items. They can also be added to wine for several reasons, including minimizing potential for spoilage while maximizing the drink's freshness.

A very limited number of individuals—less than one percent of the general population—are sensitive to sulfites. Despite the low occurrence of this allergy, legislation was passed to make it compulsory for all wines produced in the United States to mention the bottle's sulfite contents on its label if the wine contains over a certain amount of the compounds. To combat this allergy and allow sufferers the opportunity to enjoy wine, some wineries now produce wine that is labeled "sulfite free" or as having "no added sulfites." These wines do contain the naturally occurring sulfites, but none are added, resulting in a sulfite level that is significantly lower than other wines.

ALCOHOL

Although polyphenols, which are beneficial for health, are found in grapes, they cannot be absorbed from grape juice. Oxidation is required. But the presence of alcohol is *not* necessary to absorb these compounds. Therefore, dealcoholized wine is just as beneficial to health as wine rich in alcohol. In fact, for people with coronary heart disease, non-alcoholic red wine is actually more effective than its alcoholic counterpart. This important discovery is significant for people who do not drink alcohol. Dealcoholized wine also contains up to 70-percent less calories than regular wine.

Alcoholic wine, on the other hand, contains 8- to 15-percent ethanol—a type of alcohol—by weight. The effects of ethanol on overall mortality in modern, western populations follow a J-shaped curve, in that moderate ethanol intake produces a significant reduction in mortality relative to abstinence from ethanol—but beyond moderate intake, (the exact amount of which varies according to gender, age, ethnicity, and other factors,) mortality rises sharply.

Health Benefits of Drinking Wine

Various medical studies have highlighted the benefits of moderate consumption of wine with

TABLE 12.2 THE CONCENTRATION OF POLYPHENOLS IN WINE		
Component	**Concentration in Red Wine** (1 milligram/1 liter)	**Concentration in White Wine** (1 milligram/1 liter)
Nonflavonoids (hydroxybenzoic acids, hydroxycinnamic acids, and stilbenes)	240-500	160-260
Flavonoids (flavonols, flavanols, and anthocyanins)	750-1060	25-30
Total phenolic acids and polyphenols	1,000-2500	190-290

meals. Wine has been found to have a positive and protective effect on many parts of the body—both to prevent possible future disease processes and in an effort to halt or slow those that have already begun.

As always, it is important to drink only in moderation. Suggestions for staying within this limit are described in the inset on page 168. However, if you have any prior medical disorders, check with your physician before starting any wine-drinking regimen.

TREATING THE KIDNEYS

As you read on page 166, wine contains polyphenols, which have many potential health benefits. Among these benefits is kidney health. Moderate consumption of wine fights the production and progression of renal diseases such as glomerulosclerosis and tubulointerstitial fibrosis.

IMPROVING THE LUNGS

Wine can improve pulmonary function. Tests have indicated positive associations of wine intake, both short term and lifetime, with the ability to breathe deeply. Both the forced vital capacity (FVC) and forced expiratory volume (FEV) were tested and showed improvement with the consumption of a moderate amount of wine.

PREVENTING CARDIOVASCULAR DISEASE

There are hundreds of studies on the beneficial effects of red wine on the cardiovascular system. Ethanol, as well as the polyphenols found in red wine, helps to limit the onset and growth of *atherosclerosis*—a buildup of plaque in the arteries—by promoting the formation of nitric oxide, an important relaxing and protective element for blood vessels. Regular and moderate red wine consumption increases the presence of high-density lipoproteins (HDL or "good" cholesterol). This substance fights low-density lipoproteins (LDL or "bad" cholesterol), thus reducing the risk of cardiovascular incidents and heart diseases.

Atherosclerosis is a type of arteriosclerosis, which means a buildup of fatty tissue, cholesterol, and other substances on artery walls. It may result in the blockage of an artery, and in some cases lead to a stroke. Studies have shown that moderate consumption of wine can reduce the risk of this disorder.

*T*he Antioxidant Potential of Red Wine

Researchers believe that red wine, when drank in moderation, can have certain health benefits, including reducing the potentially harmful process of oxidation. One glass of red wine (5 fluid ounces or 150 milliliters) offers equivalent antioxidant effects to any of the following.

- 12 glasses of white wine
- 2 cups of tea
- 5 apples
- 1.1 pounds (or 500 grams) of onion
- 5.5 portions of eggplant

- 3.5 glasses of blackcurrant juice
- 16.9 fluid ounces (or 500 milliliters) of beer
- 7 glasses of orange juice
- 20 glasses of apple juice

Drinking to Your Best Advantage

Certain attributes of wine have the potential to help you maintain optimal health. However, it is important to understand how to increase the likelihood of receiving these positive effects, while being aware of negative possibilities.

Do not dismiss the recommended daily wine intake. In France, doctors recommend men drink no more than 15.89 fluid ounces (or 470 milliliters)—a little more than three glasses—of red wine with an alcohol by volume (ABV) of 11 to 12 percent. Women should not drink more than 12.68 fluid ounces (or 375 milliliters) of red wine.

To make your wine intake a beneficial experience, it is highly recommended to drink it with meals. A seven-year survey followed 8,647 men and 6,521 women, aged thirty to fifty-nine years. Those who drank wine outside mealtimes exhibited a higher rate of death (of all causes, including cardiovascular disease and cancer) than those who drank wine only with meals.

The recommended suggestions are important. Overindulgence in wine (or other alcoholic beverages) leads to impaired reactions that can result in changed behavior, accidents, and fatal injuries. Drunk driving is the number one cause of fatal car crashes in many countries.

Alcohol is also potentially addictive to people of all walks of life. Remaining within the recommended intake can reduce the likelihood of this problem, but not eliminate it. The acute and long-term effects of alcohol abuse or alcoholism—whether drinking hard liquors, wine, or beer—can be devastating. Usually, the brain and liver are affected first. Alcohol can also cause cancer, heart disease, and skin, muscle, and bone disorders.

Women who drink heavily during pregnancy have a 50-percent chance of birthing a child with fetal alcohol syndrome (FAS), a condition characterized by permanent mental retardation, stunted growth, learning disabilities, damage to the central nervous system, cardiovascular disorders, and abnormal facial features. Yet this can be avoided by not drinking during pregnancy. As a result, the US Surgeon General urges pregnant women—as well as women who may become pregnant—to completely abstain from drinking any alcohol, including wine, beer, and liquor.

There is a risk of gaining weight from drinking wine. However, this should not be a problem if drinking is kept within a reasonable limit. In 3.38 fluid ounces (or 100 milliliters) of dry wine, there are between 105 and 110 calories, whereas sweet wine contains between 160 and 180 calories. This is equivalent to a large piece of fruit, 1.76 ounces (or 50 grams) of bread, or 0.88 ounces (or 25 grams) of chocolate.

Cardiovascular disease accounts for almost 50 percent of deaths in the North American population. Should every person drink two glasses of wine each day, cardiovascular disease would be cut by 40 percent, and $40 billion in medical bills, medicine, and emergency services could be saved annually.

MAINTAINING LIVER HEALTH

A study conducted in 1997 separated rats into three different groups. In the first group, rats drank sweet wine that was similar to port. The second group of rats drank dry red wine. The third group of rats drank ethanol diluted in water. At the end of the study, the group of dry red wine-drinking rats showed no hepatic lesions (liver damage)—whereas the other two groups did. The implication is that dry wine consumption protects from hepatic lesions induced by ethanol.

PROTECTING THE BRAIN

Drinking wine is beneficial for the brain in several ways. It protects against stroke. The Copenhagen City Heart Study showed that drinking a small amount of alcohol at first indication of stroke risk can have a positive result. This effect is strongest among existing wine drinkers.

Wine can also help stop or even improve the deterioration of the brains of elderly people. A study on several thousand people over the age of sixty-five found that the risk to wine drinkers of developing either incident dementia or Alzheimer's disease was significantly lower than that to members of the non-drinking control group. It is believed that the polyphenols in wine protect against Alzheimer's disease by inhibiting the formation of plaque and destroying recent plaques.

More so than other types of drinks, red wine also contains the specific polyphenol antioxidants that are believed to prevent oxidative damage to the brain. Another study examined subjects over the age of sixty-five for risk of development or worsening dementia. This time, one group drank red wine while the other group drank beer. Wine intake was associated with lower risk of dementia, while beer consumption was associated with increased risk.

RELIEVING STRESS

Some naturally occurring wine flavonoids, such as chrysin and apigenin, selectively bind with high affinity to the central benzodiazepine receptor and exert powerful anxiolytic effects. Therefore, wine may be used to relieve anxiety and tension. However, other studies have shown that too high an alcohol intake in the evening leads to a significant deterioration of sleep quality, particularly during the last part of the night.

ASSISTING RECOVERY FROM BACK SURGERY

There are indications that wine may be helpful after back surgery. A study of 148 patients evaluated their pain and impairment, as well as an assessment of their operation. The study was undertaken two-and-a-half years after back surgery. Findings indicated that wine may be strongly associated with a good prognosis after first-time lumbar disc surgery.

SLOWING EYESIGHT DEGENERATION

Age-related macular degeneration (AMD), a disorder that results in the deterioration of eyesight, affects more than 15 million seniors throughout the United States. A study of more than 3,000 adults found that alcohol consumers—and particularly wine drinkers—were at reduced risk for AMD. The effects of wine as an antioxidant and on platelet aggregability are associated with reducing the chance of developing AMD.

PURIFYING WATER

A recently conducted study found that undiluted red and white wines are effective in significantly reducing the number of viable *salmonella*, *shigella*, and *escherichia coli* in approximately twenty to thirty minutes. The pathogens are killed not by the wine's alcohol content but by the presence of polyphenols—which are similarly responsible for wine's effectiveness as a digestive aid. In much the same way, wine in moderate amounts (of approximately one drink per day) inhibits the spread of certain toxins in the body.

This same test examined the effect of diluting water with bismuth salicylate—Pepto-Bismol. It found that bismuth salicylate also improved the water quality by decreasing colony counts, but was not as effective as either red or white wine.

RESISTING COLDS

Wine may protect against the viruses of the common cold. A study that compared drinkers of more than fourteen glasses of wine per week with a group of people who abstained from all alcohol found that the wine drinkers experienced a 40-percent reduction of risk. On the other hand, the intake of beer, spirits, and other alcoholic beverages did not appear to have an effect.

Another study, conducted on mice, showed that the wine's antioxidant phytochemicals—plant compounds—impact the detoxification pathway and offset the detrimental effects of ethanol on immunity.

A Danish study suggested that wine drinking was significantly associated with higher intelligence, higher parental educational level, and higher socioeconomic status. Beer drinking, on the other hand, has been associated with significantly lower scores.

For a long time, it was thought that gout was caused not only by the overindulgence of food but also by the absorption of wine and other alcoholic beverages. As it turns out, wine is the only alcoholic beverage that is safe for patients with gout—although it does not cure or treat it.

Roman soldiers conquered their world without being sickened by diarrhea because the centurion would add wine to the local water supply. Twenty minutes later, the pathogens would be killed, and the water safe to drink.

*F*lushing Syndrome

Some people's faces become flushed when they drink wine. This occurs because of an isozyme called ALDH2 that is involved in the oxidation of methanol and alcohol. A high percentage of the Pacific Rim Asian population is significantly deficient in ALDH2, especially when compared to Caucasians, Native Americans, and Asian Indians. The individuals who lack this isozyme rapidly convert ethanol to acetaldehyde, but only slowly convert acetaldehyde into acetic acid. As a result, many Japanese, Chinese, Korean, Taiwanese, and Vietnamese people tend to turn red even after having consumed only minute amounts of alcohol.

Preliminary studies have indicated that individuals who have low ALDH2 levels may be able to boost this level by ingesting fruit that releases sugar over a long digestion period. One example of such a food is bananas.

FIGHTING CANCER

Wine contains compelling anti-cancer properties. Aromatase is an enzyme that converts androgens (such as testosterone) into estrogen. This process promotes the proliferation of breast cancer cells. Red wine and red wine extract may be a *chemo-preventive*—having the ability to interfere with a certain disease path—supplement in post-menopausal women who have high risk of breast cancer, because it suppresses the aromatase activity. Red wine has been shown to be much more effective than white wine when used for this purpose.

A study found that specific components of wine—in this instance a particular clone of Pinot Noir—were found to be more active than the wine as a whole. Preliminary research indicates that certain clones of certain wines could eventually be recommended to women with a family history of breast cancer.

Wine is also active against other cancers or malignancies. Resveratrol is a substance found in the skin of red grapes which, alone or combined with quercetin (a flavonoid also found in wine), prevents harmful body elements from attacking healthy cells. Effective in the quantity found in red wine, it is an inhibitor of oral squamous carcinoma cell growth and proliferation.

Data from three prospective studies of more than 28,000 subjects confirmed that intake of wine is associated with a reduced risk of lung cancer. This seemingly protective effect may be related to the antioxidant properties of wine—but all wines are not equal when consumed for this purpose. A study in the year 2000 found that while red wine seems to protect drinkers from lung cancer, white wine actually has an inverse association and may increase the risk.

Red and white wine consumption was also associated with a decreased risk of tumors in the glands (more specifically, adenocarcinomas of the esophagus and gastric cardia) as well as a reduced risk of esophageal squamous cell carcinoma and noncardia gastric adenocarcinoma. Although both red and white wine were found to be effective, red wine has shown to be more effective because of its copigmentation.

Examining 35,000 older American women for alcohol intake and risk for non-Hodgkin lymphoma (NHL), a study found that women who averaged more than two servings of wine each month had a 79-percent reduced risk of developing this cancer. Moderate intake of red wine showed the strongest protective effects. It is also effective for men: a study of over 2,500 men showed that drinking one or more glasses of wine a day from the age of sixteen, or even earlier, decreased the likelihood of developing NHL. No associations were evident for beer or spirits.

Conclusion

Wine has been part of human culture for more than 9,000 years. During this time, it has acted as a protective agent against various disease processes and assisted matters of health in various other ways. Epidemiological research has demonstrated that people who drink wine in moderation exhibit improved cardiovascular health and, on average, live longer—and happier—lives than those who abstain. It can be concluded, therefore, that wine "works."

Yet knowledge of the potential dangers of wine consumption is prevalent throughout our society. Leading wine critic Robert Parker, Jr. responded to this concern. He said, "Part of life is to live it, and enjoy it, and seize the moments that you find particularly pleasing." He also pointed out that, "Fettuccine Alfredo is dangerous for your health. Kung pao chicken will destroy your life… These are the people who do studies that your carry-out Chinese meals are saturated in fat… I'd just like to meet them! I mean, what do they do for pleasure?"

After all, wine is not primarily a tranquilizer, antioxidant, or any other protective agent. First and foremost, wine is about pleasure. Wine lovers know that the effort put into understanding and appreciating wine—as opposed to simply enjoying it or its psychotropic effects—pays big dividends. Really tasting wine adds an extra dimension to the basic daily routines of eating and drinking. It turns obligation into pleasure and a daily necessity into a celebration of life.

Cheers!

Wine may have the potential to strengthen bones. According to several studies, those who choose wine over other alcoholic drinks tend to have a lower risk of hip fracture.

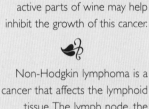

Oral squamous carcinoma is more commonly known as cancer of the tongue, usually associated with the consumption of tobacco and alcohol products. Certain active parts of wine may help inhibit the growth of this cancer.

Non-Hodgkin lymphoma is a cancer that affects the lymphoid tissue. The lymph node, the source of tissue in the lymphatic system, produces and stores lymphocytes, the white blood cells responsible for immunity against infections and diseases.

Conclusion

There is a lot of work that goes into the production of every bottle of wine. In fact, the multi-stepped process of making wine can be considered an art form. All the considerations and decisions made along the way have a tremendous effect on the final product. You may find that you have an even greater appreciation for wine now that you are familiar with the many processes involved.

As the wine industry has spread in global markets and competition has increased, the number of available bottles has expanded to include a seemingly overwhelming amount of choices. Wine-loving consumers find it beneficial to become familiar with the most popular and important grapes and producers in order to determine the right bottle for the right occasion.

There are many different wine grape varieties throughout the world. You are now familiar with the most popular and important. Although those discussed in this book by no means comprise a conclusive list, they provide a great background on a substantial number of prominent grapes.

You can now also apply your wine knowledge to practical situations. From preparing and storing the bottles to arranging a wine tasting, and from matching wine with food and reading wine labels, the information found here has prepared you for quite a future as a wine connoisseur.

Whether you began this book as a wine novice or have been drinking for many years, I hope that your understanding of our favorite beverage has been enhanced. However, your grape education should not stop here. The next step to expand your knowledge is tasting wines produced with the grapes about which you have read—unless, of course, you've been reading with a full cellar and a glass of wine in your hand. In that case, by all means, continue tasting.

Be merry and have a glass of good wine with your next meal.

Glossary

All words that appear in italic type are defined within the glossary.

ampelographer. Scientist whose area of study is the documentation and classification of grape varieties.

ampelography. The science of documenting and classifying grape varieties based on photographic evidence and genetic fingerprinting.

amphora. Ancient container used by the Greeks, Egyptians, Romans, and Phoenicians for the storage and transportation of various beverages, including wine.

anosmia. A deficiency that is characterized by an inability to distinguish smells and aromas.

aroma. Smell produced by a combination of grape-variety characteristics, *terroir, viticulture, vinification,* and aging processes.

aroma wheel. A method of classifying different aromas and smells associated with wine. The wheel was designed by a team under the supervision of Professor Ann Noble at the University of California at Davis.

astringent. A quality of wines that causes a harsh, puckering feeling in the mouth after being tasted. Astringency is a result of *tannic* wine.

barrel. A wooden container usually made from oak or chestnut wood that is used to store and transport wine. Each region has its own barrel-size specifications.

berry. Fruit of the vine. Grape berries appear as a bunch, held together by stems.

Botrytis cinerea. A fungus that causes grape berries to rot. This usually leads to grey rot, which can destroy the affected grapes. Under particular climatic conditions, however, such as those found in the Sauternes and Barsac regions, noble rot is produced instead, which leads to magnificient sweet wines by piercing the skin and allowing for evaporation of moisture. The resulting yield is dramatically reduced but produces wines with very high concentrations.

bouquet. Wine aromas developed inside the bottle. Two main families of bouquets exist: animal (game, venison, fur) and vegetal (undergrowth, mushroom, truffle).

budding. Stage of grape-vine development when the first leaves appear on the vine. Buds are delicate to spring frost and must be protected in cold climate regions.

Cahors. City located in the department of Lot, France. It is home to the world-famous wine by the same name that is made with the Malbec grape variety.

cask. See *barrel.*

château. Wine-producing estate in Bordeaux, France.

chianti. Red wine produced in the region of Tuscany, Italy. The main grape variety in Chianti is Sangiovese. Other varieties allowed for the blend are Malvasia Canaiolo Nero, Merlot, and Cabernet Sauvignon.

coulure. A vine disease that occurs when grape pollination fails, resulting in decreased yields. Pinot Noir and Merlot are particularly susceptible to coulure.

crop thinning. A *viticulture* technique in which some grape bunches are cut before maturity to improve the quality of the remaining ones. Also known as green harvest.

cuvée. 1. The quantity, usually approximately 2,000 liters, obtained after the first pressing of the grapes. 2. The best expression of a wine as found during the blending process.

disgorgement. Step in the process of sparkling wine production that removes dead yeast from the liquid.

domaine. Wine-producing estate, commonly found throughout France.

dosage. Wine and sugar added to sparkling wines after *disgorgement* to obtain a certain level of sugar. Also called "liqueur de dosage" and "liqueur d'expedition."

downy mildew. A vine disease caused by a fungus that results in an ultimate loss of all leaves, thereby significantly reducing the photosynthesis process. It looks like a cotton wool and first develops on the underside of the leaves. Downy mildew is native to North America and was not brought to Europe until the second half of the nineteenth century.

drainage. The ability of soil to eliminate its excess humidity or moisture. The soil composition plays a role. For example, gravel usually ensures good drainage while clay usually does not. The angle at which the slope stands also affects the soils ability to drain.

goblet. A vine *training* system that requires two spurs to be tied up in a circular shape atop a short trunk. It is called such because the resulting vine resembles the shape of a wine glass.

grand cru. Describes quality of wine. This term refers to different levels of quality in different regions throughout France. In Alsace and Burgundy, grand cru wines originate from *terroir* of superior quality.

grange. One of the most famous Australian red wines. A rich, deep, and dark red wine made by the Penfolds winery in South Australia, Grange is produced from the Shiraz grape.

green harvest. See *crop thinning*.

hard liquor. Alcohol that is distilled rather than fermented.

loam. A type of soil composed of equal amounts sand, clay, and silt. It allows good aeration and draining but still retains some moisture.

loess. Geological deposit of yellow or brown silt material made of microscopic particles. Coarser than clay but finer than sand, loess forms a very fertile soil.

marl. A combination of limestone and clay that can be found in the Burgundy region. It is commonly used as a fertilizer.

must. Unfermented grape juice obtained from pressing freshly gathered grapes.

New World. A host of wine-producing countries outside of Europe including Argentina, Australia, Chile, China, New Zealand, South Africa, and the United States.

oak barrel. See *barrel*.

oïdium. See *powdery mildew*.

Old World. A host of wine-producing countries located in Western and Eastern Europe. These include Austria, France, Germany, Italy, Luxembourg, Russia, Spain, and Switzerland.

olfactory. Pertaining to sense of smell.

Opus One. A rich and powerful red wine made by a joint-venture between Baron Philippe de Rothschild and Robert Mondavi, whose vineyards are located in the Napa Valley in California. The wine is based on Cabernet Sauvignon, Cabernet Franc, and Merlot grapes, the traditional Bordeaux blend.

peronospera. See *downy mildew*.

phylloxera. A vine disease caused by an insect, the *Phylloxera vastatrix*, which attacks the vine's roots. Phylloxera devastated the vineyards of Europe from 1863 until the end of the nineteenth century, at which point most European vines were grafted onto American phylloxera-resistant rootstocks.

powdery mildew. A fungal disease that affects the entire vine, including the leaves, and can destroy a harvest.

premier cru. A term for superior Burgundy wines that are one quality level below those with the *Grand Cru* distinction.

pressing. Extracting the juice from the grapes.

pruning. Cutting the past harvest vine shoots so as to control the growth of foliage as well as the *yield* of the vine.

riddling. Process that brings the dead yeasts from the bottom of the bottle to its neck so that they can then be removed through *disgorgement*. In the past, riddling was performed manually, but these workers have been replaced by machines called giro-palettes.

Romanée Conti. Producer of some of the most

expensive wines in the world. Owned by the Leroy and de Villaine families, this *domaine* has existed in its current form since the sixteenth century and produces six red wines (Romanée-Conti, Echezeaux, Grands Echezeaux, La Tâche, Romanée St. Vivant, and Richebourg) and one white wine (Le Montrachet).

rootstock. Vine roots on which shoots of existing grape varieties are grafted to render the plant resistant to some diseases, such as *phylloxera*.

scions. Vine plants at the early stage of their lives. They are brought up in nurseries and then planted in order to generate a new vine.

swirl. The act of rotating a glass containing wine to further oxygenate the wine, which enhances aromas during the sensory evaluation process.

taille. The *must* from the grapes' second *pressing*.

tannic. A quality of wine in which the taste of *tannins* is stronger than the wine's other elements.

tannins. Compounds present in the skins, seeds, and stalks of grapes that are responsible for the sometimes *astringent* taste of wine, particularly young reds. Tannins are necessary for long and graceful aging, and the astringency diminishes with time.

tartaric acid. One of the acids commonly found in wine. It is relatively rare in fruits other than grapes. Tartaric acid can be added to wine if additional acidity is needed to balance the wine's pH level, and promotes a crisp flavor and graceful aging.

tendrils. Spiral-shaped leaf structures developed by the grape vine to hook itself onto supporting material such as steel wire.

terroir. French term that has been adopted into the English language and refers to all the characteristics of a specific area that affect the grapes that are grown there. These include soil, climate, and other influential factors.

training. The art of guiding the vine shoots so as to ensure regular and controlled growth along steel wires or poles in the vineyard.

varietal. Wine produced from one type of grape variety.

vine. Name of the plant on which grape *berries* grow in bunches.

vineyard. Piece of land on which wine grapes are grown.

vinification. All activities pertaining to the art of winemaking, from the harvest of the grapes to the bottling and bottle maturation of the finished product.

viticulture. All the activities pertaining to growing grapes, from soil preparation until grape harvest.

viticulturist. A worker dedicated to selecting and growing grapes.

yield. The quantity of grapes obtained at harvest from a vineyard. Usually measured in hectoliters per hectare (HL/HA).

Bibliography

Alley, L, "King Tut was a red wine drinker, scientists say," *Wine Spectator* (March 2004).

Bowers, JE, "Development and characterization of additional microsatellite DNA markers for grape." *American Journal of Enology and Viticulture* (October 1999): 243–246.

Cernili, D, and Sabellico, M. *The New Italy: A Complete Guide to Contemporary Italian Wine.* London: Mitchell Beazley of Octopus Publishing Group, 2000.

Clarke, O, and Rand, M. *A Comprehensive Guide to Varieties & Flavours: Grapes & Wines.* London, England: Little, Brown and Company, 2001.

Clarke, O, and Rand, M. *Grapes and Wines: The Definite Guide to the World's Great Grapes and the Wines They Make.* New York, New York: Harvest Books, 2007.

Collombet, F, and Paireault, JP. *The Flammarion Guide to World Wines.* Paris, France: Flammarion, 2000.

Cooper, M. *Buyer's Guide to New Zealand Wines.* Auckland, New Zealand: Hodder Moa Becket, 2003.

Dominé, A. *Wine.* Cologne, Germany: Könemann Verlagsgesellschaft mbH, 2001.

Dubs, S, and Ritzenthaler, D. *Les Grands Crus d'Alsace.* Lorraine, France: Editions Serpenoise, 2002.

Gabriel, R, "A commentary of pharmacoge-nomics: what can it do?" *MLO-Online* (March 2005): 25–26.

Galet, P. *Dictionnaire Encyclopédique des Cépages.* France: Hachette, 2000.

Galet, P. *Grape Varieties.* France: Hachette Wine Library Cassell Illustrated, 2002.

Halliday, J. *Australian Wine Companion.* London, England: Harper Collins, 2004.

Hermacinski, Ursula. *The Wine Lover's Guide to Auctions.* Garden City Park, NY: Square One Publishers, 2007.

http://www.winespectator.com/Wine/Wine_Basics/Wine_Basics_Template/0,,3428,00.html. "The ABC's of Wine Tasting," Thomas Matthews.

Huttenbrink, KB, Schmidt, C, Delwiche, JF, Hummel, T. "The enjoyment of red wine is influenced by the shape of the wine glass." *Laryngorhinootologie* 2001;80:96–100.

Kolpan, S, Smith, BH, and Weiss, MA. *Exploring Wine: The Culinary Institute of America's Complete Guide to Wines of the World, Second Edition.* New Jersey: John Wiley & Sons, 2002.

Langewiesche, W, "The million-dollar nose," *The Atlantic* (2000): 42–70.

Lichine, A. *New Encyclopedia of Wines & Spirits, Seventh Edition.* London: Cassell, 1987.

Livingstone-Learmonth J. *The Wines of the Rhône, Third Edition.* London, England: Faber & Faber, 1992.

Moisseeff, M, and Casamayor, P. *Arômes du Vin.* Lorraine, France: Hachette, 2002.

O'Rear, Charles. *Chardonnay: Photographs from Around the World.* Ten Speed Press: Berkeley, California, 1999.

Paladini, AC, Marder, M, Viola, H, Wolfman, C, Wasowski, C, and Medina, JH, "Flavonoids and the central nervous system: from forgotten factors to potent anxiolytic compounds," *J Pharm Pharmacol* 1999;51:519–26.

Parker, RM, Jr. *Bordeaux: A Comprehensive Guide to the Wines Produced from 1961 to 1997.* New York, New York: Simon & Schuster, 1998.

Pastena, B, and Coria, G. *Guida Ai Vini di Sicilia.* Sicily, Italy: Palermo, 1991.

Peppercorn, D. *Wines of Bordeaux.* London, England: Mitchell Beazley, 2002.

Peynaud, E. *Le Goût du Vin.* France: Bordas, 1983.

Piallat, R, and Deville, P. *Oenologie & Crus Des Vins.* France: Editions Jérôme Villette, 1983.

Pitiot, S. and Poupon, P. *Atlas des grands vignobles de Bourgogne.* France, Pitiot et Poupon, 1999.

Priewe, J. *Wine: From Grape to Glass.* New York: Abbeville Press, 1998.

Renaud, S, and Gueguen, R, "The French paradox and wine drinking," *Novartis Foundation Symposium* (1998): 152–8, 208–22.

Roger, R. *Connaissance des Boissons: Beverage Knowledge.* Switzerland: Ecole Hotelière de Lausanne, 2000.

Ribéreau-Gayon, P, Glories, Y, Maujean, A, and Dubourdieu D. *Traité d'Oenologie 1. Microbiologie du vin: Vinifications.* Paris: Dunod, 1998.

Ribéreau-Gayon, P, Glories, Y., Maujean, A. and Dubourdieu D. *Traité d'Oenologie: Tome 2.* Paris: Dunod, 1998.

Robinson, J. *Vines, Grapes & Wines.* London, England: Mitchell Beazley, 2002.

Robinson, J. *The Oxford Companion to Wine.* New York: Oxford University Press, 1994.

Turin, L, "A method for the calculation of odor character from molecular structure," *Journal of Theoretical Biology* (2002): 367–385.

Turin, L, "A spectroscopic mechanism for primary olfactory reception," *Chemical Senses* (1996): 773–791.

Voss, R. *Wines of the Loire.* London, England: Faber and Faber, 1995.

Walton, S. *The World Encyclopedia of Wine.* London, Enland: Lorenz Books, 1999.

Index